16 99

Alpine Christian Fellowship
PO Box 2111
Alpine, CA 91903

San Diego Christian College
2100 Greenfield Drive
El Cajon, CA 92019

THE
GOOD
LIFE

THE GOOD LIFE

MAX ANDERS

WORD PUBLISHING
Dallas · London · Vancouver · Melbourne

THE GOOD LIFE
Living with Meaning in a Never-Enough World
Max E. Anders

Unless otherwise indicated, Scripture quotations are from the New American Standard Bible (NASB), © The Lockman Foundation 1960, 1962, 1963, 1968, 1971, 1972, 1973, 1975, 1977, and are used by permission.

Other Scripture quotations marked KJV are from The King James Version. Those marked NCV are from The Holy Bible, New Century Version, copyright © 1987, 1988, 1991 Word Publishing, and are used by permission. Those marked NIV are from The Holy Bible, New International Version, Copyright © 1973, 1978, 1984 International Bible Society, and are used by permission of Zondervan Bible Publishers.

An effort has been made to locate sources and obtain permission where necessary for quotations used in this book. In the event of any unintentional omissions, modifications will gladly be incorporated in future printings.

Library of Congress Cataloging-in-Publication Data

Anders, Max E., 1947–
    The good life : living with the meaning in a never-enough world /
Max E. Anders.
        p.   cm.
    ISBN 0–8499–1049–8
    1. Christian life—1960– .   2. Self-actualization (Psychology—
Religious aspects—Christianity.   I. Title.
BV4501.2.A455   1993
248.4—dc20   93–14756
                                                                          CIP

3 4 5 9   LB   9 8 7 6 5 4 3 2 1

Printed in the United States of America.

To Margie

My wife
My friend
My comrade in arms
My spiritual intimate

Contents

Acknowledgments

To Kip Jordon at Word, who believed in the book and in doing so helped me make it better.

To Judith Markham, whose wonderful editorial skill is exceeded only by her gracious spirit.

To Roxanne Brooks, my secretary, who labored faithfully and skillfully on the details of the manuscript.

To the people of Grace Covenant Church in Austin, Texas, whose love encouraged me as I was preaching the sermons from which this book was drawn.

I pray that the Lord Jesus will be lifted up in this book and that He will "draw men unto Himself."

Introduction

We don't buy glasses; we buy vision. We don't buy awnings; we buy shade. We don't buy a newspaper; we buy information. It isn't the product we want. It's what the product will do for us. We buy something or pursue something, not because we want the "thing" itself, but because we want what that thing will give us or do for us.

Most people today are pursuing one thing above all: the good life. This usually translates into one, or all, of the following:

- We want to be wealthy.
- We want to have purpose.
- We want to love and be loved.
- We want to be powerful.

Wealth, purpose, love, and power. If we have those, we say, we have it all. Unfortunately, instead of the "real thing," we too often settle for a substitute. We are content with cheap—and dangerous—imitations. Instead of wealth, we grab money. Instead of purpose, we settle for ambition. Instead of love, we accept sex. Instead of power, we take clout.

No matter how appealing, of course, the substitute never really satisfies.

Imagine yourself cast adrift on the ocean without a supply of fresh water. After hours under the blazing sun you look longingly at the endless platform of water beneath your raft. "Water, water everywhere," the poet's refrain burns through your mind. If only you could take a drink. But if you do, your platform will soon become your grave, for drinking salt water will dehydrate and, eventually, kill you.

The human body needs water. If we go too long without it, we develop a deep, driving, natural thirst. But it is thirst for the real thing—for a drink of pure water. Salt water can never satisfy the thirst that drives us to drink it in the first place. Instead, it will hasten us to our grave. Our only hope is to hold out for pure water.

And so it is with our desire for wealth, purpose, love, and power. Let no one apologize for wanting these; they are the very things for which we were created. But let us understand what those longings really are. They are longings for immortality. God has created us to value and long for these things. But He has also created us so that He, and He alone, can satisfy these desires. True wealth, purpose, love, and power are gifts God wants to give us in Christ, so when we feel these longings, it is really God we want.

In this world we find ourselves adrift in life amid a sea of money, ambition, sex, and clout. We think that by drinking them we can slake our thirst for wealth, purpose, love and power. Not so! None of these will satisfy our thirst. Instead, they will dehydrate our souls and drive us to the grave. Our only hope is to hold out for the Water of Life, Christ Himself.

If we are looking for a guide to "the good life," a yellow pages directory for "the real thing," there is no better place to look than the book of Ephesians in the New Testament. There we learn that:

- God wants us to have wealth (Eph. 1–3).
- God wants us to have purpose (Eph. 4:1–5:17).
- God wants us to have love (Eph. 5:18–6:9).
- God wants us to have power (Eph. 6:10–24).

That is our destiny—our inheritance. In heaven we shall possess more wealth than our finite minds can possibly imagine. We shall have a complete sense of purpose. We shall love and be loved fully. And the power we shall enjoy will be beyond our wildest imaginations. C. S. Lewis said that if we were to see our glorified selves walking down the street, we would be tempted to fall at our feet and worship ourselves.

But we don't have to wait for heaven. As children of God, we can begin to delve into our spiritual treasures and our heavenly inheritance right now. In a world of pain, frustration, and death, we can rejoice in sorrow, love in the face of hate, and triumph in defeat.

Now, I can hear some of you saying, "Those things don't sound very exciting. They don't sound very satisfying." In fact, if you were honest, you'd probably say, "I'd take a load of money, great opportunities, a beautiful woman (or a handsome man), and personal power over this other stuff any day of the week." I understand. Those things can look pretty good . . . for the moment.

Unfortunately, no matter how good they sound, those things don't satisfy. Not completely, not unendingly. Rich men and women have an empty longing in their souls that money cannot satisfy. When the powerful retire, they are forgotten overnight. Ask anyone in a nursing home or in an emergency room how important sex or ambition is to them. When death comes, as it does to all, we do not call for any of these to comfort us.

If this life were all there is, we could say, "Well, grab all you can while you can, because in the end it all turns to ashes anyway. Enjoy it while you can." This life, however, is merely an introduction to immortality. And that changes everything.

Wealth, purpose, love, and power—those longings are very real. But remember what those longings really are. They are longings for immortality. They are longings for deliverance from this world. It is heaven we long for. It is God we seek. Let's not settle for inferior substitutes.

Part 1

Wealth

God wants us to have wealth. We must be careful not to settle for money.

1

The Vault Is Open
(Ephesians 1:1–3)

We are half-hearted creatures, fooling about with drink and sex and ambition when infinite joy is offered us, like an ignorant child who wants to go on making mud pies in a slum because he cannot imagine what is meant by the offer of a holiday at sea. We are far too easily pleased.

C. S. Lewis

People spend a fortune today trying to discover who they are. They get color-coordinated on the outside and psychoanalyzed on the inside. Tracing back to their earliest memories and beyond, they search for self-identity. This is not surprising, of course. It is the natural longing of the human heart, the seeking of the human soul after God. We long to know who we really are!

This is true for us even as Christians. We do not understand who we are and who we have become. We do not see ourselves as God sees us. Instead of accepting and comprehending who we have become in Christ, we identify with the person we used to be. So we must be imprinted with the proper identity. Otherwise, we'll be like the duck who thought he was a dog.

Sounds like a Disney cartoon or a Dr. Seuss story, doesn't it? But it is nothing so fanciful. It is something that happens in real life.

Imprinting. The dictionary defines it as "a rapid learning process that takes place early in the life of a social animal and establishes a behavior pattern as recognition of and attraction to its own kind or a substitute." Ducks, for example, attach themselves to the first thing they see after they hatch. Now normally this works just fine because the first thing they see is Mama Duck. They attach themselves to her and begin thinking and acting like her. Which is fine. They are like her. They are ducks.

Occasionally this early attachment backfires, however. Like the duckling that hatched under the watchful eye of a collie dog. The first thing the

17

baby duck saw was the collie, and a bond was forged. The duckling took one look at the collie and decided that it, too, was a collie. It followed the dog around, ran to it for protection, spent the hot part of the day under the porch with the collie, and slept with it at night. After the duckling grew up, most of the time it acted like a duck, except that it spent the hot part of the day under the front porch. And when a car pulled into the driveway, the duck would explode from wherever it happened to be, quacking viciously and pecking at the tires. After all, that was what the "other" dog did.

The duck had an identity problem. It didn't see itself as a duck; it saw itself as a collie. Yet that couldn't change the fact that it was a duck. So sometimes it acted like a duck, and sometimes it acted like a dog.

This type of confusion is seen much more dramatically in the cases of children who have been reared by wild animals. During the last several hundred years there have been fifty-three documented cases of "feral children"; that is, children who have been lost in the wild and have survived by being nurtured, protected, and cared for by wild animals such as wolves, bears, antelopes, monkeys, and pigs.

In the February 1987 edition of *Sierra* magazine a story entitled "Uganda's Wild Child" told of a "monkey child" who was found in a jungle in Uganda and was believed to have been living with a tribe of monkeys for as long as four or five years. The boy, estimated to be five or six years old at the time, was taken to an orphanage, where he grunted and squealed, jumped around with his hands clenched, and preferred to eat grass. He seemed to be afraid of people and tried to scratch anyone who approached him.

Another example was a boy who had somehow become part of an antelope herd in Southern Morocco. "Antelope Boy" lived with the antelope, ate grass with them, drank from the same pools of water, and ran with them. Several attempts were made to capture him to no avail, and he was observed living in this natural habitat over a period of ten years.

Those who have studied these wild children have determined that if a child lives with animals beyond the age of four to six years of age, he cannot be reclaimed as a normal functioning human. These children are "imprinted," their brains impressed indelibly and permanently with animal behavior; they lose their human identity. They do not understand that they are human, not animal. And the results are usually tragic.

While these are extreme and bizarre examples, all of us suffer from a certain kind of imprinting: negative spiritual imprinting. We have all grown up in a fallen world. The world was the first thing we saw, and we identified with it. We became like it. But when we are born again, we become children of God. We are no longer what we were. "If any man is in Christ, he is a new creature; the old things passed away; behold, new things have come" (2 Cor. 5:17)!

Too often, however, we don't see it that way. As a result we act like the world, rather than like who we really are. We are ducks acting like dogs. We believe the right things and try to do the right things, but the imprint of the world is strong. We forget our true identity. Instead of swimming around in clear, blue lakes, bobbing for seaweed, preening our feathers, and laying eggs, we're quacking at cars or harassing the cat.

Seeing Ourselves as God Sees Us

Fortunately, we are not permanently imprinted like the duck or the monkey child. We can change. We can begin to act more consistently with our true identity. God has promised to change the willing mind and to work supernaturally from within us to accomplish change. In fact, that's our biggest challenge as believers.

So how do we find our true identity? We must begin by seeing ourselves as God sees us, and in his letter to the Ephesians, the apostle Paul offers us help with that. The epistle to the Ephesians was addressed to ordinary Christians like you and me, but notice how Paul addresses them. He calls these ordinary Christians "saints":

> Paul, an apostle of Christ Jesus by the will of God, to the *saints* who are at Ephesus, and who are faithful in Christ Jesus.
>
> Ephesians 1:1, italics added

All Christians are saints, in the biblical sense of the word. "Saint" comes from the Greek word *hagios,* which means "set apart for God." It does not necessarily mean a saintly lifestyle, such as that of Mother Teresa. It simply means anyone who has become a Christian, anyone who has believed in and received Christ as his or her personal Savior. So, if you are a Christian—if you believe in Christ and have committed your life to Him—you are set apart for God. You are *hagios.* You are a saint, and *everything that the Lord says to the Ephesian believers through Paul, He says to you!*

What, then, does Paul say to the Ephesian believers? Well, first of all, he uses a phrase that is particularly important—so important, in fact, that he uses it, and related phrases, twenty-seven times in his letter. The phrase is "in

Christ." And if we are going to understand how God sees us, we must understand what it means to be "in Christ."

That's not always easy with our finite minds, so an analogy might help. For example, substitute the word "Congress" for "Christ." If you were a senator or a representative, we would say that you were "in Congress." What would that mean?

Well, if you are "in Congress," you have been elected to that position. All the power, privileges, and responsibilities of that position are yours. You are a member of Congress. You have a place there. You are accepted there. You got there through required means, so you are worthy to be there. When you walk into the congressional chambers, no heads jerk up in surprise. Nobody says, "What are you doing here?" Why? Because you belong there.

To be "in Christ" means you belong in Christ. You have been elected. All the power, privileges, and responsibilities of that position are yours. You are a member of His body. You have a place there. You are accepted there. You got there through required means, so you are worthy to be there. When you walk into heaven, no heads will jerk up in surprise. Nobody will say, "What are you doing here?" Why? Because you belong there.

Since we are dealing with infinite things, however, we must move beyond this finite analogy. For while there is no mystery about Congress— well, none except how they ever manage to get anything done—there is always something about the spiritual that is just a bit beyond our human understanding. And while a member of Congress is only as secure as the next election, being "in Christ" means that everything that is His is ours forever. Just as He is holy and righteous, so we are holy and righteous in Him. All His holiness, righteousness, goodness, glory, power, and wealth are ours!

"But wait," you say. "There must be something wrong here. I don't feel holy, righteous, good, glorious, powerful, or wealthy. In fact, just between you and me, I'm not always good. I do some ugly things. I'm selfish. And sometimes I know what I'm doing is wrong, but I do it anyway. What you are saying may be true for other Christians, but it's not true for me. There's something wrong with me."

I know how you feel. If you were a fish, you'd be under the limit; you'd have to be thrown back. If you were a car, you'd be recalled.

One of the most common negative feelings among Christians is that "there must be something wrong with me . . . things work for others, but not for me." But central to understanding what it means to be a saint, central to overcoming the negative spiritual imprinting of the world and reidentifying with who we really are, is this understanding: We are in Christ.

That means God sees us through Christ's righteousness. He is satisfied with Christ, and He is satisfied with us because we are in Christ. It is true that we must accept His offer of salvation. But after we have, our security does not depend on who we are; it depends on who He is. We are secure in God's love because it is

His will, not ours (1:5)

His grace, not ours (1:6–7)

His good pleasure, not ours (1:9)

His purpose, not ours (1:11)

His power, not ours (1:12, 14)

His calling, not ours (1:18)

His inheritance, not ours (1:18)

His love, not ours (2:4)

His workmanship, not ours (2:10)

"But I don't deserve it," you say. And, in a sense, that's true. You don't. But in another sense, you do. You don't have a right to it, and you don't deserve it because of any of your own actions. But you have inherent worth, which explains why God offers salvation to you. Do you think He would waste His time on you—send Christ to die for your sins—if you weren't worth it?

You do not earn salvation.

You cannot earn it.

But you are worth it, *because you are created in the image of God.* God is the highest value in the universe, and anything made in His image has the next highest value in the universe.

Not because of anything you do, but *because you are a living, breathing soul bearing the likeness, the image, of God.*

Once we begin to get an accurate image of who we really are and how God really sees us, light begins dawning in our darkened understanding. Then we stand a greater chance of acting more consistently like who we have actually become. We stand a greater chance of acting more like God than like the world. Our guarantee of this astounding truth is that phrase "in Christ."

What Christ has, we have. We are "fellow heirs" with Him (Rom. 8:17). He is not ashamed to call us brothers and sisters (Heb. 2:11). What Christ possesses, we possess: an inheritance that is imperishable and undefiled and will not fade away, reserved in heaven for us (1 Pet. 1:4). And God has "blessed us with every spiritual blessing in the heavenly places in Christ" (Eph. 1:3).

Now, you may be saying at this point, "I don't feel all that blessed." I used to feel that way. I thought that, as a Christian, I ought to have a continuous sense of being blessed . . . but I wasn't even sure what those blessings were. However, I have learned that Paul did not leave that to our imagination. He enumerated our spiritual blessings in Christ.

He chose us to be holy and blameless (1:4).

He predestined us to adoption (1:5).

He freely bestowed His grace on us (1:6).

He redeemed us and forgave our trespasses (1:7).

He gave us an inheritance (1:11).

To gain a more personal sense of what this means to us, read these same truths as personal affirmations.

I am chosen by God.

I am holy and blameless before Him.

I am adopted through His Son.

I am a recipient of His grace.

I am redeemed.

I am forgiven of all my sins.

I have been given an inheritance.

Our Response

What is a fitting response to such overwhelming largess? First, I think a "thank you" would be in order. Not just a one-time "thanks," but an ongoing attitude of gratitude.

> Oh give thanks to the Lord, call upon His name;
> Make known His deeds among the peoples.
> Sing to Him, sing praises to Him;
> Speak of all His wonders.
> Glory in His holy name;
> Let the heart of those who seek the Lord be glad.
>
> 1 Chronicles 16:8–10

A second fitting response is obedience. Not grudging obedience. Not obedience with gritted teeth, but with thankful hearts!

Everything God asks of us is for our good. So when we are tempted to be dishonest or unethical or immoral or lazy or selfish, God says, "Don't do it! It will only hurt you!" Remember who you are. Remember your identity. You do not belong in the world anymore. You are in Christ. "Don't do these things," He says. "Not just for My sake, but for yours! I hate sin because I love you! And sin hurts you."

When we understand who we are, we begin acting like who we are, not who we were. And when we begin to see ourselves as God sees us, we can begin to relax and enjoy God. Certainly there is still work to be done, responsibilities to be assumed, reverence to be maintained. But, as the Westminster Catechism reminds us, "Man's chief end is to glorify God and to enjoy Him forever." Not until we enjoy God have we entered into the fullness of what He wants to give us *in Christ.*

In *Desiring God,* John Piper writes:

1. The longing to be happy is a universal human experience, and it is good, not sinful.

2. We should never try to deny or resist our *longing* to be happy, as though it were a bad impulse. Instead we should seek to intensify this longing and nourish it with whatever will provide the deepest and most enduring satisfaction.

3. The deepest and most enduring happiness is found only in God.

4. The happiness we find in God reaches its consummation when it is shared with others in the manifold ways of love.

5. To the extent we try to abandon the pursuit of our own pleasure, we fail to honor God and love people. Or, to put it positively: the pursuit of pleasure is a necessary part of all worship and virtue. That is,

The chief end of man is to glorify God

by

enjoying Him forever.[1]

I have heard many earnest and well-meaning Christians say, "I don't know why Jesus would die for me." Let me say, gently and kindly, that is a works-oriented statement, not a grace-oriented statement.

It fails to recognize our inherent value: we were created in the image of Christ at birth and placed in Christ at the second birth. It recognizes only our human failures: why would God die for such an unworthy person? But He did not die for us because we were good. He died for us because we are created in His image and have infinite and inherent worth.

We must stop seeing ourselves as ducks or dogs or monkeys—or children of the world. We are children of God! We must begin seeing ourselves as God sees us. We must enter into His joy. Enter into His glory. Dare to accept what He is promising to give. Dare to accept the riches that are ours because we are *in Christ.* The vault is open and the treasures of His blessings are there for *all* who are *in Christ.*

Focus Questions

1. Before reading this chapter, how did you see yourself? What negative imprinting had you experienced?

2. After learning how God sees us, how do you see yourself now?

3. What would you say to a person who says, "I don't know why Jesus would die for me"?

2

Treasures from God the Father
(Ephesians 1:4–6)

A man can no more diminish God's glory by refusing to worship Him than a lunatic can put out the sun by scribbling the word "darkness" on the walls of his cell.

C. S. Lewis

I have a mystery I'd like you to solve. Here are the facts.

One evening, late in 1941, Colonel Robert Montgomery of Scotland Yard stood before the members of the London Mystery Club, a group that enjoyed discussing mystery novels. However, he wasn't there to discuss a Sherlock Holmes story. He was there because he needed help in solving a mystery.

"Recently a stranger arrived in London from South America," the colonel told the group. "Our intelligence sources inform us that this man is probably a Nazi agent, and we believe his principle mission is to smuggle in the currency needed to finance espionage in the United Kingdom.

"A few hours after he stepped off the boat," the colonel continued, "we arranged an automobile accident that sent him to the hospital with a fractured arm. While he was being treated, our staff searched his clothing and his luggage, which consisted of a briefcase containing only some letters from his friends in British Guiana. We discovered nothing else. Either this man is not an enemy agent, or he is an exceedingly clever one.

"We considered a number of possible ploys. He could have mailed counterfeit British currency to himself, but the irregularity of wartime mail makes this rather unlikely. He could have had diamonds implanted in his body surgically, but when we x-rayed his body in the course of determining the extent of his injuries, that possibility was eliminated.

25

"Tomorrow morning this man will walk out of the hospital and merge with our populace. Do you have any suggestions as to how he might be concealing what could amount to thousands of pounds?"

Could you have solved this mystery? When I first read it, I turned my brain inside out but couldn't crack it. Then, after hearing the solution, I thought, "Of course! It's so simple. So obvious. Why didn't I think of that."

Many things in life are like that. We cannot understand them. They have us totally puzzled. Yet when we hear the explanation, we smack our foreheads and say, "Of course."

This Scotland Yard mystery is an example. When the colonel finished talking, the club members turned to one another, whispered for a few moments, and several heads nodded.

Then the president of the club said, "Colonel, we think you have overlooked a rather obvious possibility—the letters in the briefcase. The stamps on them could be rare editions, worth thousands of pounds each."

As it turned out, that was exactly right. So simple . . . so obvious. Why didn't I think of that?

Criminal mysteries are not the only things that stymie me. *Lots* of things in life stymie me. Like . . . how I can lose a pencil when I haven't moved from my desk . . . how accountants figure out the tax laws . . . how nuclear physicists work with the theory of relativity . . . how computer experts program computers . . . how poets understand modern free verse. I know I am not without some mental capacity, and yet I cannot understand many things that other humans seem to comprehend readily. So it should come as no surprise to find that I cannot understand everything about God. And yet one day I will stand before Him with all the difficult and unanswerable questions I have today, and I will smack my glorified forehead with the palm of my heavenly hand and say, "Of course. It's so simple. Why didn't I think of that?"

Early in the book of Ephesians we come up against one of the greatest head-smackers of all time—the first great treasure in the vault of God. It's what theologians call the doctrine of election. Someday we will understand it completely. But for now we just have to take Scripture at face value and understand it as best we can.

This treasure from God the Father has two facets: (1) We are chosen, and (2) we are adopted.

> He *chose* us in Him before the foundation of the world, that we should be holy and blameless before Him. In love He predestined us to *adoption* as sons through Jesus Christ.
>
> Ephesians 1:4–5, italics added

We Are Chosen

God chose us to become His children before the world was even created, Paul says.

Now that raises many questions. Don't we choose to become Christians? How can it be a choice if God has already predetermined it? Does that mean some people cannot become Christians because they are not chosen? How can we have a free will if God is sovereign? And so the struggle goes between the doctrine of the free will of man and the sovereign election of God.

The reality is that the Bible teaches both, without reservation or qualification: God is sovereign (John 6:44; Rom. 8:29–30; Eph. 2:5), and we have a true choice (Matt. 11:28; John 3:16; 1 Tim. 2:1, 4; 2 Pet. 3:9). People have tried to explain this in various ways, but the tension between the two cannot be resolved. Any attempt to do so results in imbalance at best and error at worst. So for us the question is: How do we begin to make sense out of these seeming contradictions?

We begin by recognizing a fundamental principle found in Isaiah 55:9: "For as the heavens are higher than the earth, / So are My ways higher than your ways, / And My thoughts than your thoughts." There is no actual contradiction, for God would never contradict Himself. The apparent contradiction exists either because we do not have full information or because we, as fallen creatures, cannot understand the issue. With our limited human intelligence we cannot and should not expect to understand the Bible completely. The Bible is infinite revelation. It contains truths so simple that a child can understand them and mysteries so complex that even a theological Einstein could not comprehend them.

However, despite the great gap between our finite mental capacity and the Lord's infinite knowledge, God can communicate with us, and has. But when it comes to equally valid truths that seem to contradict each other, we should not try to force the two ideas together. It is not intellectual suicide to simply believe them both. We do it all the time with the rest of creation.

Take light, for instance. Matter cannot be energy and energy cannot be matter. Yet light has properties of both energy and matter. Impossible, but true. We do not, however, question the existence of light.

This is what we call an *antimony,* "a contradiction between two equally valid principles or between inferences correctly drawn from such principles."

Unexplainable things exist all around us in the world of science and nature; so why not in the spiritual realm?

Furthermore, our ability to comprehend God's truth has been radically affected by the Fall. "For now we see in a mirror dimly, but then face to face;

now I know in part, but then I shall know fully just as I also have been fully known" (1 Cor. 13:12). When we stand before God in heaven, we will smack our foreheads and say, "Oh . . . I understand." Until then, we must suspend our finite judgment and hold His infinite truths in tension. It's all part of understanding who God is and who we are.

When we do that, when we accept both truths fully without letting one diminish the other, we can glory in the fact that we have been known and chosen by God from before the creation of the world . . . and at the same time we can commit ourselves unreservedly to the spread of the gospel message, knowing that among those who hear, some may choose salvation.

One is always chosen "for" something, of course. And when it comes to God's elect, we are chosen to be "holy and blameless before Him" (Eph. 1:4). This has both positional and practical dimensions.

When we were born again spiritually, our old self was crucified with Christ, and Christ's righteousness was placed in our heavenly bank account (Eph. 4:24). We have become one with Christ. His righteousness is now our righteousness. Spiritually, therefore, we are holy and blameless in God's eyes because we are "in Christ." This is a positional reality.

But practically speaking, are we really holy and blameless? (In answering this question, we'd better roll up our pant legs, because we have to walk through some deep water. But if we take it slowly and carefully, we'll make it all right.) We don't feel holy and blameless, do we? Why? Because we confuse "blameless" with "sinless."

Holiness means "being set apart for proper use"—or, specifically, being set apart for God. In a practical or functional sense, then, we are holy when we have committed our daily thoughts and actions to God's service. And though we may—and will—serve Him imperfectly, we are holy as long as we set ourselves apart to serve Him. Should we stray, we can repent, recommit ourselves, and once again be functionally holy.

How about blameless though? While we live in a society where nobody wants to take the blame for anything, we know, in fact and indeed, that we have done things for which we ought to be blamed. We have deliberately made wrong choices. We have purposely done things we shouldn't have done. We are to blame.

But that's not what God means by "blameless." He doesn't mean "sinless." Never having done anything wrong is sinless—and we know that's not us. But we can be sinful and still be blameless. How? By handling our sin the right way.

What can we do about our sins? We can't take them back. What's done is done. By contrast, when we do something that injures someone else (we've all been guilty of that), we can acknowledge it, apologize to the person, and do whatever is necessary to make reparation or restitution. We can't do that with sin. No, but we can confess our sins to God, acknowledge our need for His forgiveness, accept His forgiveness, and then leave it in His hands to straighten out the results of our sin. When we've done that, we become blameless.

In Christ we can be holy *and* blameless . . . both positionally *and* practically.

We Are Adopted

Those of you who are old enough will remember G. Gordon Liddy, the menacing mastermind of the Watergate burglaries that toppled President Richard Nixon back in the 1970s. Gordon Liddy was, and still is, a colorful and complex character.

As a sickly and easily frightened child, Liddy resolved to become strong and conquer his fears by facing them down. Because he feared heights and electricity, for example, he would climb to the top of electrical towers. Because he feared rodents, he roasted and ate part of a rat. His will, he determined, would become stronger than anything he confronted.

To Liddy, the world was always a challenge to be conquered. He became a pilot, an FBI agent, an attorney, and a White House aide. Then the Watergate scandal was uncovered—and Liddy was right in the midst of it. But he would not be broken. Subpoenaed to testify in court, he was asked to swear to "tell the truth, the whole truth, and nothing but the truth."

"No," responded Liddy.

He was eventually given a twenty-one-year sentence, served four years, and was paroled. He returned home to his wife and family, started several businesses, and became a popular lecturer. He even accepted some acting roles on television.

One evening during a guest appearance on "Late Night with David Letterman," the talk-show host asked Liddy, "What happens when we die?"

"We are food for the worms," replied Liddy.

Gordon Liddy had conquered every challenge set before him, but he couldn't shake the memory of that casual exchange with Letterman. It created a deep sense of uneasiness—and he didn't know why. He started thinking about God.

"By definition, God is infinite, and we are finite," Liddy reasoned. "It is contrary to the rules of logic for a finite being to be able to apprehend the infinite. So . . . there has to be some communication. That infinite being is going to have to tell me. I am never going to be able to apprehend that myself."

But was there any communication?

"Then," he says, "a light went on in my head. That's what the Bible is all about!" The Bible was not merely a historical record; it was God's means of communicating with finite man.

But since it would be impossible for a finite being to be worthy of the infinite, there must be something more. So that must be where Christ comes in, thought Liddy. God must have sent His Son to win that which we cannot win for ourselves and to continue the communication.

At that point he realized Christ was who He claimed to be, and Gordon Liddy became a Christian. Drawing on the first great treasure in the vault of the Father, he discovered the second: He became a member of God's family.[1]

> He predestined us to adoption as sons through Jesus Christ to Himself,
> according to the kind intention of His will, to the praise of the glory of
> His grace, which He freely bestowed on us in the Beloved.
>
> Ephesians 1:5–6

When God chooses us, we become part of His family—a process the apostle Paul likened to Roman adoption. In his commentary on Ephesians, William Barclay writes: "When the [Roman] adoption was complete it was complete indeed. The person who had been adopted had all the rights of a legitimate son in his new family and completely lost all rights in his old family. In the eyes of the law he was a new person. So new was he that even all debts and obligations connected with his previous family were abolished as if they had never existed."

That, Paul says, is what God has done for us. We were absolutely in the power of sin and of the world. We belonged to the family of Adam. But God, through Jesus, took us out of that family and adopted us into His; and that adoption wipes out the past and makes us new.

Just as a child has no capacity to grasp how much love it takes for a parent to change its diapers and clean up after its messes . . . to chauffeur it around . . . to cope with the demands of adolescence . . . so we have a limited capacity to grasp how much God loves us. But when we do begin to understand all that He has done for us, the only natural response is galloping gratitude.

Why do parents put up with the tears and tantrums, disobedience and demands of children? Because our children bear our image and have our blood pulsing through their veins. Because we love our children and value our relationship with them. We want them to love us and enjoy their relationship with us.

I remember the first time I wrote to my parents and really thanked them for all they had done for me. Later they told me how much that meant to them. And so it is with God—to an infinite degree, of course. He is our spiritual Father, and He longs for the time when we will have some comprehension of what He has done for us . . . when we will have enough understanding to say, "Thank You, Father" . . . when we will rejoice in our relationship with Him.

Often that is easier said than done, because we feel guilty. Like a kid with a messy room. We know the corners of our heart are still cluttered with foolishness and selfishness. Because of our inconsistent lifestyle, we can't shake our sense of inadequacy and unworthiness. We don't dare to believe the freedom of the grace of God.

Yet God chose us before the foundation of the world to be holy and blameless. Knowing full well every sin we would ever commit, He adopted us anyway, clearing our name of all the debts of our old family Adam, through the blood of His beloved Son on the cross.

These things are true, whether we feel like they are or not. Just as the earth is round, even though the landscape before you looks flat. You have learned to accept that fact, despite your feelings. And that is exactly what God asks you to do. Accept the fact that He has chosen you in Christ to make you holy and blameless.

When all is said and done, that's what the great mystery is all about—the sovereignty of God's choosing and adopting, drawing us to Himself. And the free will of men and women responding, praising God for His mercy and grace.

Focus Questions

1. When you became a Christian, did you think it was because of God's sovereignty or because of your own free will? What do you think now?

2. When God adopted you into His family, He paid the debts of your old family Adam and gave you the riches of your new family in Christ. What, specifically, are you most grateful for as a result of your adoption?

3. What would you say if someone asked you what this sentence means: Good people don't get to heaven; perfect people do? (This will be explored more in the next chapter.)

3

Treasures from God the Son

(Ephesians 1:7–12)

*Alexander, Caesar, Charlemagne, and I myself have founded
great empires. . . . But Jesus alone founded His empire upon
love, and to this very day, millions would die for Him. Jesus
Christ was more than a man.*

Napoleon

I have a friend in Indiana who sometimes travels to North Carolina to dig for
emeralds. After studying available geological information, he selects a site, rents
a backhoe, and in a fairly short period of time unearths a huge pile of rock and
rubble. Then he spends hours and days on his hands and knees sifting through
it. Not because he loves rock and rubble, but because he loves emeralds.

In their natural state, emerald crystals are embedded in rock, nonde-
script and indistinguishable to the casual observer, so firmly embedded that
it is difficult to tell where rock leaves off and emerald begins. Once you break
off the foreign deposits, however, you get a glimpse of a crystalline form. Cut
and polished, that crystal becomes a beautiful and valuable jewel.

We're a lot like emeralds. Embedded in the rock and rubble of sin, we
look at ourselves and ask, "What does God see in me? How could He love
me?" But God looks at us and sees the potential. He knows He can break
away the clay—the earth suit in which we are housed—and polish our redeemed soul into a beautiful gem. If we are to enter into the freedom and joy
that God intends for us to have in our salvation, we must understand the
nature and extent of that redemption.

Redemption

In the Roman Empire, of which the apostle Paul was a citizen, slavery
was an accepted institution. Slaves were bought and sold like horses and

cattle. At the height of that civilization, some estimates put the number of slaves at over six million. Slaves could be set free, however. Anyone who wanted to do this could buy a slave—pay the purchase price—then set him or her free. It was called *apolutrosis,* "to buy back for the purpose of setting free." *Apolutrosis* is the word Paul used here for "redemption."

Slavery is not unlike our predicament. We are all enslaved to sin (John 8:34; Rom. 7:14). Sin is our master. If we are to be released from its bondage, someone must pay the price, and the price is death (Rom. 6:23). The only person who could pay that price was Jesus, the Son of God.

We have all sinned. We all deserve to die. Therefore, no other human could die for us, because every other human being deserves to die. Someone who did not deserve to die had to die in our place. That was Christ, which is why it was so important that He was both God and man. If He were not man, He could not die for our sins; if He were not God, it would not have mattered that He died for us. It was essential that He be both God and man.

The price of our redemption was His blood, shed on the cross (1 Pet. 1:18–19). Thanks to the Son of God, we have been redeemed, bought back for the purpose of setting free. And the result of that redemption is the forgiveness of sin.

But why would God love us enough to send His Son to die for us? How could He see anything in us worth dying for? Because God looks past the outer person (the flesh) to the inner person (the spirit). The outer person is the rock and rubble. The inner person is the emerald.

God does not look at rubble and pretend it is emeralds. He sees things as they are: rubble is rubble and emeralds are emeralds. The emeralds are destined for heaven; the rubble will never make it.

The Bible clearly teaches a distinction between the material and immaterial parts of us, and we must look at the relationship and distinction between the two as it relates to salvation (John 3:1–7). We have been born once physically. Now we must be born again spiritually. Thus, the Christian has two dimensions. The immaterial has been born again. The material has not. The immaterial has been redeemed. The material has not.

In Romans 7, Paul refers to the flesh as the outer man and the spirit as the inner man. The outer man is the rubble; the inner man is the emerald.

God looks at us now and is pleased with us in Christ. Not because He overlooks our sin. Not because He doesn't see it. Not because He doesn't care if we sin. But because the spiritual part of us has been born again and is fit for heaven right now, and that is who God is looking at.

We can't look at things the way God does, of course. Left to our own perception, we get confused. Thinking that what we experience, which includes sin, is the only "us" there is, we don't feel redeemed; and sometimes because of that we don't act redeemed. But going beyond our natural perception to the revealed Word of God, we can begin to see the difference and accept, by faith, that we are redeemed.

That is why, though we are not wild about going through it, we must die. We must die, because that is how we shed our bodies. Dying is merely having the redeemed spirit leave behind the fallen body. The redeemed spirit is joined with a holy body in heaven, and our redemption is complete.

Now I am not saying that the spirit is good and the flesh is bad, in the sense of Platonic dualism. I am not saying that it is wrong, for example, to do something that will benefit the flesh, such as physical exercise. Augustine said, "We must care for our bodies as though we were going to live forever, and we must care for our souls as though we were going to die tomorrow." Nor am I saying it is wrong to take pleasure in something physical, such as athletic competition or good food or even the divinely given gift of sex within the institution of marriage. It is good to enjoy that which is good about our physical beings; it is bad to pander to the illicit desires of the flesh.

God gave us our bodies before the Fall, and though they will one day be redeemed, they are not yet redeemed; they are fallen. Somehow, mysteriously, the power of the spirit dwells in our bodies. So when we say that God is pleased with us because we are in Christ, it refers to the spiritual part of us that is totally and fully redeemed when we believe in and receive Jesus as our personal Savior.

God is not playing games with us when He says He is pleased with us . . . that we meet His standards in Christ. We don't have to hoodwink ourselves into believing that we are holy and righteous. While it is true that we are a walking civil war right now—and will be until we die or the Lord returns—the spiritual part of us, the inner man, stands before God today as holy and righteous . . . acceptable, in Christ.

That is what it means to be redeemed. Our sins are gone. Completely, forever. Right now, we are acceptable to God, because we are in Christ, and Christ is acceptable to God.

Forgiveness

According to the March 1991 *U.S. News & World Report,* 78 percent of all Americans believe in heaven and 60 percent believe in hell. Yet there are several misconceptions about both places, and all of them are linked to how good we are. The most common misconception is that when we die, God puts all our good works on one side of a scale and all our bad works on the other side, and if our good works outweigh our bad works, we get into heaven.

The fact is, how good we are on earth has absolutely nothing to do with whether we get to heaven. Goodness isn't the issue. Perfection is.

Goodness isn't enough. God demands perfection. Other than Christ, the best person who has ever lived was not perfect. A broken window cannot be unbroken. And a person who sins cannot unsin. Regardless of how good we are in the eyes of other people, we are unacceptable for heaven. We cannot make ourselves acceptable.

In Old Testament times, once each year the Israelites celebrated a Day of Atonement (Yom Kippur), a day of fasting and sacrifices when the priests and people were cleansed from their sins. On that day the priests killed a goat, its shed blood symbolizing a sacrificial covering for sin. Then they laid hands on another goat, symbolically transferring all the sins of the people to that goat, which was then taken far out into the wilderness so that it could never find its way back. This vividly portrayed to the Israelites that the sins covered by the blood and placed on the scapegoat were gone, never to return.

The Son of God became the ultimate scapegoat. He was sacrificed—His blood shed—and upon Him were laid all of our sins forever (Ps. 103:1–2, 12; Isa. 44:22; Mic. 7:18; Rom. 8:1). He redeemed us—bought us back and set us free—and made us acceptable to God.

Now some people say, "I know that when I became a Christian, He wiped my slate clean. But now I have to help keep the slate clean." That is a noble gesture, but you can't do it!

The issue is forgiveness. If we are not forgiven of every single sin, we die. That means being eternally separated from God. If we have any hope whatsoever of making it to heaven, it will only be because God forgives every one of our sins. Period. Past, present, future.

All.

Not a few, but all.

Not some, but all.

Not most, but all.

All.

When God created the world, all your sins were in the future. He created the world anyway.

When Jesus died on the cross, all your sins were in the future. Jesus died for you anyway.

When you were in the womb, all your sins were in the future. God gave you life anyway.

There is nothing you have ever done or can ever do that will surprise an omniscient God.

And there is nothing you have ever done or can ever do that will earn your acceptance with God. That acceptance comes only through Christ.

There is nothing we can do to enhance it, there is nothing we can do to detract from it, because it depends on Christ, not on us.

When we grasp that fact . . . that salvation is totally free . . . that we can do nothing to earn it, nothing to lose it . . . what an exhilarating, freeing truth it is! Our redemption, our acceptance, our forgiveness—past, present, future—are totally *in Him.*

A man named Jake led me to Jesus a long time ago, and for many years he was my spiritual mentor. In the summer of his seventy-first year, Jake's body succumbed to the assault of cancer, and he graduated to his heavenly home. He had one word of epitaph carved on his tombstone: FORGIVEN. Jake understood, and he helped me understand.

Inheritance

Imagine that the year is 1875, and you are prospecting for diamonds in the remote mountains of South Africa, far from the nearest civilization. Somehow a courier finds you and tells you that your rich uncle has died in San Francisco and left you a vast fortune. To collect it, however, you must present yourself to his estate attorney in that city.

At that moment you discover you are fabulously wealthy. You now own a mansion in the city and a summer home in the country. Fine clothes, concerts, exhibits, powerful connections—all these and more are suddenly and wonderfully yours.

There's only one problem. You're not in San Francisco to collect it and enjoy it.

Oh, there is some joy now in the anticipation, in just knowing it's true. And the courier has brought you a good sum of money to pay for your return trip. But it will take three weeks of hard travel just to get to Cape Town, and three months over rough seas to get to New York, and another six months of bone-jarring travel across the United States to San Francisco.

Wealthy? Beyond measure. But you have to endure at least ten months of hard living before you get to experience your wealth.

The Christian is in a similar situation. The Bible presents a picture we can barely imagine. Wealth, purpose, love, and power await us in heaven. For now, however, the limitations of earth are very much with us. Yet we are no longer just earthlings. We have been chosen and adopted into a royal family. We are children of God, citizens of heaven, and we must learn what is expected of us and begin to act like it. We have been chosen and adopted by the Lord and King, who has, through His Son, bestowed upon us redemption, forgiveness, and a rich inheritance.

Someday we will understand things that are now incomprehensible (John 16:23). Our minds, now darkened by the presence of sin, will be free to function clearly. Our true desires will be fulfilled, for God alone can perfectly complete us. "Thou hast formed us for Thyself, and our hearts are restless till they find their rest in Thee," declared Augustine in the first chapter of *Confessions*. It is heaven we long for. It is God we seek.

Emotionally, our passions will be pure and sinless. Our fellowship and love for God will be reflected in intimate love and complete unity with other believers.

Physically, the troubles and distractions caused by the constant demands of weak and dying bodies will disappear. We will not get tired or diseased. We will not have to worry about clothing or food.

Throughout the Scriptures, the doctrine of the resurrection provides genuine hope for the future. Now we know God by faith, but then we will know Him face to face. Now we suffer, but then we will realize that the "sufferings of this present time are not worthy to be compared with the glory that is to be revealed to us" (Rom. 8:18). Now we are surrounded by death, but then death will be swallowed up in victory. By faith, believers can say with Paul, "O death, where is your victory? O death, where is your sting?" (1 Cor. 15:55).

This is our inheritance. Great, glorious, and good. It takes us beyond our wildest imaginations . . . to full knowledge, glory, and enjoyment of God.

Many of us struggle with our feelings about this. We may not feel holy and righteous. We may not feel valuable. We wonder why God would love us.

We look at our performance, rather than God's perfection.

We look at our circumstances, rather than God's promises.

Let me ask you a question. "Why would you love a baby?"

A baby causes a mother more physical pain than most women experience at any other time in their lives.

A baby screams demandingly for hours on end and soils its clothes at random but persistent intervals.

Then that baby, who is part of you and carries your image, begins to grow. It starts to recognize you and respond to your love. It begins to express love and obey love. And suddenly all the pain and sleepless nights and work and worry and love are worth it.

This finite parent-child relationship is merely a reflection of our relationship with our heavenly Father. We are made in His image, and God sees what we truly are underneath our body of sin. He sees what we will become when we are conformed to the image of Christ. He knows that someday we will be able to love and obey and worship Him perfectly. So for now, when we tell God that we love Him in our imperfect way, I believe He smiles and says, "It's all worth it. It's tough, but it's worth it."

A newborn baby does not have to earn a mother's or a father's love, and we do not have to earn God's love. He gives it to us simply because we are in His image.

We are redeemed, not because of what we have done but because of what Jesus has done.

We are forgiven, not because of who we are but because of who He is.

We have inherent and infinite value, not because of who we are but because of who God is.

We are celestial royalty. We must recognize and rejoice in this. For if we do not see ourselves as royalty, we will not act like royalty.

And if we want to see what we are worth to God, we only have to look at the cross.

Focus Questions

1. Do you have any difficulty accepting the fact that God sees you as acceptable in Christ? If so, why?

2. How would you answer our earlier question now: What does good people don't get to heaven, perfect people do mean?

3. What part of your inheritance in Christ are you most looking forward to? What part of being a Christian do you enjoy most now, even before getting to "San Francisco"?

4

Treasures from God
the Holy Spirit

(Ephesians 1:13–14)

This third Person is called, in technical language, the Holy Ghost or the "spirit" of God. Do not be worried or surprised if you find it (or Him) rather vaguer or more shadowy in your mind than the other two. I think there is a reason why that must be so. In the Christian life you are not usually looking at Him: He is always acting through you. If you think of the Father as something "out there," in front of you, and of the Son as someone standing at your side, helping you to pray, trying to turn you into another son, then you have to think of the third Person as something inside you, or behind you.

C. S. Lewis

*A*lexander the Great, it is said, once sent an emissary to Egypt. This representative of the great ruler traveled without weapons or military escort, carrying only the seal of Alexander.

The emissary met with the mighty king of Egypt, who stood with his army behind him, and communicated the message from Alexander the Great. "Cease hostilities against Alexander's interests," he said. The king of Egypt, wishing to save face, said that he would consider the request and let the emissary know.

At that, Alexander's man drew a circle in the dirt around the king of Egypt and said, "Do not leave this circle without informing me of your response."

Talk about nerve! The emissary was unarmed and alone. The king of Egypt had an entire army at his back. Yet the king dared not touch the man because he carried the seal of Alexander the Great. To touch the emissary was

41

to touch Alexander. To disobey the emissary was to disobey Alexander. To give affront to the emissary was to give affront to Alexander.

Realizing this, after a long, tense moment in which the king assessed his options, he said, "Tell Alexander he has his request," and then stepped out of the circle.

We Are Sealed

Today we wear signet rings as jewelry. But in the ancient world the ring bearing the insignia of an official was a form of power, authority, or validation. When stamped into hot wax, the ring transferred a seal or insignia. If a letter or a public proclamation bore the seal of a king or a governor, for instance, it was immediately recognized as carrying all the weight of that office.

In the Scripture we see several instances when seals play a prominent role. For example, when King Darius had Daniel thrown into a lions' den, the king had his servants block the entrance with a stone and place the seal of his signet ring on that stone. No one dared break the seal without incurring the wrath of the king (Daniel 6).

In the book of Esther, when King Ahasuerus gave Haman power and authority, "the king took his signet ring from his hand and gave it to Haman. . . . Then the king's scribes were summoned . . . and it was written just as Haman commanded . . . being written in the name of King Ahasuerus and sealed with the king's signet ring" (Esther 3:10, 12).

When the Roman soldiers rolled the stone over Jesus' tomb, they sealed it with Pilate's seal. No one dared break the seal without incurring the wrath of Pilate.

An official seal gave the bearer power and authority, but the power and authority were only as significant as the person behind the insignia.

In Ephesians 1:13, Paul promises believers that, "after listening to the message of truth" and "having also believed," they have been "sealed in Him with the Holy Spirit of promise." The Holy Spirit is *our* seal. The God of the universe has stamped His mark on our lives.

Belief is a spiritual watershed. It is that mysterious and wonderful instant in which we cross from death into life.

Before we believe, we are not Christians.

After we believe, we are.

Before we believe, we are not redeemed.

After we believe, we are.

Before we believe, none of the blessings in Christ are ours. After we believe, every spiritual blessing in Christ is ours. Upon belief, the blessings of the Holy Spirit come to us because:

> . . . having also believed, [we] were sealed in Him with the Holy Spirit of promise, who is given as a pledge of our inheritance . . .
>
> Ephesians 1:13–14

We Are Secure

In addition to being sealed—which is a sign that we are God's own possession, and thus protected by His power and authority—we are also secure. That is, nothing can ever happen to remove us from God's ownership and protection. We know this because Paul writes that the Holy Spirit was given to us as a pledge. A pledge is a down payment, guaranteeing the rest of the payment in full at a later date.

In ancient documents, the word translated here as "pledge" was used to refer to earnest money exchanged in the purchase of an animal or even a wife. In the New Testament, this word also occurs in 2 Corinthians 5:1–2, 5:

> For we know that if the earthly tent which is our house is torn down, we have a building from God, a house not made with hands, eternal in the heavens. For indeed in this house we groan, longing to be clothed with our dwelling from heaven. . . . Now He who prepared us for this very purpose is God, who gave to us the Spirit as a pledge [or down payment].

The point is this. When we believe in and receive Jesus, we are born again spiritually. But we are not born again physically. In order to go to heaven, we have to get rid of this body we are in and get a new body. That happens when we die or when Jesus comes back, whichever is first. So we are not yet fully redeemed. We are redeemed spiritually, but not physically.

God has left us on earth to advance His cause. As a guarantee that He is actually going to complete the redemption process, He has given the Holy Spirit to live in each of us. That is His down payment . . . His assurance to us that the day will come when He will give us a new body and receive us into heaven (Rom. 8:23). Because God would never enter into an agreement without being true to the agreement, and because God will never lack the resources to make the full payment after He has made a down payment, we are as secure as the character and riches of God.

In summary, then, we can say that we are sealed in the Holy Spirit. We have been identified as God's own possession, and we are protected by His authority. We are secured by the down payment of His Holy Spirit who lives in us and who is the guarantee that God will ultimately give us a new body and receive us into heaven, completing our final redemption.

But What About . . . ?

A couple of predictable questions come up any time you study or examine this passage.

The first one is, *What do you do with passages of Scripture that seem to suggest that you can lose your salvation?*

What do we do, for example, with verses such as, "it is the one who has endured to the end who will be saved" (Matt. 10:22)? Or what about those people who seem to have a conversion experience and then return to a degenerate lifestyle? Or those who claim to believe in Christ but evidence no change at all in their lives? And what about verses like Galatians 5:19–21, where the apostle Paul is talking to believers?

> Now the deeds of the flesh are evident, which are: immorality, impurity, sensuality, idolatry, sorcery, enmities, strife, jealousy, outbursts of anger, disputes, dissensions, factions, envying, drunkenness, carousing, and things like these, of which I forewarn you just as I have forewarned you that those who practice such things shall not inherit the kingdom of God.

Is there a contradiction here or what?

Ultimately, of course, such questions have led to a number of different theological beliefs on the matter.

As is usually the case, the truth lies somewhere in the middle. It is true that once we are saved, we are always saved. There is no way to reverse the treasures that are ours once we are in Christ (Rom. 8:31–39). But it is also true that if a person's life evidences no ongoing change, there is no biblical basis for assuming the person was ever saved in the first place. We cannot say to someone who claims to be a Christian but is living in flagrant, willful sin, "I know you are not a Christian." But we can say, "Your lifestyle gives you no comfort from Scripture to assume that you are a Christian" (Luke 3:8; 2 Cor. 13:5).

If a person truly believes (in the biblical sense of the word, which means not just head knowledge but also heart response), then he is not only sealed by the Holy Spirit, but also has been given the Holy Spirit as a pledge. Thus, he is secure.

The second major question that often comes up is, *Is it possible to be a Christian and live in sin?*

In answer to that, let's look at 1 Corinthians 5:1–5:

> It is actually reported that there is immorality among you. . . .
> And you have become arrogant, and have not mourned instead. . . . I
> have decided to deliver such a one to Satan for the destruction of his
> flesh, that his spirit may be saved in the day of the Lord Jesus.

The Corinthians Paul is addressing here were Christians, yet they were living in terrible sin. So, yes, Christians can sin and still be Christians. The apostle John has written:

> If we say that we have no sin, we are deceiving ourselves, and the truth
> is not in us. If we confess our sins, He is faithful and righteous to forgive
> us our sins and to cleanse us from all unrighteousness.
>
> 1 John 1:8–9

However, if we, as Christians, live in prolonged, willful sin, the Lord feels free to bring sorrow, unhappiness, and even calamity into our lives to convince us of the error of our ways and bring us to our senses. He may even take our lives (1 Cor. 11:27–32; 1 John 5:16–17). Our body may be destroyed, but our soul will be saved.

So, once saved, always saved? Yes.

Why? Because having believed, we have been sealed by the Holy Spirit, who has been given as a down payment for our final redemption in heaven.

True belief involves commitment to the truth and a personal embracing of that truth. True belief has colossal consequences: salvation, redemption, forgiveness, and inheritance. When we are sealed with the Holy Spirit, all these treasures are secure. The vault, the entire panorama and promise of God, lies open before us.

In the Father
   we are chosen;
   we are adopted.

In the Son
   we are redeemed;
   we are forgiven.

In the Holy Spirit
>   we are sealed;
>   we are secured.

All of these riches are on deposit in our eternal bank account, safe-guarded by something much more sound than the FDIC. We won't end up like the family of the rich old man who, gathered for the reading of the will, heard the attorney say: "I, Charles Smith, being of sound mind, spent it all!"
As Peter writes:

> Blessed be the God and Father of our Lord Jesus Christ, who according to His great mercy has caused us to be born again to a living hope through the resurrection of Jesus Christ from the dead, to obtain an inheritance which is imperishable and undefiled and will not fade away, reserved in heaven for you.
>
>   1 Peter 1:3–4

I read a story one time of a man named Frederick Nolan, a believer living in North Africa, who was fleeing from his enemies during a time of persecution. Relentlessly, they chased him on foot through the African countryside until he fell exhausted into a small cave. He expected his enemies to find him soon, but he was not able to keep running, and there was no place else to hide.

Sitting there, waiting for death, he noticed a spider weaving a web. Within minutes, the little insect had woven a beautiful pattern across the small mouth of the cave. When the pursuers arrived, they saw the spider's web and assumed that he could not be in the cave. If he had entered, they figured, he would have broken the web. So they went on, and Nolan was safe.

Later, Nolan wrote:

> Where God is, a spider's web is like a wall,
> Where God is not, a wall is like a spider's web.

That is like the Holy Spirit and our security in Him. The Holy Spirit takes up silent residence within us. He is soft and quiet. His presence in us seems like a delicate thing, easily broken, perhaps, like a spider's web. But not so. "Where God is, a spider's web is like a wall." God has woven the web of the Spirit over the doorway of our life.

He has sealed us with the Holy Spirit of promise, claiming us as His own possession and protecting us with His power; and He has pledged himself to giving us a new body and receiving us into heaven.

Focus Questions

1. If you made a down payment with the most valuable possession you have—even a family member—what would your down payment be? What insight does that give you into the fact that the Holy Spirit is God's down payment for our redemption?

2. What would you tell someone who doubted his or her salvation because of sin in his or her life?

3. If God failed to finalize our redemption, it would mean that He would forfeit the down payment He put on us—the Holy Spirit. What does that tell you about your security in Him?

5

The Giver Behind the Gift
(Ephesians 1:15–23)

Why are individual Christians weak? . . . because they have forgotten what God is like and what He promises to do for those who trust Him. Ask an average Christian to talk about God. After getting past the expected answers, you will find that his god is a little god of vacillating sentiments. He is a god who would like to save the world but who cannot. He would like to restrain evil, but somehow he finds it beyond his power. So he has withdrawn into semi-retirement, being willing to give good advice in a grandfatherly sort of way, but for the most part he has left his children to fend for themselves in a dangerous environment. Such a god is not the God of the Bible . . . the God of the Bible is not weak; He is strong. He is all-mighty. Nothing happens without His permission or apart from His purposes. Nothing disturbs or puzzles Him. His purposes are always accomplished.

James Montgomery Boice

*W*e are information addicts. We have newspapers and news magazines and news programs. We have ABC and NBC, CBS and PBS, and now the round-the-clock sources of CNN and C-Span. In an instant we can have the halls of government, Senate hearing rooms, political candidates, and world leaders in our living rooms. We are probably the most well-informed people who have ever lived. Information can be translated into knowledge, and knowledge, as they say, is power.

But when it comes to our eternal destiny, all this wisdom of the world fades away. It is spiritual knowledge and spiritual wisdom we need—and that is quite another matter.

As we have already said, we need to understand who we are. If we don't see ourselves as beloved children of God, chosen in Him before the foundation of the world and adopted into His heavenly family . . . if we don't see ourselves as the object of the cosmic affections and attentions of the Creator of the universe, redeemed, forgiven, enriched, sealed, and secure . . . if we don't see ourselves as holy and righteous beings destined for glory above, we won't act like it. That is why Paul began his letter assuring us that these things are true.

The common misconception is that Christian growth makes God like us better. But what we do or don't do has no effect on our position before God.

We can't do anything to make Him love us more . . . we can't do anything to make Him love us less . . . because He already loves us totally and perfectly in Christ.

We can't do anything to make Him forgive us more . . . we can't do anything to make Him forgive us less . . . because He has already forgiven us everything in Christ.

Positionally we are secure in Him, because we are in Christ. We are already accepted, forgiven, in His favor, in His grace.

We must believe that, accept that, and live accordingly, or we will not have the Christian experience God wants us to have.

Grasping this is not merely a matter of human understanding, however. Having these truths penetrate our hearts must include the ministry of the Holy Spirit to us, illumining our mind to the spiritual truth. Perception of these dramatic realities is usually a gradual dawning of understanding as we focus on the truth and as God works in us to bring about that understanding. That is why, after telling us the blessings that are ours in the Father, Son, and Holy Spirit, Paul prays that we will "get it"—that we will comprehend it all (Eph. 1:15–19). Since we cannot comprehend it by ourselves, Paul's prayer is logical.

Our Understanding

Knowing God is central in the life of a Christian. Not knowing *of* God . . . not knowing *about* God . . . but knowing God. Not a superficial or even an intellectual or philosophical knowledge, but a personal, intimate, and experiential knowledge of our Author and Creator. So much of living a satisfying Christian life boils down to whether or not we do the things God asks of us—obedience, if you will. But to obey God, we must trust Him. And to trust Him, we must know Him.

In that spirit, Paul prays "that the God of our Lord Jesus Christ, the Father of glory, may give to you a spirit of wisdom and of revelation in the knowledge of Him" (Eph. 1:17).

This is truly a great prayer to be prayed for the Christian. It is a prayer we can pray for each other. It is a prayer we can pray for a struggling teenage child or a struggling new Christian. It is a prayer we can pray for ourselves.

The word *sophia,* translated "wisdom," is equivalent to "insight into the true nature of things." This is not the cause-and-effect wisdom of the world; it is true knowledge and understanding of things as they really are. The word "revelation," whose root word is *apocalypsis,* meaning "to unfold or unveil," has nothing to do with the giving of new revelation, as in the Scriptures. It means grasping or understanding that which already exists. In other words, we need insight into the true nature of things as they exist and really are.

So when Paul prays that we might have a spirit of wisdom, he is praying that we might be given a capacity for spiritual discernment. When he prays that we might have a spirit of revelation in the knowledge of Him, he is praying that we might experience, through the ministry of the Holy Spirit, an unfolding or unveiling of the person and work of God to us.

Paul's whole point here is that we should come to a personal and experiential knowledge of the wonderful person who bestowed on us all the spiritual blessings which he had just mentioned. Since God is the only One who can make this spiritual truth known to us, Paul asks God to have that ministry in us.

Our Enlightenment

Then Paul goes on to pray that we might have more than just a personal knowledge of God. He prays that we might be enlightened—to know what this wonderful person has done for us. In this regard, his prayer encompasses three things.

First, he prays that we may know the "hope of His calling"—that is, the assurance of our salvation. As the hymn writer penned it:

> My hope is built on nothing less
> Than Jesus' blood and righteousness. . . .
>
> When all around my soul gives way,
> He then is all my hope and stay.

Paul wants us to grasp that hope, for without it, life is hard.

Second, he prays that we may know "the riches of the glory of His inheritance." Do you think the Kennedys are rich? Do you think Ross Perot is rich? Do you think the queen of England is rich? Well, in eternal accounting, they are paupers. *You* are rich. Everything Jesus has, you have. The cattle on a thousand hills? Yours. A mansion in heaven? Yours. Acres of diamonds? Yours. Paul prays that you will begin to understand just how great your inheritance in Christ really is.

And finally, the apostle prays that we may know "the surpassing greatness of His power toward us who believe."

This is not the power God gives to believers, but the power He exercises in our behalf, assuring our salvation. In fact, everything Paul mentions in these verses is an example of the power God used in raising Christ from the dead. Thus, in a sense, God is saying: "Because I did all that for Jesus, it is assurance that I can exercise whatever power is necessary to assure your complete salvation. If I did this for Jesus, I can do this for you!"

We must pace ourselves, however. This knowledge, this understanding is continuous and progressive. It does not come in quick and complete packages. You can't pray for it today and have Federal Express deliver it to your door tomorrow.

We need a new attitude, a new disposition, a new mindset if we are to become spiritual scholars. We need to be constantly testing our spiritual health. And that means knowing who we are and what we have been given, not merely as an intellectual exercise or theological theorizing, but with every bit of our heart, soul, and mind.

As Paul himself later told the Philippians:

> Not that I have already obtained it, or have already become perfect, but I press on in order that I may lay hold of that for which also I was laid hold of by Christ Jesus. Brethren, I do not regard myself as having laid hold of it yet; but one thing I do: forgetting what lies behind and reaching forward to what lies ahead, I press on toward the goal for the prize of the upward call of God in Christ Jesus.
>
> Philippians 3:12–14

Knowing God

How well do we know God?

Isn't it true, more often than not, that the God you picture in your mind is old, has a long beard—and maybe leans on a cane? . . . He wears a robe . . . sandals. He's not too sure about modern things like advanced nuclear physics, dense packs, laser beams, and electronic computers. He's more of a kind old grandfather that is gonna be there when you need Him, and you can trust Him because He is wise and generous. He could handle most things today. But He's sort of losing touch.[1]

There are very few prayers in the Bible in which people asked God for *things*. And those there are do not offer prayers for material goods or for personal well-being, but for intangible "things" like spiritual enlightenment and enablement—that the recipient might know God, serve God, and become more like Him.

No man has seen God at any time. Yet Paul prays, "That I may know Him, and the power of His resurrection and the fellowship of His sufferings, being conformed to His death" (Phil. 3:10).

What were we made for?

To know God.

What aim should we set ourselves in life?

To know God.

What is the eternal life Jesus gives?

Knowledge of God.

What is the best thing in life?

Knowledge of God.

What gives God the most pleasure?

Our knowledge of Himself.

What gives us the most pleasure?

Our knowledge of God.

What is the chief end of man?

To know God and enjoy Him forever.

Graduating summa cum laude in the spiritual realm isn't easy, of course. We have trouble even imagining what it is like to know God. Yet something deep within us realizes that all true and lasting meaning in life is found in knowing the God who is there.

But how do we do this?

In James Packer's classic work, *Knowing God,* he writes: "Knowing God involves, first, listening to God's word and receiving it as the Holy Spirit interprets it, in application to oneself; second, noting God's nature and character, as His word and works reveal it; third, accepting His invitations and doing what He commands; fourth, recognizing, and rejoicing in, the love that He has shown in thus approaching one and drawing one into this divine fellowship."[2]

What does it mean to know God? It means we

- read and believe His Word,
- recognize His character,
- accept His Son,
- obey His commands,
- rejoice in His love.

We know God by faith in Christ. "He who has seen Me has seen the Father" (John 14:9).

We know God by spending time with Him in prayer.

We know God by faith, assent, consent, commitment, prayer, and obedience.

Oswald Chambers wrote, "The best measure of the spiritual life is not its ecstasies but its obedience."[3]

Listen to the call of God in your life. Listen to that still, small voice whispering truth in your ear, telling you that

there is more to life than you are experiencing;

meaning in life does not come by accumulating possessions or receiving recognition;

unless God fixes the center of your life, all those relationships you have or long to have are just planets without a sun;

you are inherently flawed and will never taste the longings of your soul unless He remakes you.

life has no satisfaction unless it is lived with Him and for Him.

Listen to God calling you to Himself.

Everything else is just a pot of gold at the end of the rainbow. When you get to where it was supposed to be, it disappears.

Answer the call of God to know Him better. Nothing else . . . nothing . . . will satisfy.

Focus Questions

1. What could you do to cooperate with God's work in giving you "a spirit of wisdom and of revelation in the knowledge of Him"?

2. Paul prays that we might grasp the "hope of our calling," "the riches of our inheritance," and "the greatness of His power." But our grasp of these is dependent on God's ministry of enlightenment to us. That being true, what should be our attitude toward the acquisition of these insights?

3. Re-read James Packer's presentation of what it means to know God. What is the most important first step you can take to know God better?

6

Masterpieces on Display
(Ephesians 2:1–22)

Looking forward to the eternal world is not . . . a form of escapism or wishful thinking, but one of the things a Christian is meant to do. . . . If you read history you will find that the Christians who did most for the present world were those who thought most of the next. The Apostles themselves, who set on foot the conversion of the Roman Empire, the great men who built up the Middle Ages, the English Evangelicals who abolished the slave trade, all left their mark on earth, precisely because their minds were occupied with heaven. It is since Christians have largely ceased to think of the other world that they have become so ineffective in this.

C. S. Lewis

Some time back my wife, Margie, and I enjoyed the opportunity of viewing the works of two major artists: a display of the etchings of Rembrandt at the University of Notre Dame and an exhibit of the major works of Georgia O'Keefe at the Chicago Museum of Art. These great artists lived centuries and continents apart, and their work is very different. Masterful, but different. Distinctive. In fact, every great artist has a unique style that sets him or her apart.

When you see weird little cubes of color like pieces of a puzzle put together wrong, you know you are looking at a Picasso. When you see limp objects draped like wet laundry over foreboding landscapes, you have a Dali. Elongated figures, stretched to two or three times their normal height, mean an El Greco.

You can also tell a great deal about an artist by studying his or her style and subject matter. In his succession of self-portraits, Van Gogh depicts his descent into madness. Michelangelo's sculpture reveals his idealism. Norman

Rockwell's celebration of Americana exudes his optimism. Look closely at the art, and you will discover the artist.

You and I are works of art, too, intended to display the glory of our Creator. (You are probably tempted to say, "Well, if I'm a work of art, it isn't going to be much of a display!")

When a Southern sculptor was asked how he created his stone master-piece of Robert E. Lee, he said, "I just got a big block of marble and chipped away everything that didn't look like Robert E. Lee."

A sculptor will tell you that he sees his final creation in detail before he ever begins to work the stone. So, in a sense, he really does chip away everything that doesn't look like what he is creating.

When we become Christians, we are like blocks of marble. God already knows how He wants us to look, and He begins chipping away everything that doesn't conform.

All we can see is ourselves, however, before He is finished with us, so we conclude that this is all we will ever be.

We say . . .

I'm not beautiful. I'm not a work of art.

He says . . .

But I'm not finished with you yet.

This big corner over here doesn't look like it belongs.

But I'm not finished with you yet.

This part is chipped and rough.

But I'm not finished with you yet.

This section hasn't even been touched.

But I'm not finished with you yet.

This surface needs to be sanded, smoothed, and polished.

But I'm not finished with you yet.

When He is finished, we'll be perfect, flawless—a tribute to the glory of our Creator. The universe will take one look at us and cry out, "Glory to God."

But why would God do this? Why would He fashion us into works of art through whom He can bring glory to Himself and to whom He can express His kindness forever?

What Do We Look Like?

The greatest motivating force in the universe is love—and it all origi-nates and culminates in God. "For God so loved the world, that He gave" (John 3:16). Love gives. If it doesn't give . . . it isn't love. It may cause chills to run up and down your spine. It may take your breath away. But if it doesn't give . . . it isn't love.

God looked at our hopeless condition and, motivated by His love for us, He gave us a way out.

"And you were dead" begins the second chapter of Ephesians.

We were dead. Are we clear about this? *We were dead.* Without hope. Lost. Destined for an eternity separated from God. If we do not fully comprehend this, we will never understand why the power of God is so essential in our lives. Or how great that power is. Or what that power has done for us.

"And you were dead." Spiritually dead. Separated from God.

Why? Because of sin.

Sin kills. And we are sinners.

We do not become a liar when we lie; we lie because we are liars. We do not become a thief when we steal; we steal because we are thieves. Sin is part of us (Matt. 15:18–19; Rom. 3:23; 5:12; 6:23).

Give people the most ideal conditions, and they will still go wrong. No one has ever yet produced a Utopia, and no one ever will. Because as soon as you let people in, you let sin in.

Man didn't fall in hell. He fell in Paradise!

All of us are born with a spiritual birth defect! No one has to teach two-year-old Johnny to be selfish. "Come on now, Johnny, say 'No! Mine!'" Selfishness comes naturally to Johnny. All of us start with a bias toward evil, with a will that is in bondage to and under the dominion of Satan, with lusts and evil desires waiting for an opportunity to demonstrate themselves.

But God—two of the greatest words in the New Testament—but God did not leave us in our lost and hopeless condition.

> But God, being rich in mercy, because of His great love with which He loved us, even when we were dead in our transgressions, made us alive together with Christ . . . and raised us up with Him, and seated us with Him in the heavenly places, in Christ Jesus, in order that in the ages to come He might show the surpassing riches of His grace in kindness toward us in Christ Jesus.
>
> Ephesians 2:4–7

He made us alive with Christ.

He raised us up with Christ.

He seated us with Christ.

"Sitting down is a sign of completion," writes Martyn Lloyd-Jones. "When a man has finished his task he sits down. And Christ has sat down. What else does it mean? No longer labour, but rest. But still more important, victory! . . . A sign of victory! He sits down victorious. And you and I are in Christ, and symbolically, we are seated with Him in the heavenly places. The work of your redemption is already complete, you need nothing further, it has all been done."

We have become His masterpiece, His work of art. And just as a masterpiece hanging in the Louvre brings glory to its creator, so we bring glory to God.

Many of our problems and struggles in the Christian life stem from the fact that we do not comprehend the significance of what we have become in Christ. We still identify with earth more than we identify with heaven; we live more like "earthlings" than "heavenlings." We need to transfer our affections and values to heaven, to spend more time cultivating a heavenly mindset.

If we do not understand who we have become in Christ and do not identify with that new person, then doing the right thing becomes even more difficult. When the going gets rough, we get weary. We are tempted to do wrong more than we want to do right. Doing the right thing becomes a matter of unconvinced willpower, and unconvinced willpower doesn't last long in the crunch. It is hard enough to do the right thing when you believe deeply. It's nearly impossible when you don't.

If we do not understand who we became when we accepted Christ, we'll have a diminished capacity to live a proper lifestyle. The commands and practical teachings of Scripture, for example those in Ephesians 4–6, become a matter of gritting our teeth and trudging into a legalistic set of do's and don'ts.

But if we understand who we have become, we say, "I'll do this because it is consistent with who I am, and my life will be more satisfying in the long run because of it."

Everything God asks of us, He asks based on something He has already done for us. And everything He asks of us, He asks in order to give something good to us. When we embrace these two truths, obedience becomes much easier.

What Does Our Family Look Like?

In the second chapter of Ephesians, the apostle Paul moves from the individual's life to corporate life, and we begin to get our first glimpses of the mystery he calls the church.

In eternity past God created something for eternity future—namely, a people to enjoy and glorify Him forever. In eternity present—what we know as earthly time and history—God is in the process of summing up all things in Christ. To do that, He had to do two things: He had to make alive that which was dead and to bring together that which was separate.

After God brought life to that which was dead, as we have just discussed, His second great challenge was bringing together that which was separated.

During the Old Testament period, if you were born a Jew, you had immediate access to the message of salvation. God did not choose the Jewish nation to the exclusion of all the other nations of the world; He chose the Jewish nation in order to reach all the other nations of the world. As the psalmist said, "God blesses us [Israel], / That all the ends of the earth may fear Him" (Ps. 67:7).

The covenant of promise was given to the Jewish nation—namely, that God would send them a Messiah, a Savior. The Abrahamic Covenant was the supreme covenant God made with the nation of Israel: "I will make you a great nation, / And I will bless you, / And make your name great; / And so you shall be a blessing; / And I will bless those who bless you, / And the one who curses you I will curse. / And in you all the families of the earth shall be blessed" (Gen. 12:2–3). Later, other more specific covenants flowed out of this one, but this covenant with Abraham surrounded and determined all of God's dealings with Israel.

Gentiles were strangers to this covenant because they were not a part of God's dealings with Israel. The separation was so great that, in obedience to the Mosaic Law, Jews could not even eat with Gentiles, enter their homes, or socialize with them. The two were completely segregated.

Gentiles worshiped many gods, but they did not worship the true God. The Gentile world was without God because they did not want Him. Though they knew about God, they did not honor Him as God, and their foolish hearts were darkened (Rom. 1:21).

But God did not leave the Gentiles in this lost and hopeless condition. He sent a Messiah, a Savior—His Son—not only to bring them salvation, but to tear down forever the separation between Jews and Gentiles. Through the substitutionary death of Christ, both Jews and Gentiles could be saved. Through Christ the system of separation established in the Mosaic Law was abolished, and Jews and Gentiles were united. Through Christ, the redeemed of God became fellow citizens with all the saints.

This was not some big organization, some Saints Incorporated. Rather, God established a new spiritual entity called the church, where all believers had equal standing, where there was no distinction between Jew and Gentile, male and female, slave and free.

That which was dead had been made alive, and that which was separate had been brought together—in Christ. When He did this, He created something totally new: the church.

"I will build my church," Jesus said to His disciples, "and the gates of hell shall not prevail against it" (Matt. 16:18 KJV).

World leaders come and go, countries ebb and flow, political systems wax and wane. Yet the church remains constant, and the affairs of God remain dominant in the affairs of men. The dictatorship in Ethiopia didn't stamp out the church. The Communist regime in China didn't stamp out the church. The oppression of Stalinism in the Soviet Union didn't stamp out the church. The God-is-dead movement in the United States and Europe didn't stamp out the church.

I remember well when John Lennon proclaimed that the Beatles were more popular than Jesus Christ. Though I was a new Christian at the time, I remember shaking my head and thinking, *What a profoundly limited perspective. The church will be alive and well when the Beatles are not even a footnote in history.*

Paul uses three images to describe this unique entity. The church, he says, is like a kingdom, a family, and a temple.

> So then you are no longer strangers and aliens, but you are fellow-*citizens* with the saints, and are of God's *household*, having been built upon the foundation of the apostles and prophets, Christ Jesus Himself being the corner stone, in whom the whole building, being fitted together is growing into a holy *temple* in the Lord.

A Kingdom

When you travel abroad and cross borders from country to country, you quickly become aware of how important your own citizenship is and how valuable your passport is. As a citizen of one country, you are separate and distinct from citizens of other countries.

But in addition to the nations of earth, with their temporal authority, there are two spiritual kingdoms in this world. Each of us belongs to one or the other. Either the kingdom of Satan or the kingdom of God has ultimate dominion over our lives.

When we become Christians, we move out of the kingdom of Satan into the kingdom of God (Col. 1:13). As members of this spiritual kingdom, we have allegiance to our monarch, Christ the king. As members of this kingdom, we are bound by the laws of the kingdom. We share the resources of the kingdom, and we enjoy the protection of the king.

If you travel abroad, you will soon become very grateful to be a citizen of the United States. U.S. influence around the world is considerable, and were you to have any trouble, help and protection are as near as the American Consulate.

As Americans, we can be proud of our heritage . . . proud to be part of a nation that has produced the likes of George Washington, Thomas Jefferson, and Abraham Lincoln. But in the kingdom of God we become "fellow citizens with the saints." Someday we will sit down with Abraham and Moses and David, Luther and Calvin and Wesley.

A Family

As part of the church, we move beyond citizenship, however, to a much greater level of intimacy as members of God's own family. The apostle John could not get over this. "See how great a love the Father has bestowed upon us, that we should be called children of God; and such we are" (1 John 3:1)!

A child always outranks any ambassador or governor or senator. The story is told of a meeting Abraham Lincoln held with his cabinet during the Civil War. At a crucial point in their discussion, a knock came at the door. It was Willie, the president's ten-year-old son, wanting to see his father. Lincoln laid aside all the affairs of state to ask what his son wanted. When it came to gaining access to his father, Willie outranked everyone.

Members of a family have unique relationships, privileges, and responsibilities.

—As members of God's family, Jesus is our brother (Rom. 8:29).

—As members of God's family, we are fellow heirs with Christ (Rom. 8:16–17), who willingly shares all His glory, majesty, wealth, and position with us.

—As members of God's family, we must act like it. When we live like children of God, people can tell who our Father is and we bring glory to Him (Matt. 5:16).

A Temple

The purpose of the Old Testament temple was to reflect—in a literal, material way—the glory of God. If you were to reproduce that temple today, it would cost billions of dollars. It was all gold, silver, ivory, and tapestry— a stunning sight. When Solomon showed the temple to the queen of Sheba, she fainted, overcome with its visual glory. Then she burst out in spontaneous eulogy to God: "Blessed be the Lord your God."

Not only was the temple a physical picture of the glory and beauty of God; it was also His dwelling place. God localized a manifestation of Himself within the inner sanctum of the temple, the Holy of Holies, where only the high priests were allowed access to His presence.

When Christ died on the cross, "the curtain of the temple was torn in two from top to bottom" (Matt. 27:51 NIV), signifying that Christ had made it possible for all believers to go directly into God's presence. From that point on, the temple was not a building made with hands; the temple was people (1 Cor. 3:16; 2 Cor. 6:16). The Old Testament temple was designed to be a physical representation of God; now God's people became His temple, a spiritual representation of the Lord. Just as the people could go to the temple and see what God was like, so people should be able to look at the Christian and see what God is like. We have become the dwelling place of God in this world. We make up His body on earth . . . His church.

As a result, we see the inevitability of duty flowing out of doctrine . . . the inevitability of practice flowing out of principle . . . the inevitability of behavior flowing out of belief. Because . . .

—if we are citizens of a kingdom, it matters how we act;
—if we are members of a family, it matters how we act;
—if we are living stones in a temple, it matters how we act.

It matters, it matters, it matters!

We must understand who we are. Once we do, we will want to live like who we are. Then the specific life commands we find in Ephesians 4–6 will be welcomed as light in the darkness, water for the thirsty, bread for the hungry. We will welcome them rather than resent them, because we hunger, we thirst, and we want to see.

Focus Questions

1. What parts of the "statue" of your life look most unfinished to you? Are you resisting God's work in these areas? If not, what should be your response to the unfinished work?

2. God's great work is to make alive that which was dead (our spirits) and to bring together that which was separated (Jews and Gentiles) into the church. What do these two truths tell us about (1) the evangelization of the lost and (2) our regard for those in other churches who are not like us?

3. Paul uses three images to portray the church: a kingdom, a family, and a temple. That means that we are citizens, family members, and living stones. How should each of these images affect our actions?

7

The Great Mystery
(Ephesians 3:1–13)

Why is the church significant to the world? Because the church represents penetrating light and undiluted salt in a lost, confused, insipid society.

Chuck Swindoll

As you look out my mother-in-law's back door in New Mexico, you see the grand Florida mountain range. The profile of the Floridas against the deep blue southwestern sky is ruggedly handsome. Their jagged edges and sharp formations seem to be one gigantic, unbroken rock sculpture dropped onto the flat New Mexico wilderness.

One day when we were riding horseback near the base of the Floridas, however, we noticed that the mountains were not unbroken. The closest rock formation jutted higher than a skyscraper, and behind it was the bulk of the mountain range. In between the two was a beautiful grassland of gentle slopes, which from a distance was completely hidden. From the patio of my mother-in-law's home, you would never know that secret valley was there.

For thousands of years, there was a secret in the heart of God. It was hidden from the world, from the priests, from the patriarchs, from the prophets, even from the angels until the time came for Him to reveal it through His Son to His holy apostles.

This secret was that there was to be a new creation, a new living temple, a new spiritual body through whom God was going to work to carry the message of salvation to the ends of the world. This new creation was to be comprised of both Jews and Gentiles, and it was to be called the church.

The church was not foreseen by anything written in the Old Testament. It was a total surprise, like that little valley at the base of the Floridas. In his letter to the Ephesians, Paul calls it a mystery . . . a *musterion* . . .

something previously unknown which has now been revealed (Eph. 3:3–5) by direct revelation from the Lord Himself.

So What's the Mystery?

So Jews and Gentiles are joined as one in a new spiritual entity called the church. That's the mystery? What's the big deal? you may ask. Why is Paul making so much of this?

If we take this attitude, it's because we have absolutely no comprehension of the degree of separation that existed between these two groups of people.

It would be something like saying there is no longer going to be a University of Texas and a Texas A&M University. There is now going to be a new university called Lone Star State University, and all Aggies and all Longhorns will become a part of Lone Star State and get the same degree. There will be no more Aggies or Longhorns. Now there are only the Lone Star State Prickly Pears. If you were an Aggie, this would be tough to handle; and the same would be true if you were a Longhorn. But if you have difficulty imagining the union of the Aggies and the Longhorns, think of what it would have meant to a Jew to become one with a "Gentile dog."

This is why Paul belabors the point, emphasizing the three levels of unity that now exist between Jews and Gentiles: we are now fellow heirs in all the eternal riches God has to bestow on His people; we are now fellow members of the body of Christ; we are now fellow partakers of the blessings of God (Eph. 3:6).

What Do We Do About It?

Blacks and whites united in South Africa . . . Protestants and Catholics united in Northern Ireland . . . Christians and Muslims united in Lebanon . . . Arabs and Jews united in Israel. Paul's message of Jews and Gentiles united in Christ was more earthshaking than any of those and met with even more resistance. Yet the apostle was willing to go wherever necessary to proclaim this message of reconciliation.

When Paul wrote his letter to the Ephesians, he was sitting in a Roman prison, awaiting trial before Caesar. He did not consider himself a prisoner of the Romans or of the emperor, however; he was a "prisoner of Christ Jesus for the sake of you Gentiles" (Eph. 3:1). God was unifying Jews and Gentiles into this new thing called the church, and it was Paul's primary responsibility to spread the message of the gospel to the Gentiles.

What a God of irony we have! Prior to his conversion, Paul had been a rabid defender of Judaism and a persistent persecutor of the followers of Christ. He even watched and gave his approval when the Jews stoned Stephen to death. After Paul's conversion, God revealed to him that he was the apostle who was to proclaim the message that there was no longer a distinction between Jews and Gentiles.

Paul knew he had a responsibility to tell others about this mystery, and he was not going to let circumstances keep him from it. Like Paul, each of us has a responsibility to minister to others. Each of us has been given knowledge of truth that will help others prepare for their eternal destiny. We are not to keep that truth to ourselves. We have a responsibility to spread it to others. All of us.

I have heard many people say, "I don't know what my spiritual gift is," and have seen them use that as an excuse to do nothing. Yet the Bible talks much more about our responsibility to others than it does about spiritual gifts.

Each of us has a responsibility to minister. To do something. Setting up chairs for a morning worship service or stuffing church bulletins may not seem like a ministry, until you realize that those activities are an important part of the worship service. Eliminate those ministries, and you shut down the worship services. When you realize this, you are on the way to discovering the secret to finding your spiritual gift: involvement.

Get involved. When you do, God will guide you, through experience, to your place of most rewarding and fruitful service. There are no little people and there are no little jobs; there is only faithfulness to God.

As imperfect as it is, the church is what God has chosen to further His kingdom on earth. To the degree that we are involved and contributing to the church, we are involved in the work God is doing in the world.

When the church denounces sin, people are influenced to stand against it. When the church speaks out on moral issues, people learn to penetrate the fog of compromise and gain the courage to stand alone against the tide of immorality.

"You are the salt of the earth," said Jesus. You are the light on a hill. That's your role, Christian!

Though many in the world around us will not enter the doors of a local church, they see us living in their midst, standing for the truth. As the old saying goes, we may be the only sermon they ever hear. So . . .

Let's stand against sin;
Let's stand against unrighteousness;
Let's stand against encroaching worldliness;
Let's stand against the darkness;
Let's stand for love;
Let's stand for goodness;
Let's stand for truth;
Let's stand for light;
Let's be His church!

The Heart of the Mystery

There are probably few people in the United States who have never tasted a Coke. It's the same with hundreds of millions of people around the world. They've tasted "the real thing," and it's all Robert Woodruff's doing.

Woodruff, while president of Coca-Cola from 1923 to 1955, had vision. During World War II he promised, "We will see that every man in uniform gets a bottle of Coca-Cola for five cents wherever he is and whatever it costs." After the war, he stated that in his lifetime he wanted everyone in the world to have a taste of Coca-Cola. With vision and dedication rarely matched in corporate American culture, Woodruff and his colleagues reached their generation around the globe for Coke.

Woodruff was more committed to giving each person in the world a drink of Coke than most of us are to giving each person in the world a drink of the water of life.

As the church, our collective mandate is to take the gospel to the world. As individual members of the body, our mandate is to do what we can to contribute to that overall goal. We must ask, then, what we can do individually.

At the very least, we can pray that God will raise up laborers for the spiritual harvest—and pray for those laborers. At the very least, we can give our finances, our time, and our talents to take the gospel to the world. And some of us can go . . . for life . . . for a few years . . . even for a summer or a couple of weeks.

The Great Commission is a personal assignment for each of us. So each of us must ask the Lord, "Heavenly Father, what do You want *me* to do?"

At the heart of the mystery that is the church lies another mystery—the wisdom of God. The totality of the wisdom of God includes the outpouring of His grace and His saving power and the fact that we are kept not by how faithful we are but by how faithful God is—the fact that God takes the fallen, the broken, the earthbound and raises them up, heals them, and makes them heavenbound.

The mystery of the wisdom of God turns things backward, upside down, and inside out.

Elevating yourself lowers you;
Lowering yourself raises you.

To keep what you have is to lose it;
To give it away is to keep it.

To find your life is to lose it;
To lose your life is to find it.

Abundance can bring poverty;
Poverty can bring abundance.

Freedom leads to slavery;
Slavery leads to freedom.

Cleverness is folly;
Foolishness is wisdom.

Strength leads to weakness;
Weakness brings strength.

The first shall be last;
The last shall be first.

While the wisdom of God is beyond the comprehension of our natural mind, the Holy Spirit does illumine the receptive mind with the Word so that we can begin to understand the mystery of the ages. And, amazingly enough, the church is God's great instrument in history to display His wisdom to the world.

Jay Kessler, president of Taylor University and former president of Youth for Christ, gives five reasons why he believes in the church.

1. The church is the only institution dealing with the ultimate issues. Death. Judgment. Relationships. Purpose. Lasting priorities. Meaning in life. Identity. Heaven and Hell.

2. The church provides perspective that gives dignity to mankind. We live in a day in which man has become a means rather than an end. This creates a desperate sense of inner worthlessness. The church counteracts this insidious message.

3. The church provides a moral and ethical compass in the midst of relativism. Like a swamp of murky, slimy water, our society has either rethought, resisted, or completely rejected absolutes. Not the church! It still stands on the timeless bedrock of Scripture.

4. The church is the only place to find true community, healing, compassion, and love. It is here people care. Really care. Not because of status or money. But because the Spirit of God is at work, weaving together the lives within the Body.

5. The church (like no other institution) has provided motivation for the most lasting, unselfish, essential, courageous ministries on earth. Schools. Hospitals. Halfway houses. Orphanages. Leprosariums. Missions.

So, as Chuck Swindoll writes,

Up with the Church! That's where the Body and the Head meet to celebrate this mysterious union . . . when ordinary, garden-variety folks like us gather around the pre-eminent One. For worship. For encouragement. For instruction. For expression. For support. For the carrying out of a God-given role that will never be matched or surpassed on earth— even though it's the stuff the world around us considers weird and weak.

No, the church isn't perfect. After all, we're a part of it. And it hasn't always practiced what it preached. Still, it is the only vehicle God has for working out His eternal will in the world.

Focus Questions

1. A spiritual gift is something we enjoy doing and something that accomplishes ministry (Rom. 12:4–8; 1 Cor. 12:1–11). Each believer is gifted and is responsible to use that gift in serving others (1 Pet. 4:10). What evidence do you have of your spiritual gift? Have you become involved enough in ministry to have given the Lord a fair chance to help you see your gift? What more might you do in this regard?

2. What could you do to help spread the message of the gospel as far as possible?

3. If you were Robert Woodruff and you wanted to reach the world with the gospel instead of Coke, what would you do?

8

The Riches of Our Spiritual Resources

(Ephesians 3:14–21)

A prayer is nothing but a cry of helplessness: "God help me."
When we ask on that level, God promises to give.

Ray Stedman

I have been a Christian for many years now, but I still remember vividly my frustration with my own immaturity during the early days of my Christian faith. When I was in Bible college, I would talk to everyone about it: the president, the dean, visiting speakers and missionaries, other students, fellow Christians. I read books about the mature Christian life and agonized over how far my life fell short. I drove myself to distraction because I couldn't get to where I wanted to be.

Now that I am older and perhaps a little wiser, if I were counseling myself, I would say:

Max, be patient. You can't be holy in a hurry. You are not old enough in the Lord yet to be spiritually mature. God understands your immaturity, just as a parent understands the immaturity of his six-year-old. A six-year-old is a six-year-old, and you cannot expect him to act like a thirty-year-old. You must wait for him to become thirty before you can expect him to act like thirty. This doesn't mean that God doesn't care if you sin. He does. But He has provided for you. God's grace is greater than all your sin. When you sin, confess it, and be restored to fellowship. Hold on to your desire to be more than you are. God will honor that. But be patient. It will take time. Accept where you are in your spiritual growth. God does. He understands. He takes it into account (Ps. 103:8–14).

Oh, how I needed to hear that, but no one ever told me. Some of you probably need it, too. So I say to you: Don't be harder on yourself than God is. Pray for Him to strengthen you. Be as faithful as you can be to what you understand God to be asking of you. Then be patient (Phil. 2:12–13).

The mature Christian life doesn't come about by popping ourselves into some spiritual microwave. God's means are much more subtle—and they aren't instant. "For this reason," Paul said:

> I bow my knees before the Father, from whom every family in heaven and on earth derives its name, that He would grant you, according to the riches of His glory, to be strengthened with power through His Spirit in the *inner man;* so that Christ may dwell in your hearts through *faith;* and that you, being rooted and grounded in *love,* may be able to comprehend with all the saints what is the breadth and length and height and depth, and to know the love of Christ which surpasses knowledge, that you may be filled up to all the *fulness* of God.
>
> Ephesians 3:14–21, italics added

This is a marvelous prayer in which Paul asks the Lord for a logical succession of things: that we might (a) be strengthened with power, so that (b) we may experience faith and love, so that (c) we may experience the fullness of God. In this chapter, we want to look at each of these spiritual blessings.

Inner Strength

Paul prays first that we might be strengthened with power through God's Spirit in the inner man. This inner strength is not self-discipline or the power of positive thinking. It is not self-talk or inner renewal. It is not getting a grip on yourself or turning over a new leaf.

Inner strength is not a spiritual muscle we can build by working out at the gym or jogging ten miles a day. It is a gift of God that comes to us through prayer. It is a spiritual strengthening that enables us to do what needs to be done. But it is not personal power. It is a fundamental work of God from His Spirit to our spirit.

The Source and Nature of Our Strength

In their book *Fearfully and Wonderfully Made,* Dr. Paul Brand and Philip Yancey describe the importance and significance of the white corpuscles, "the

armed forces of the body which guard against invaders." When damage
threatens the body at any point,

> an alarm seems to sound. . . . As if they have a sense of smell . . .
> nearby white cells abruptly halt their aimless wandering. Like beagles on
> the scent of a rabbit, they home in from all directions to the point of
> attack. Using their unique shape-changing qualities, they ooze between
> overlapping cells of capillary walls and hurry through tissue via the most
> direct route. When they arrive, the battle begins. . . . a shapeless white
> cell, resembling science fiction's creature "The Blob," lumbers toward a
> cluster of luminous bacterial spheres. Like a blanket pulled over a corpse,
> the cell assumes their shape; for a while they still glow eerily inside the
> white cell. But the white cell contains granules of chemical explosives,
> and as soon as the bacteria are absorbed the granules detonate, destroy-
> ing the invaders. In thirty seconds to a minute only the bloated white
> cell remains.[1]

When the body is attacked, it resists. To do this, it must be strengthened
from within. When Christians are attacked by the forces of the evil one, we
too must resist. And to do this, we need reinforcements. We need to be
strengthened from within. That is why Paul prays that God, according to the
riches of His glory, may strengthen us with might by His Spirit in the inner
man.

No matter what form the attack takes, we can be "more than conquerors." In fact, that's the only way we can keep coping and functioning and living in a world such as this. Not by eliminating our temptations and problems,
but by being strengthened by God to live above them. Not without pain and
suffering, but in spite of pain and suffering.

What is the source of this power or inner strength? God the Father.

How do we get it? We ask Him for it in prayer.

What kind of power is it? It is not physical power . . . it is not intellectual power . . . it is not emotional power. It is SPIRITUAL POWER.

All my Christian life I have wanted that kind of power. Power to do what
I knew I should do, and power not to do what I knew I should not do. Power
to close that gaping chasm between what I ought to be and what I am.

When I began my Christian life many years ago, I read this passage in
Ephesians for the first time. And for years after that, I asked, *So, where's the
power? What does it look like? How do I get it? Why haven't I felt it?*

I saw demonstrations of miraculous power in the Bible, and I thought,
"There's no reason why Christianity today ought to be inferior to the

Christianity of the Bible. If people had the power of God then because of the intensity of their zeal and commitment to the Lord, then the same power should be available to me if I am equally intense and zealous and committed."

I wanted to pray and have the rain stop, and then pray and have it start raining again. I wanted to pray and heal someone. I wanted to pray and have multitudes saved. I wanted signs and miracles. I wanted to always do right and never do wrong. I wanted to always be happy and to always believe God. I wanted control over my life. As I looked around at the gross godlessness, the sickening sin, the ever-present evil, I wanted to prevail against it. I wanted spiritual power . . . real power.

I didn't have that kind of power, of course. Neither did anyone I knew. Oh, some claimed to have it, but I knew they didn't.

Then, as I studied the Bible, I began to realize that the signs and miracles of faith were concentrated within relatively short time frames: periods of rapid or crucial change, such as the deliverance of the Israelites from slavery in Egypt; or the era of the prophets when God was trying to get the nation of Israel to repent so that He would not have to send them into captivity; or the life and ministry of Jesus and the era of the early church when God changed His entire way of relating to His children. As the message of the Messiah was established and began to spread, exciting displays of supernatural power began to subside. Trace the chronology of the epistles in the New Testament (which is different than their order of appearance in the Bible), and you see the Christian faith take on a deeper, quieter tone.

In the lives of believers you see hope, contentment, thankfulness, joy, peace, praise, humility, steadfastness, patience, and love. While none of these are flamboyant manifestations, they are subtle but miraculous evidence of the power of God strengthening the inner man. For without the power of God, we cannot grow and become more like Christ; we cannot be motivated to selflessly serve others; and we cannot be content in Him.

God does not promise us the power to overcome all circumstances or the power to change immediately. What He does promise is the strong underlying power of a gradually changed life.

There are times, of course, when the power of God seems to be more obvious—times when I have been almost overwhelmed by the presence of God, or gripped by a spiritual truth, or astounded by the realization that I had just been used in an extraordinary way. And I admit that I would like to have that kind of power all the time. But if I did, you see, I would get used to that kind of power, and pretty soon it wouldn't be enough. I would want greater power. I would want ax heads to float on water. I would want to be able to call down fire out of heaven. Perhaps even throw a lightening bolt or two. POWER!!!

The point, of course, is that the power resides in God and not in us. And to see signs of it, we must look through eyes of faith. God is at work in us and through us. We just don't always recognize it because we're looking frantically in the wrong direction or for the wrong thing.

Faith

Paul prays that we might be strengthened with power, so that Christ may dwell in our hearts through faith. When I was a child, I believed Jimminy Cricket, Pinocchio's little friend, who sang, "When you wish upon a star, your dreams come true." I wished on the evening star; I wished on birthday candles. I was sure if I believed hard enough, my wishes would come true. (Needless to say, I had lots of disappointments.)

Unfortunately, many "grown-up" Christians operate under a similar kind of Magic Kingdom illusion: If you pray long enough and hard enough—some would even say, "claim the result"—it will happen. The only thing that will keep it from happening is if your belief falters. In other words, if you believe something will happen, it will.

This is not faith. It's wishful thinking.

Faith is strong and solid and active. Faith is believing what God has said and acting accordingly.

Many people today say, "It doesn't matter what you believe, as long as you believe it sincerely." Others say, "Faith is believing in spite of the fact that there is nothing to believe." Or worse yet, "believing in spite of the evidence to the contrary."

But faith is only as good as the object in which it is placed.

We place our faith in an airplane every time we go to the airport. We place our faith in an elevator every time we head for the twenty-fifth floor. We place our faith in a steel structure every time we cross a bridge.

Faith by itself is absolutely worthless. Faith will not get us off the ground. Faith will not get us to the second floor. Only a flight-worthy airplane will get us across the United States. Only an intact cable system will get us to the twenty-fifth floor. Only solidly engineered steel and concrete will get us across the Straits of Mackinac.

And when it comes to power for daily living, the object of our faith must be Jesus Christ.

Once we have invited Christ into our hearts, we must allow Him to settle down and be at home there. That requires the strengthening power of His Spirit. Robert Munger has given us a very clever and helpful illustration of what this means in his classic booklet, "My Heart, Christ's Home."

The Christian life, he says, is like a house. When we invite Him in, Jesus moves from room to room. In the library of the mind, He throws out the trash and replaces it with His Word. In the dining room, He replaces our sinful appetites for prestige, materialism, and lust with the virtues for which believers are to hunger and thirst: humility, meekness, and love. He moves on into the living room, where He finds many worldly companions and activities, and even into the closets where we keep our hidden sins. Only when He has cleaned every room, closet, and corner in the entire house can He settle down and be at home.

Christ takes up residence in our hearts when we accept Him. But to have Christ dwell in our hearts through faith means He is at home in every corner of our lives, because we believe His promises and, therefore, become obedient to His Word (John 14:23).

Abundant Love

Paul prays that we might be strengthened with power through His Spirit in the inner man so that Christ may dwell in our hearts through faith . . . and so that we may experience abundant love.

In his book *Lessons from a Sheepdog,* Phillip Keller tells of a border collie he bought to herd sheep on his ranch in Canada. The collie was inexpensive because it was ill-tempered and unpredictable, but Keller was short on funds and hoped the animal would work out until he could afford a better one.

When Keller got the dog back to his ranch, it quickly became clear that the animal had been beaten, starved, and neglected. It was wild and nervous, filled with fear and suspicion. Keller spent several days just trying to win the dog's trust. He spoke repeatedly and gently to the animal, never moved quickly, tried cautiously to pet it. Nothing worked. The dog remained suspicious and unpredictable and refused to eat.

After nearly a week of this, Keller realized that the dog was going to starve to death unless he let it go free. So he released the collie and watched it disappear over the hill into the brush-dotted pastureland. Although he figured he would never see the animal again, he continued to put out food and water and frequently let his eyes roam the horizon, hoping to catch a glimpse of it.

One day Keller spotted the dog watching him from the distance. He spoke to the animal softly. It disappeared. The next day the dog appeared again, and that evening some of the food was gone. For several days this pattern was repeated as a distant bond of trust began forming.

Then the impossible happened. One morning as Keller sat on a large rock overlooking his grazing sheep, he noticed, out of the corner of his eye, a black-and-white form coming up behind him. The man sat motionless, his hands braced behind his back. Suddenly he felt a cold, wet nose on his hand.

After a moment, Keller turned slightly. The dog stayed. The man put his hand on the dog's head. The hint of a wag stirred the end of the dog's tail. And at that moment the bond was sealed between man and dog.

The collie became Keller's constant companion, shadowing him in unwavering devotion and instant obedience. When Keller left the ranch, the dog refused to eat. The animal became an extension of Keller himself, working the sheep with uncanny instinct and precision, loyalty, and devotion.

Keller's experience with the collie is a picture of the healing, enriching, and transforming process and progress of love. And that process—between God and man—is exactly what Paul is talking about:

> that you, being rooted and grounded in love, may be able to comprehend with all the saints what is the breadth and length and height and depth, and to know the love of Christ which surpasses knowledge.
>
> Ephesians 3:17–19

We are like a tree, Paul says, sinking our roots deeply into the soil of God's love. Tapping into this love—experiencing this love—gives us life and strength and enables us to stand with security, stability, and permanence. When the winds of adversity blow, the love of God holds us steady.

The Character of Love

Paul prays that we may be able to comprehend the magnitude of this love: "the breadth and length and height and depth"—what I like to call "the great cube of God's love." This is not always easy, because as human beings we naturally have a distorted view of love.

Remember that romantic moment in *My Fair Lady* when lovesick Freddie wanders the street in front of Eliza Doolittle's house, lamenting "that overpowering feeling" he has for her? That's what love is today—"that overpowering feeling." And if we wake up the next morning and don't have that overpowering feeling, we assume love is gone; so we dump that relationship and move on, searching for another emotional experience we are deluded into thinking is love.

Or we buy into the view Elvis made famous: "It's now or never, come hold me tight. / Kiss me, my darling, be mine tonight. / Tomorrow may be too late. / It's now or never, my love won't wait." That isn't love. It's the world view of a tom cat. Love can always wait; lust can't.

Does God hate the world's concept of love? Without a doubt. But not for legalistic reasons. Not because He wants to spoil our fun. He hates it because the value system of the world is totally opposed to His value system. The value system of the world says: love isn't forever . . . it isn't unconditional . . . we can leave any time we want to . . . we can be totally self-absorbed and selfish . . . nothing is permanent . . . everything is relative. And every time we accept and act on these worldly definitions of love, we sow the seeds of our own destruction—pain, emptiness, and dissatisfaction.

God mirrors the true definition of love: He loves us forever . . . He loves us unconditionally . . . He will never leave us or forsake us . . . He sacrificed His beloved Son for our salvation . . . He only does what is best for us. And the more we become like Him, the more joy, meaning, and satisfaction we have in life.

How do we "comprehend" His love? One important way is through the evidence of that love in the lives of His children. When we experience the love of Christ demonstrated by His people, a capacity to comprehend the meaning and importance of God's love is awakened in our hearts.

Why else would Christ have commanded us to love others as He has loved us?

The Fullness of God

Paul prays that we might be strengthened by His Spirit in the inner man so that we might experience supernatural faith and love . . . and so that we might experience the fullness of God.

J. Wilbur Chapman, a minister from a previous generation, used to tell the true story of a man who, after years of estrangement from his family, had become destitute, dispirited, and reduced to begging for a living. One day, positioned near a train depot, he touched the shoulder of a disembarking passenger.

"Mister," he said, "can you give me a dime?"

The man turned around, and the beggar started to hold out his hand. But when he saw the passenger's face, he went white with shock. It was the father he had not seen for years.

"Father, Father, do you know me?" he cried.

With tears in his eyes, the father threw his arms around his son. "Oh, my son, at last I've found you! I've found you! You want a dime? Everything I have is yours."

How like that we are. We go around tapping the world on the shoulder, begging for a dime, when our heavenly Father wants to give us everything He has. We are content to scrounge for crumbs, when we've been invited to a banquet. We settle for the emptiness of the world, when we can "be filled up to all the fullness of God."

What is that fullness? Some state of nirvana where all troubles cease? Some charismatic ecstasy of "blessedness" in which we are free of all pain and problems?

Not really.

We begin to taste the fullness of God as, through the process of prayer, the exercise of faith, and the experience of love, we are transformed more and more into the image and character of God . . . as we become more and more like Him.

God does not force Himself on anyone. He does not storm the walls of our hearts and take control of our lives. Like a Cosmic Gentleman, He asks for control through the revealing truth of His Word and the piercing conviction of the Holy Spirit. And when we see the wisdom and the goodness of this Faithful Friend, we say, "Yes, I give You control of my life."

The thought of anything or anyone controlling us is another concept despised—at the very least misunderstood—by the world around us. We want to think we are totally in control and totally free. But we aren't. Nobody is. Total freedom doesn't exist. We can be free from the toothbrush and a slave to cavities, or we can be a slave to the toothbrush and free from cavities. We can be free from God and a slave to the world, or we can be a slave to God and free from the world. We cannot be free from both.

When we do choose to turn over control to God, He fills our mind, our emotions, and our will. The mind of God influences our thoughts, the love of God warms our heart, and the will of God becomes stronger than the pull of the world. We are filled up with God. We begin to think His thoughts, make His decisions, feel His emotions.

This is our inheritance . . . our real wealth.

Focus Questions

1. What evidence of spiritual power in the inner man have you seen in your life?

2. What "room" in your life needs the most attention if Christ is to be at home there?

3. To what degree have you experienced true love—love that gives, instead of takes? To what degree do you express true love—love that gives, instead of takes?

Part 2

Purpose

God wants us to have purpose. We must be careful not to settle for ambition.

9

The Worthy Walk
(Ephesians 4:1–3)

Imagine yourself a living house. God comes in to rebuild that house. At first, perhaps, you can understand what He is doing. He is getting the drains right and stopping the leaks in the roof and so on. . . . But presently He starts knocking the house about in a way that hurts abominably and does not seem to make any sense. What on earth is He up to? The explanation is that He is building quite a different house from the one you thought of—throwing out a new wing here, putting on an extra floor there, running up towers, making courtyards. You thought you were going to be made into a decent little cottage; but He is building a palace.

C. S. Lewis

*A*s a joke and challenge to its readers, *Saturday Review* magazine hides a nonsense ad in its classified section in each issue. I enjoy trying to spot these clever notices. One month this one appeared:

> COMPUTER ERROR has resulted in large supply of electric-powered chairs that make approximately 150 high-speed revolutions per minute automatically as soon as body weight hits the seat. Excellent bargain for people who are nausea-resistant. SR Box SC

Nonsense or not, some of us feel that our lives are like that chair . . . lots of high-speed stress, but going nowhere. Whether we are schoolchildren struggling with mathematics or workers wrestling with seemingly meaningless jobs, we all long for purpose. We want our lives to have some significance. Without purpose, nothing is worth doing.

God gives us that purpose in Christ. He calls us to live for Him. He calls us to join the Great Cause of the Ages: manifesting the character and proclaiming the name of Christ, reflecting the spiritual rebirth that has taken place inside us. If our lives are to have meaning, we must live for the Christ who has given us new life. Identity and actions go together. What we do is an integral part of who we are. This becomes evident from early childhood onward.

Four-year-old Johnny falls down on the sidewalk as he runs to greet his father who has just pulled into the driveway. Johnny is tired and hungry, and his two-year-old sister, Susie, has just snatched his favorite toy. Because of all this, he cries harder than is really warranted. Daddy picks him up and says, "There, there. You're a big boy, Johnny. Act like it."

Who Johnny is (a big boy) should affect how he acts.

A princess sits beside her mother, the queen, at the princess's presentation to the public as heir apparent to the throne. When it is time for the princess to stand and walk to the microphone and say a few words to the gathered dignitaries, the queen leans over to her and says, "You are a princess. Walk like one!"

Who she is (a princess) should affect how she acts.

Eighteen-year-old Chuck has gone through five tough weeks of Marine boot camp in South Carolina. During the last week the recruits are forced to crawl under rolls of barbed wire with live machine gun fire blazing just inches over their heads. Chuck freezes. He begins to sweat. His hands dig into the red clay beneath him as panic sweeps his soul. Just then a buddy crawls up beside him and says, "Get hold of yourself, man. You're a Marine. Act like one!"

Who Chuck is (a Marine) should affect how he acts.

Throughout our life, from beginning to end, our actions are linked to our identity. Who we are—how we see ourselves—affects how we act.

This is the basic principle to which Paul refers in the opening sentence of chapter four of Ephesians.

> I, therefore, the prisoner of the Lord, entreat you to walk in a manner worthy of the calling with which you have been called.

In essence he says, "You are a child of God. Act like one."

Paul has spent the first three chapters of Ephesians telling us who we are; now he begins spelling out how we are to act. The first three chapters of Ephesians give us doctrine; the last three give us duty. The first three give us principle; the last three give us practice.

One of the greatest difficulties in the Christian walk arises because we never really understand, or never really believe, who the Bible says we are. The Bible says that we are children of God; but because we see ourselves as children of the world, too often that is how we act.

We are chosen by God to be holy and blameless.

We have been adopted by Him into His holy family.

We have been forgiven of every sin—past, present, future—because of the death of Christ.

We have been redeemed.

We have been given a fabulous inheritance that will be ours throughout eternity.

We have been sealed and secured by the Holy Spirit.

We have been made alive in Christ and seated in the heavenlies with Him.

We have been made fellow citizens with all the saints of God.

We have been made into a dwelling place of God.

Because we are created in the image of God, we have infinite and inherent value. And if we see ourselves as God sees us, it will exalt us without inflating us, humble us without debasing us. We are children of God, destined for the throne.

Now, Paul says, "Act like it."

Worthy to Walk

"I want to believe all this," you may be thinking, "but I'm having trouble. I don't feel like I have infinite worth. How could I? Look at all the things that have happened to me. Look at all the things I've done. With all my faults and inherent deficiencies, how can God love and value me?"

Ah, but He can. He does! Let me use a little analogy that might help you see and understand why.

Suppose you inherit a gold mine. You're overjoyed. You love that gold mine. You can hardly wait to get out there and get to work in it. But the first time you go out to inspect your treasure, the gold says, "How can you love me? I'm all dirty. I'm all mixed up with that awful iron ore, and I have that rotten clay all over me. I'm contaminated with bauxite and mineral deposits. I'm ugly and worthless."

"Oh, but I do love you," you say to the gold. "You see, I understand what you really are. I know you have all these imperfections, but I have plans for you. I am not going to leave you the way you are now. I am going to purify you. I am going to get rid of all that other stuff. I see your inherent worth. I know that the iron ore, the clay, and the mineral deposits are not part of the true you—you are just temporarily mixed up with them.

"I warn you, it won't be easy. You will go through a lot of heat and pressure. But look at this piece of gold jewelry. Isn't it beautiful? That's what you are. Left to yourself, you would remain in this dark place, buried in the dirty ore. But I know how to change you from what you are now to what you can be. I will make you beautiful, and you will make me wealthy."

God is not blind. He knows all about our imperfections. But He also understands our inherent worth, and He knows how to change us from what we are now to what we can be. Once this process is completed, God will have made us beautiful, and we will have given Him joy.

Understand who you are.

Believe who you are.

Act like who you are!

We can't repeat this too often. We can't overemphasize this. Much of our failure to trust . . . to believe . . . to obey stems from the fact that we do not see ourselves as God sees us. We do not understand who we have become in Christ. We see ourselves as children of the world, bound by the cause and effect of flesh and blood. But that is not who we are. And if we are to enter into the joy of who we have become in Christ, we must change how we see ourselves.

This is what Paul is trying to tell us in Ephesians. He has spent three chapters telling us who we are in Christ. Now He begins to tell us, in detail, how we should live.

Characteristics of the Worthy Walk

"Therefore," Paul says, "based on all that I have told you about who you are in Christ, this is how you should live. Walk in a manner that is worthy of your calling." Our walk is our life; our calling is all the spiritual blessings we have in Christ. Certain characteristics are fundamental to this worthy walk.

Humility

Walk in a manner worthy of [your] calling . . . with all humility.

Ephesians 4:1–2

Humility does not mean you must see yourself as a pitiful excuse, a lowlife, a piece of refuse at the bottom of the human pile. Rather, it means you see yourself as God sees you: you have infinite and inherent value, but no more value than anyone else. It means being willing to accept God as the authority over your life, rather than insisting on being your own supreme authority. And since you accept God as the supreme authority over your life, and because you are of equal value but no greater value than everyone else, you are willing to order your life in such a way as to be a servant to others.

When Christians do this, we meet each other's needs in a context of harmony and love. When we fail to subordinate ourselves to others and are concerned only with meeting our own needs, we live a life of individualism and isolation—a state in which the Christian cannot be satisfied. We are not created to be loners. We are part of a *family*.

Gentleness/Meekness

> . . . and gentleness.
>
> Ephesians 4:2

Someone has said that if you think meekness is weakness, try being meek for a week. Then you will soon realize that it takes strength to be meek. Meekness literally means "power under control."

In the ancient world, soldiers rode war horses into battle. These animals were trained to submit to their master-riders, surrounded by the ferocious heat of battle. Though strong, noble, and beautiful creatures, these war horses were meek; their strength was under total control.

Moses was described as the meekest man who ever lived, yet his dynamic, charismatic leadership challenged the powerful throne of Egypt. Meekness is not weakness; it is strength under control.

Patience

> . . . with patience.
>
> Ephesians 4:2

"O Lord, give me patience . . . and hurry!" is a common prayer. Most of us have offered it at some point. Yet patience rarely comes quickly—and those who need it most find it the slowest in coming. Here, perspective is all-important, for it is often in the waiting that we find the reality.

Throughout the Scriptures, patience is a characteristic of God's mature people. And patience means *patience*. It doesn't mean that if I am patient now, maybe the Lord will see I have learned my lesson and will give me what I want sooner. No. Patience is believing that God's timetable is good, no matter what time it is.

Abraham received the promise of God but had to wait many years to see its fulfillment. "Thus," the writer of Hebrews tells us, "having patiently waited, he obtained the promise." Noah was told to build an ark; 120 years later his patient obedience was rewarded.

Those who have the ability to tolerate ambiguity, tension, and delay are the ones who will "run and not get tired . . . walk and not become weary" (Isa. 40:31).

Forbearance in Love

> . . . showing forebearance to one another in love.
>
>   Ephesians 4:2

Finally, Paul calls us to forbearance in love, which is the willingness to put up with something or someone in a spirit of love—*agape* love. It is the commitment of our will to benefit another.

Paul amplifies this concept in 1 Corinthians 13 when he writes, "Love is patient, love is kind, and is not jealous; love does not brag and is not arrogant, does not act unbecomingly; it does not seek its own, is not provoked, does not take into account a wrong suffered" (13:4–5). This is what Paul means when he says we are to be "showing forebearance to one another in love."

Consequences of the Worthy Walk

When we walk the worthy walk, we preserve unity in the body of Christ, which is one of the great goals of the church of Christ:

> . . . being diligent to preserve the unity of the Spirit in the bond of peace.
>
>   Ephesians 4:3

Paul's use of the word "preserve" implies that unity already exists. We don't have to create it; we just have to manifest it and keep it alive. We must demonstrate on the outside the inner unity that exists among all Christians.

Organizations such as the World Council of Churches and the National Council of Churches often point to a verse like this to justify their existence. But this passage is not referring to structural or organizational unity; it is talking about spiritual unity.

All those who have received the spiritual blessings of Christ in the heavenly places . . . who were dead and have been made alive . . . who were separate and have been made one . . . who have become a dwelling place of God in the Spirit . . . are united in Christ. To try to force unity among those who have not entered into these realities or to impose it through some organizational structure is both a flagrant misunderstanding of the meaning of this passage—and an impossibility.

Why is unity such a major issue? First, because without this kind of unity, Christians will not enjoy the rich relationships of other Christians and thus will not have the mutual ministry to one another that leads to a full and satisfying life. And second, because without this unity the world will look at Christians and doubt, on the basis of what they see of their relationships with one another, whether Christ is real. Remember Christ's prayer for His disciples:

> [I ask] that they may all be one; even as Thou, Father, art in Me, and I in Thee, that they also may be in Us; that the world may believe that Thou didst send Me.
>
> John 17:21

If the world sees unity among Christians, it has a basis for concluding that Christ is sent from God. If the world does not see unity among Christians, it has a basis for assuming that Christ is not sent from God. So unity is not incidental; it is a vital and strategic part of the witness of God in the world.

Our challenge is to live like who we have become: children of God, the apple of God's eye, with inherent and infinite value. Our challenge is to pay the price for what we want: a life filled with purpose and a sense of participation and communion with the God of the universe and the work He is doing in the world.

This challenge is a call to commitment, dedication, and sacrifice. It isn't easy, but nothing worth having ever is. I learned this some years ago from one of my favorite sports, basketball—which is not surprising, since we Hoosiers love our basketball!

When I was in college in Indiana, I was privileged to play for a coach who made it one of the greatest experiences of my life—although I didn't always think that. Our coach was midway through his career and had already won over four hundred games. Why? Because he was a disciplinarian. In fact, if there were such a thing as reincarnation, I'm sure he would have been Attila the Hun in a previous life.

Most Indiana basketball is "run and gun," and our coach wanted us to be able to run for the entire forty minutes of the game. To facilitate this he used a conditioning drill he called "go-go's." In this drill we started at one end of the floor, ran to the first foul line, then ran backward to the starting point; then to the half-court line and backward to the starting point; then to the far foul line and back; and then clear down to the other end of the floor and back. That was *one* go-go. We had to be conditioned to the point where we could run *twenty* go-go's full speed. And if you didn't run fast enough, the penalty was running *another* go-go.

Any horseplay or laziness, and you got fifty push-ups. Then, before we could quit practicing, we had to shoot a hundred foul shots and run a lap for every foul shot we missed.

Coach "discussed" things with us in a very loud voice—the veins sticking out in his neck and his eyes bulging. (Our mothers thought he was yelling at us. I can't imagine why!)

He didn't treat us like this because he disliked us . . . or because he wanted to punish us . . . or because he wanted us to quit the team in disgust and discouragement. Quite the contrary. We had made his team. He had chosen us. He believed we were the ones who, when pressed to the wall, would respond and become the kind of team he wanted. He was counting on us.

"I want you on the team," he was saying. "You are valuable to me. But I am going to work you within an inch of your life. Because this is how you become the kind of player I want you to be—and that you want to be. And when I am finished with you, you will have the freedom, through discipline, to rise above the pain to a place of honor."

My senior year we blew most of our opponents off the floor. We ended with a 20–6 record; we scored over a hundred points in twelve of those games; we went to the final playoffs; and our coach was selected coach of the year in our conference.

Now there were times back then when I wondered if I would live through it. After our twentieth go-go, when we were all leaning against the gym wall in synchronized wheezing, I'd think to myself: *This isn't worth it. He can't drive us like this. It's inhumane. It's dangerous. I'm quitting.* But I didn't. And today I consider that one of the most significant experiences of my life. No pain, no gain.

Conditioning and commitment. Dedication and sacrifice. That's what Paul calls us to in Ephesians. We are on the team, he assures us. God has picked us. He wants us. He loves us. He is going to push us within an inch of our lives to make us the kind of people He wants us to be. And when He is finished and the game is won, we will praise and worship Him forever.

God loves you.

He wants you on His team.

By His grace, you can do anything He asks of you.

He will make you into the kind of person you want to be.

It will be the greatest experience of your life!

Focus Questions

1. If true humility means "seeing yourself as God sees you, no more—no less," how would you describe yourself?

2. Turn to 1 Corinthians 13:4–7 and read the verses, substituting your own name in place of the word "love." What new insights does this exercise give you?

3. If unity is such an important characteristic in the church, why do you think there is so little unity? What could we do to promote greater spiritual unity?

10

Enjoying People and
Using Things
(Ephesians 4:4–10)

*Only when the church recognizes its unity and strives more and
more to preserve it, each member co-operating with all the others, will the gospel move mightily forward among the nations,
will the church itself rejoice, will Satan tremble, and will the
name of God be glorified. However, this unity makes allowance
for diversity of gifts among the many members of the one body.
In fact this very diversity, far from destroying the unity, will, if
properly used, promote it.*

William Hendricks

*E*arlier in this century, American businessman Howard Hughes was one of
the richest men in the world—and possibly one of the unhappiest.

> Howard Hughes was the world's ultimate mystery—so secretive, so re-
> clusive, so enigmatic, that for more than fifteen years no one could say
> for certain that he was alive, much less how he looked or behaved.
> . . . He lived a sunless, joyless, half-lunatic life. In his later years he fled
> from one resort hotel to another—Las Vegas, Nicaragua, Acapulco—
> and his physical appearance became odder and odder. His straggly beard
> hung down to his waist and his hair reached to the middle of his back.
> His fingernails were two inches long, and his toenails hadn't been
> trimmed for so long they resembled corkscrews. . . .
>   Hughes often said, "Every man has his price or a guy like me
> couldn't exist," yet no amount of money bought the affection of his as-
> sociates. Most of his employees who have broken the silence report their
> disgust for him.

Why was Hughes so isolated and so lonely? Why, with almost unlimited money, hundreds of aides, and countless beautiful women available to him, was he so unloved? Because he chose to be.

It is an old axiom . . . that God gave us "things" to use and "people" to enjoy. [Hughes got it turned around.] Hughes never learned to enjoy people. He was too busy manipulating them. His interests were machines, gadgets, technology, airplanes, and money . . . interests so consuming as to exclude relationships.[1]

For human beings, created in God's image, isolation and loneliness are a special kind of torture. Why? Because God is a social being who lives in unity and love, and He created us in His image to live in unity and love.

There is one body and one Spirit, just as also you were called in one hope of your calling; one Lord, one faith, one baptism, one God and Father of all who is over all and through all and in all.

Ephesians 4:4–6

This passage presents the basis for Christian unity, created by the Holy Spirit among all true Christians. This unity already exists as a result of God's sovereign work, and we are obligated to preserve and manifest it to the world through our relationships with other Christians.

God gave us things to use and people to enjoy. Like Howard Hughes—although perhaps to less bizarre degrees—we often get it turned around. We tend to use people and enjoy things. This leads to a barren life. We were created by God to be fulfilled only when living in unity and harmony with others. He created us to be interdependent, and the church is the ultimate expression of this. As we live in love and harmony with each other and use our gifts in serving one another, we experience the corporate joy and purpose God intends for His people.

The Unity of the Holy Spirit

Martin Lloyd-Jones spoke eloquently of the body of Christ in his commentary on Ephesians:

The church or body of Christ consists of people of all types and kinds and colors, from many continents and climates. The early Christians are in this body. The martyrs of the Reformation are in this body. The Puritans, the Covenanters, the first Methodists, they are all in this body;

and you and I are in this body if we are truly in Christ. The Church spans the continents and the centuries. Natural abilities play no part in this matter. It matters not what you may be, whether you are ignorant or knowledgeable, clever or lacking in faculties, great or small, wealthy or poor. All these things are utter irrelevancies. . . . The one thing that ultimately matters for each one of us is that we belong to this body. We can be members of a visible church and, alas, not be members of this mystical unseen Church.[2]

Just as the physical body is made up of countless different parts, all of which function as an organized whole, so the body of Christ is made up of countless individual parts, all of which contribute to the whole. Thus, it is extremely important that we see ourselves not as individuals in an unrelated sea of humanity, but as distinct and vital members of a great spiritual body which wants us and needs us.

I have ministered in all but a few of the fifty states, as well as in several foreign countries—often to people who could not speak the same language I was speaking. Yet there was an almost immediate bond between us because we were together in Christ.

My wife's parents once lived in an isolated little town just thirty miles north of the Mexican border in south-central New Mexico. Once while we were there, Margie and I were invited to participate in a cattle roundup at a ranch forty-five minutes' drive to the southwest. Between this ranch and Mexico there was nothing but several hundred thousand square miles of grass and a range of rugged, forbidding mountains. The prairie stretched to the mountains on the horizon.

After the roundup, Margie and I sat in the kitchen of the ranch house talking to our hosts as lunch was being prepared. Picking up on several of their comments, Margie finally asked, "Are you Christians?"

"Yes," they said, "are you?"

Suddenly we were on a whole new wavelength. We were no longer unrelated dots on the human horizon; we were brothers and sisters.

I'm sure at one time or another you've had similar experiences—moments when you realize just how much you are a part of one body.

Whether we are from Asia or Africa, Europe or Australia, South America or North America, when we are spiritually mature Christians, we all look alike. We all look like Christ, exhibiting His love, joy, peace, patience, kindness, goodness, faithfulness, gentleness, and self-control. We are one in the Spirit, and we have one hope: "the blessed hope and the appearing of the glory of our great God and Savior, Christ Jesus" (Titus 2:13).

The Unity of the Son

In the days of the early church, when the Roman Empire ruled the world, people worshiped a pantheon of gods. The Romans had gods for every occasion. Yet there was one God they resisted. In fact, rather than acknowledge this God, they brutally spilled the blood of His followers on the sand of their coliseum.

Why? Because this God said: "There is only one Lord, and that's Me! And there is only one way to salvation, and that is through My Son, Jesus Christ. He is the way, the truth, and the life."

In some parts of Africa a broom on the roof of a thatched hut or in the dirt yard of a primitive dwelling means that someone inside is ill. The occupant has placed a broom outside to drive away the demon of disease.

Louis Pasteur, however, proved that disease is caused by bacteria and can be prevented with sufficient caution and procedures.

People may have different views about disease, but that does not make these views equally valid. One person's concept of disease and cure is not as good as another person's because there is such a thing as objective truth in the world of medicine.

People also have different views about religion, but that does not make all views equally valid. One person's god is not as good as another's because there is objective truth, and the source of that truth is the Bible—God's revelation to man.

Truth is not what you think it is or what you feel it is. Truth is not relative. It does not change with circumstances or with the people involved. Truth is what God says it is. And He says there is "one Lord, one faith, one baptism, one God and Father of all" (Eph. 4:5–6).

The Unity of the Father

"One God and Father of all" is not intended to suggest the Fatherhood-of-God universalism which suggests that all men and women are children of God and therefore will eventually be saved. The context speaks of those who are in the body of Christ: those who have believed in and received the one Lord, confessed the one faith, and been placed into the one body of Christ. In John 8:44, Jesus says to the Pharisees, "You are of your father the devil, and you want to do the desires of your father." That is clear testimony that God is not the father of everyone. God is, however, supreme over all creation;

it is His plan that Jesus and the Holy Spirit are executing. Jesus said, "I come to do the Father's will. The Father is over all and through all."

His power pervades and sustains the whole life of the church. The energy of God brought the church into being and will keep it going until the consummation of His plans for this world. "For it is God who is at work in you, both to will and to work for His good pleasure" (Phil. 2:13). God works in us as individuals and as His collective body.

His presence is through all and in all. As John says: "If anyone loves Me, he will keep My word; and My Father will love him, and We will come to him, and make Our abode with him" (John 14:23). God dwells within each of His children.

These doctrinal truths are the foundation upon which our lives are built. But we also need to apply these truths to specific areas of need.

When we think of our purpose in life, we tend to think of putting food on the table and clothing on our backs . . . paying the rent or the house payment . . . going after job promotions or preparing for retirement . . . providing for our children . . . and on and on it goes.

All these are important. They are part of this life and part of our responsibility to those around us and to ourselves. But we have a purpose and responsibility above and beyond all this, and that is our part in the body of Christ. The purpose and calling of the body of Christ is to do, collectively, what Jesus did individually when He was on earth.

—He came to glorify the Father.

—He came to seek and save that which was lost.

—He came not to be served, but to serve.

So that's what we are to do.

It is okay if we put food on the table, pay the rent, buy clothing, work hard, prepare for our retirement, and provide for our children, but while we do, we must also

glorify God,

seek to save those who are lost,

serve others.

We must learn to distinguish between a life built on biblical principles and a life controlled by Christ. Even the world can recognize the value and use of biblical principles. Right now I have three books on my desk: *A Passion for Excellence, Swim with the Sharks without Being Eaten Alive,* and *Thriving on Chaos.* None of these are Christian books, yet all three are brilliant applications of the book of Proverbs to the working world. Honesty, integrity, hard work, regard for others, and commitment to excellence—all principles taught in the Scriptures—work in the marketplace. Yet a person can admire these principles—and even, within limits, adopt them—without being a Christian. Just as a person can go to church and read the Bible without being controlled by Christ.

I don't say this to point fingers. Most of us want to live a committed life. Unfortunately, many have not been taught what that means or have not had good role models.

We must begin to see ourselves not just as Americans . . . not just as Texans or Hoosiers . . . not just as Smiths or Joneses . . . but as members of the body of Christ. When we begin to grasp our true identity in Christ, it affects not only what we do, but the attitude and spirit with which we do it. It enables us to see more clearly the reasonableness of selling out totally to the Lord.

The straightest line between us and purpose and fulfillment in life is total obedience to Christ, which includes acting consistently with the reality that we are members of the body of Christ . . . united with Christ and with all other Christians . . . with a common destiny and a common purpose:

to glorify the Father,
to save the lost,
to serve others!

Unity with Diversity

While there is one Spirit, one Lord, one faith, one baptism, and one God and Father of us all, each member of this spiritual body is different. The Scripture makes this clear time and again, often by using the metaphor of the human body. World-renown surgeon Dr. Paul Brand understands well the implications of this image. In *Fearfully and Wonderfully Made,* he writes:

> Inside, my stomach, spleen, liver, pancreas, and kidneys, each packed with millions of loyal cells, are working so efficiently I have no way of perceiving their presence. Fine hairs in my inner ear are monitoring a swishing fluid, ready to alert me if I suddenly tilt off balance.
>
> My body employs a bewildering zoo of cells, none of which individually resembles the larger body. Just so, Christ's Body comprises an unlikely assortment of humans. Unlikely is precisely the right word, for we are decidedly unlike one another and the One we follow.

When my cells work well, I am hardly conscious of their individual presence. What I feel is the composite of their activity known as Paul Brand. My body, composed of many parts, is one.[3]

While the human body works as a unit, within it is great diversity. And just as there is unity and diversity in the human body, so there is unity and diversity in the spiritual body, the body of Christ. Nowhere is this more evident than in the gifts Christ has given to His church.

But to each one of us grace was given according to the measure of Christ's gift.

Ephesians 4:7

When I became a Christian, I wanted to be an evangelist. If I could have had my choice, I would have been another Billy Graham. To me, evangelism seemed such an important gift. And it was so measurable! If you had the gift of teaching, you never knew when your job was done. If you had the gift of evangelism, your work was completed when a person became a Christian.

In pursuit of this gift, I attended training seminars on "How to Witness." I read books on evangelism and how to share my faith. I witnessed to everybody, including every non-Christian I had ever known. I passed out tracts, did cold-turkey evangelism. I went to Florida during spring break and witnessed to the kids on the beach. Yet even though I did everything right, not much happened. Everyone I witnessed to was either a Christian already or wanted nothing to do with Christianity. Actually, that's been largely my experience with one-on-one evangelism for my entire Christian life.

On the other hand, I have a friend who hasn't read any of the books. He never took any evangelism training. And he does everything wrong: He comes on too strong, and he offends a lot of people. Yet he has won more people to Christ than I can begin to count. Why? Because he has the gift of evangelism. I don't.

We can't choose our spiritual gifts. Christ distributes them as He sees fit. "Now there are varieties of gifts, but the same Spirit. . . . distributing to each one individually just as He wills" (1 Cor. 12:4, 11). And the results are in His hands too.

While we must be faithful in using our spiritual gifts, the results are up to the Lord. We cannot claim credit when the results are good, nor do we need to feel guilty when we see few visible results. We have no idea what might be happening far beyond our view or comprehension or even our lifetime.

"All that's fine," you may be saying. "But let's go back to the beginning on this: I haven't the foggiest idea what my gift is." Well, here's more good news: You do not need to know your gift before you can begin serving the Lord.

If you list the primary spiritual gifts—the nonmiraculous "serving" gifts listed in Romans 12:6–8—you will see that each person is responsible to do all the things in the list.

> And since we have gifts that differ according to the grace given to us, let each exercise them accordingly: if prophecy, according to the proportion of his faith; if service, in his serving; or he who teaches, in his teaching; or he who exhorts, in his exhortation; he who gives, with liberality; he who leads, with diligence; he who shows mercy, with cheerfulness.

—Some have the gift of evangelism, but every believer is to evangelize.
—Some have the gift of teaching, but every believer teaches something to someone in the classroom of life.
—Some have the gift of generosity, but every believer must give.

So we must not become obsessed with "discovering" our spiritual gifts. Instead, we should just get busy doing the things the Bible commands God's children to do. Then we will find that some of the things we do have better results than others . . . some of the things we do are more enjoyable or come more "naturally" to us than others. And before long, by observing the results of what we have already been doing, we get insight into our own spiritual gifts and can begin to direct more of our energies into those areas.

Everyone is responsible to do something. When you are given a beautifully wrapped birthday present, what do you do with it? Tuck it away on the shelf? Hide it in the closet? Ignore the gift and the giver? No. You unwrap it and you use it and enjoy it. And you thank the person who gave it to you.

God does not give us the spiritual capacity to do something and then say, "You don't have to use it if you don't want to." Along with the gift comes the responsibility to use it well in the service of others.

And remember, there are no insignificant people and no small gifts. There is only faithfulness and unfaithfulness to what God asks of us. Billy Graham is not the teacher's pet. We are all of equal value to God. We are all important to the work and functioning of His body.

Before you are qualified to serve the Lord and minister to others, you need only two things:

—You must be a human being—in which case, you are created in the image of God.

—You must be a Christian—in which case, you are already gifted and called by God to do something important for Him.

The "I am" determines the "I can!"

We are Christ's orchestra here on earth. We each have a part to play. I may play the trumpet and you may play the violin, but each of us is vital. We are part of something larger and greater and grander than our individual selves. We are creating a symphony of praise to the glory of God. And though we do not hear the full score now or see all the musicians, the time will come when we will sit in heaven beside the Great Maestro and listen to His music for all eternity.

Focus Questions

1. Are you well integrated into a fellowship of serious Christians whose example and encouragement help you in your Christian walk? If so, how specifically has it helped you? If not, what steps could you take to fill the void?

2. What is the difference between seeing yourself as an American and seeing yourself as a Christian? What difference would it make in some of your choices and decisions if your commitment to being a Christian was greater than your commitment to being an American?

3. Though Christians are united in the Lord, they are diverse in their gifts. What contributions could you make to others? What is the most important thing you might be able to do to serve the Lord?

11

Building a House of Bricks, Not Sticks

(Ephesians 4:11–16)

The best neighbors I know are my two hands. They have lived on opposite sides of the street for many years, and they have never had a "row." If my left hand is hurt, my right hand immediately drops all other business and rushes across the way to comfort it and help it out of its trouble. If one happens to hurt the other, the one that is hurt doesn't get in a huff and say, "Here, I will not stand for that; you can't treat me that way," and get in a fight. No, no, no. They are good neighbors. My two hands are members of one another. And Christians should be like that. They are members of Christ's body. They should be as loving, as forbearing, as sympathetic and helpful toward each other as are my two hands.

Samuel Brengle

*T*he church has often been likened to a jigsaw puzzle, with each member being an individual piece. Each puzzle piece has protrusions and indentations. The protrusions represent our strengths (gifts, talents, abilities), and the indentations represent our weaknesses (faults, limitations, shortcomings, undeveloped areas). By themselves, the individual pieces may look a bit strange at times; but joined together, they produce a beautiful picture or pattern.

The apostle Paul said that there is one body, one Spirit, one hope, one Lord, one faith, one baptism, one God and Father of us all—one picture. And each of us makes up his or her part.

Have you ever spent hours putting a puzzle together, only to find, at the end, that a few pieces are missing—sometimes only one or two? Frustrating, right? If the picture is to be complete, each individual piece is vital. Each makes an irreplaceable contribution. And when each piece is in place, no one is conspicuous. Together, they blend to form the whole picture. And so it should be in the body of Christ.

Thus far in his letter to the Ephesians, Paul has been telling us that all Christians are united in Christ. We are part of a dwelling place of God in the Spirit, called the body of Christ. Now in chapter 4 he calls us to manifest or display that spiritual unity in our relationships, explaining that there is a direct correlation between that call to unity and the spiritual gifts Christ has given us. Spiritual gifts are at the heart of Christ's strategy for building His church: They establish the foundation of the ministry, they form the heart of the ministry, and they achieve the goal of the ministry.

The Foundation

And He gave some as apostles, and some as prophets, and some as evangelists, and some as pastors and teachers, for the equipping of the saints for the work of service, to the building up of the body of Christ; until we all attain to the unity of the faith, and of the knowledge of the Son of God, to a mature man, to the measure of the stature which belongs to the fulness of Christ.

Ephesians 4:11–13

This verse ties directly back to verse 7: "But to each one of us grace was given according to the measure of Christ's gift." Speaking of those gifts, Paul says, God has gifted some as apostles, some as prophets, some as evangelists, and some as pastors and teachers.

Actually there are two types of spiritual gifts: some are spiritual capacities given to each individual, and some are spiritually gifted individuals who are given to the church. Elsewhere in Scripture we read of individual gifts such as mercy, faith, exhortation, administration, and generosity. But here we read of gifted individuals who are given to the whole body: apostles, prophets, evangelists, and pastor-teachers. Of these four categories, only two are still in existence.

The apostles (meaning "sent ones") existed during a specified period of biblical history. These "sent ones" were the twelve men chosen by Christ to follow Him and be eyewitnesses of the Resurrection—along with Matthias who was chosen later to replace Judas. The term *apostle* was also applied in a more general sense to a few other outstanding leaders in the early church, including Paul, Barnabas, and Timothy. Individuals in both groups were authenticated by "signs and wonders and miracles" (2 Cor. 12:12), but neither group was self-perpetuating. As these original apostles died out, the gift of apostleship disappeared.

The prophets were also specially gifted people, and they differ from those who had the gift of prophecy. The ministry of the prophets went far beyond the ministry of the gift of prophecy described in 1 Corinthians 12. Sometimes the prophets spoke revelation from God (Acts 11:21–29) and sometimes they simply expounded upon revelation that had already been given. Like the office of apostle, the office of prophet phased out as the written record of the New Testament phased in—just as the Old Testament prophets phased out four hundred years before the birth of Christ.

The apostles and prophets filled in the gap, ministering the gospel and the revelation of God for about a hundred years after the crucifixion of Christ as the New Testament was completed (the apostle John completed his epistles, including Revelation, about A.D. 90). After the New Testament Scriptures were completed, there was no more need for the apostles and prophets, for God's revelation was complete and had literally been placed in the hands of His people.

The cornerstone of the church was Christ Jesus, upon whom the foundation was laid by the apostles and prophets. When those functions were completed, there was no more need for these gifts. Next came the building of the church itself—which meant the spreading of the gospel and the teaching of the saints, calling for the gifts of evangelism and pastoral teaching.

To evangelize is "to proclaim the Good News," hence those who are gifted and called to do so are called evangelists. In the days of the early church, when the message of the gospel was unknown outside of Jerusalem, evangelists were traveling missionaries and church planters. They led people to Christ, taught new believers the Word, established and encouraged the local body, and moved on to a new territory—not unlike our missionaries today.

Once there were believers to be taught and local bodies to be led, pastors and teachers were needed. Actually, there is strong evidence in the original language that these two words refer to one person: the pastor-teacher—one who both shepherds and teaches. However, it is important to understand that pastors are not to do all the work of the church. The pastor-teacher's responsibility is to equip the saints to do the work of the ministry. Ministry belongs to the church as a whole, of which the pastor-teacher is only one small part.

Unfortunately, many in the church take the view evidenced by a member of one of my fellow seminarian's churches. My friend had been called to a small pastorate in the rural midwest, and after conducting his first Wednesday evening prayer meeting, he asked one of the deacons to close in prayer. The deacon replied, "Pastor, that's what we pay you to do."

An extreme example, granted. Yet many do view ministry as the sole job of the pastor-teacher; that's what they hire him to do. Churches who take this perspective will strangle, abbreviate, and retard the ministry of their particular church.

In the church I pastor, it takes four hundred volunteers to do all the ministry carried out in a typical week. Look around in your own congregation. You could not possibly afford to hire enough people to do the work. Add to this the fact that God has gifted a multitude of His people to minister; and He wants to enrich and fulfill us by using us in those ministries for which He has gifted us. Plus, ministry does not take place solely within the context of local church activities. Ministry occurs in the workplace, in the marketplace, in the neighborhoods, in the government, and in the schools.

Our mandate is to move beyond ourselves, to reach out to the world around us. As we continue to grow, therefore, we must expand the number of people who accept personal responsibility for ministry, so that we will have the people resources necessary to accommodate not only our own growth but also to reach out into the world around us. Only then will we grow into local fellowships that are doctrinally stable, emotionally healthy, and mobilized for effective mutual ministry.

The Heart

The primary task of the pastor-teacher and the church is to equip the saints.
—We need to be equipped in what we know.
—We need to be equipped in how we live.
—We need to be equipped in what we can do.
From the saints who are equipped, God raises up elders, deacons, teachers, counselors, helpers, administrators, disciplers, givers, evangelists, and every kind of worker needed for the Lord's service. When believers are equipped, the whole body is built up in the unity of the faith, spiritual maturity, and knowledge of Christ.

Knowledge of Christ does not mean salvation. It means a deeper, experiential knowledge that comes from walking with Christ and getting to know

Him as Lord. Even Paul, after walking with the Lord for many years, said, "I count all things to be loss in view of the surpassing value of knowing Christ. . . . Not that I have already obtained it, or have already become perfect, but I press on . . ." (Phil. 3:8, 12). While it can and must begin to characterize our lives, knowledge of Christ is really a lifelong pursuit.

As believers, we want the fullness of Christ in our lives. We want peace, love, and joy. We want to love God with all our heart, soul, and mind. We want to be spiritually mature. That is a given. With the fullness of Christ, our lives would be richer, fuller, more meaningful, and would give more glory to God. That, too, is a given.

But . . . we cannot know the fullness of Christ in our lives unless we become part of a vital group of Christians. And we cannot experience the fullness of Christ in our lives unless we become involved in ministering to others. This doesn't mean we have to teach a doctrine class. We can greet people at the door of the church during services, we can take meals to shut-ins, we can visit prisoners, we can help someone learn to read . . . the possibilities are endless. We can

help those who cannot return the favor;
give to those who cannot repay;
care for those who cannot care for themselves;
teach those who lack knowledge;
counsel those who need guidance;
cheer those who are lonely;
encourage those who are discouraged.

I won't promise that if you do these things, you will automatically and always have joy, peace, and love. But I will tell you that you cannot have joy, peace, and love without ministering to others.

And remember: One congregation cannot meet everyone's needs. It takes the body of Christ at large; it takes unity with diversity. Not every church can sponsor a recovering-alcoholics' support group, but some can; not every church can support an overeaters' anonymous, but some can; not every church can offer a day-care ministry, but some can. Working together, employing our diversity of gifts and resources, we can support and minister to each other, even as we reach out to minister to the world around us.

A Healthy Spiritual Body

In 539 B.C. Cyrus, king of Persia, massed his army on the border between Persia and Babylonia, swept down from the mountains, and conquered the awesome Babylonian empire. As the Persians moved into the territory, they made an amazing discovery: thousands upon thousands of Jews living in Babylonia.

Seventy years earlier Nebuchadnezzar and his Babylonian army had swept across the entire eastern end of the Mediterranean Sea, crushing every civilization in its path. Among them was the nation of Judah and its capital city of Jerusalem. In a brutal strategy common at the time, the Babylonians destroyed the city and enslaved anyone who might make a valuable contribution to their culture—educators, artists, craftsmen, and others. Transported as slaves to Babylonia, these Jews lived in captivity and multiplied for the next seventy years.

Then Cyrus burst upon the scene, and within twenty-five years the Persian empire stretched from India to Ethiopia, from the Caucasus Mountains in the north to the Arabian Sea in the south. But their philosophy of government was even more impressive than their military deeds, for the Persians fostered peaceful coexistence among the nations of the empire through a policy of tolerance.

In keeping with this policy, Cyrus not only permitted the displaced Jews to return to Jerusalem, but allowed them to rebuild their city and reinstate their temple worship and the sacrificial system of the Mosaic Law.

One of these Jews of the Dispersion was a well-educated young man named Ezra, son of one of the families taken into captivity years earlier. Knowing the prophecies of Nehemiah, which had predicted the captivity, the seventy-year exile, and the return, Ezra was thrilled at the hope of restoring the temple, reinstating the sacrifices, and reviving the worship of Jehovah.

Before the city and the temple could be rebuilt, however, Ezra knew that the returning Jewish people would have to be rebuilt. They needed both a knowledge of the Mosaic Law and an understanding of their national heritage before they would have the courage and commitment for such a monumental undertaking. So Ezra dedicated himself to the task of restoring the people of Israel and to becoming the kind of person who could be used by God to rekindle national pride and spiritual fire in his people.

In order to do this—to be used by God in the lives of other people—Ezra studied the Law of the Lord, practiced the Law of the Lord, and taught its statutes and ordinances throughout the land. Studying the Law gave him biblical knowledge; practicing the Law gave him a biblical lifestyle; and teaching the Law gave him a biblical ministry. Ezra knew what he needed to know, became what he needed to be, and did what he needed to do.

There's a lesson here for us, too: If we want to be people God can use to rebuild the lives of others, we need biblical knowledge, a biblical lifestyle, and a biblical ministry. Ezra's lifestyle grew out of his knowledge, and his ministry flowed out of his lifestyle. Our lifestyle will never go beyond our knowledge, and our ministry will never go beyond our lifestyle.

Moving this principle from the individual to the corporate, we see that a healthy church must be doctrinally sound (knowledge), have balanced spiritual growth (lifestyle), and have committed and mobilized members (ministry).

Growing Up

As a result, we are no longer to be children, tossed here and there by waves, and carried about by every wind of doctrine, by the trickery of men, by craftiness in deceitful scheming; but speaking the truth in love, we are to grow up in all aspects into Him, who is the head, even Christ, from whom the whole body, being fitted and held together by that which every joint supplies, according to the proper working of each individual part, causes the growth of the body for the building up of itself in love.

Ephesians 4:14–16

We all begin life as children—indeed, as babies. But we immediately begin growing, and eventually we become adults. We mature. This is so obvious, yet when it comes to the Christian life, we seem to forget it.

The Christian life is a totally new life. A birth. And we are not born as adults; we are born as babies—no matter what "earth age" we may be when our new birth occurs. The Christian life is not an addition to or continuation of a former life; nor is it some kind of spiritual evolution. We don't gradually move from being a non-Christian to being a Christian; we don't begin as a non-Christian and just keep getting better and better until we finally evolve into a Christian.

So it is not wrong to be a spiritual baby. In fact, it is unavoidable. The day we become a Christian we may be a great intellect, a capable professional, or a strong leader, but we enter the Christian life as a spiritual infant.

The single greatest frustration to me as a young Christian was that I wanted to be more mature than I was. It seemed that no matter what I did, I could not speed up the process significantly. I was certain God was sick and tired of me for being so immature.

Everyone starts out as a child. We must accept that. However, everyone must grow out of childhood.

When it comes to spiritual maturity, you can start growing wherever you are. Perhaps you have been a Christian for a while but have been rebellious or lazy, or perhaps you haven't had anyone to teach and disciple you. So you are still immature. That doesn't matter. Just start where you are and begin growing. This is the right place, and now is the right time.

How do you know if you are immature? Well, the characteristics of spiritual childhood are fairly predictable: "children [are] tossed here and there by waves, and carried about by every wind of doctrine, by the trickery of men, by craftiness in deceitful scheming. . . ."

For the above read: unstable, fickle, changeable, ignorant, gullible, susceptible, indiscriminate, and undiscerning.

A number of years ago when Margie and I were living in Phoenix, Arizona, we were walking down the street of a pleasant neighborhood subdivision with several of our friends. It was a lovely summer evening, and one of the group started trotting out ahead of the rest of us, laughing and happy. Suddenly he was swallowed up by the darkness. Alone and frightened of the dark, he came running back, crying.

"That guy's unstable," I said to Margie. "One minute he's laughing, the next he's crying."

"Of course he's unstable," she said. "He's only two!"

Children are unstable . . . fickle . . . changeable. Have you ever tried to reason with an enraged two-year-old? You might as well reason with a cactus.

Another time we were visiting with friends whose three-year-old was, well, to say the least, volatile. When her parents asked her to do something, she erupted like a little Mt. Vesuvius, filling every corner of the room with vibrations from her overdeveloped vocal cords.

"Susie," her mother said, "if you are going to cry, please go to your room so we don't have to listen to you."

Susie stormed to her room, slammed the door so hard that pictures tilted on the wall, and let out a bloodcurdling scream. There was a moment of silence . . . then another scream . . . then more silence. We didn't know if she had died or if she was just inhaling. Moments later she appeared in the living room, tears streaked down each cheek and a beatific smile on her face. "I'm done," she said.

Children are tossed about by their emotions and by circumstances.

Children tend to believe whatever they are told and are therefore susceptible to unscrupulous persons.

Children are ignorant and have limited reasoning ability. They need someone older and wiser to teach them and protect them.

Children are impatient. They want everything right now. They don't want to practice for hours to learn the piano; they're bored with scales; they want to play "Moonlight Sonata."

Children dislike repetition and discipline.

Children overestimate their own ability and knowledge.

This is understandable. They are children. But if they are to become mature, functioning adults, they must grow out of these and other characteristics. And the same is true for us as newborn Christians: We must grow up. We can and we will if we will just keep

eating the Word of God,

breathing prayer,

exercising faith and resting in Christ,

from running into the street of carelessness or rebellion.

In recent years a host of unscrupulous radio and television preachers have ravaged the reputation of the church and wreaked havoc on the lives of their followers. Some are puzzled by this. "Why?" they ask. Why would anyone let these electronic hucksters pick their pockets and tamper with their theology?

Why? Because immature Christians are susceptible. They have no discrimination . . . no discernment. And many remain that way because they do not immerse themselves in the Scripture, memorizing it and meditating upon it; they do not place themselves under the tutelage of reputable teachers so that they become doctrinally stable.

If it takes at least twelve years of elementary and secondary schooling to be fully educated, why should we think our spiritual education would happen overnight? Yet in the average church the education for the new believer is hit and miss. The average ninety-day wonder from one of the cults can take apart the average Christian because the cultist has been trained with a purpose and a strategy.

Christian education with strategy and purpose equips us and grounds us with the foundation of knowledge we need to grow to maturity. And as individuals grow up in Christ—becoming more and more like Him—the local congregation gains balanced spiritual growth and doctrinal stability.

Then, committed and mobilized, the people of God—the whole body, with each individual making a contribution—use their spiritual gifts as God intended, building up the body in love.

Lewis Timberlake writes:

> While on a tour of California's giant sequoias, the guide pointed out that the sequoia tree has roots just barely below the surface of the ground.
>
> "That's impossible," I said. "I'm a country boy, and I know that if the roots don't grow deep into the earth, strong winds will blow the trees over."
>
> "Not sequoias," said the guide. "They grow only in groves and their roots intertwine under the surface of the earth. So, when the strong winds come, they hold each other up."[1]

God's people are like the giant sequoias. We grow in groves, our roots intertwined in Christ. And when the strong winds of life blow, we stand upright against them, reaching toward the Son.

Focus Questions

1. Realizing that we can't hire enough pastors to do everything, in what ways have you taken personal responsibility for ministering in the church or outside the church?

2. Following Ezra's example of gaining biblical knowledge, biblical lifestyle, and biblical ministry skills, what could you do to further yourself in each of these areas?

3. Are you a spiritual infant, adolescent, or adult? What do you need to do to progress to the next stage?

12

Walk Which Way?
(Ephesians 4:17–24)

When we are tempted, we do not say, "I hate God and God hates me." Rather, we simply forget about God and act as though He didn't exist, or we had never known Him.

Dietrich Bonhoeffer

*I*t's amazing how many people are afraid to fly—even some seasoned travelers. They are scared to death of dying in a plane crash. Yet with odds like a hundred thousand to one, a person is more likely to be kicked to death by a donkey than die in a plane crash. People also fear the possibility of being murdered in our crime-ridden society. Yet a person is eight times more likely to die while playing a sport than to be shot by a stranger. People are afraid of dying on the operating table. Yet we are at greater risk getting in our car every day than we are in surgery. One in forty thousand die in surgery; one in four thousand die in auto accidents.

> When it comes to taking risks, most of us are curiously irrational. Millions of people buy lottery tickets, even though we are three times more likely to be struck by lightning than to strike it rich in a lottery. It is ironic that we spend money on extremely long and improbable odds, and blithely ignore the relatively short odds that concern our health and well being, such as smoking, or eating high cholesterol foods, or worrying excessively, or placing ourselves under constant and serious stress.
>
> We don't appreciate what are the big risks and what are the small ones. Put another way, when it comes to risk, we are idiots.

Many people also fear the "risk" of making a total commitment to Jesus. What if He sends us to some isolated mission field? Or what if He keeps us here and makes an idiot out of us at work or with our friends? What if He asks us to give up things that are important to us? What if He takes away everything we enjoy so that our lives become empty, stark, and joyless?

Yet, if we take the Bible even halfway seriously, we see that those fears are unfounded. And even a cursory observation of the things the world looks to for meaning and purpose must cause us to admit that they don't satisfy. Both faith and reflection bring us to the same conclusion: It is not dangerous to commit ourselves to Christ. Yet we fear it anyway.

Paul calls us to break with our past and commit ourselves totally to following Christ. We are to
—put off the old self;
—put on the new self.
The old self is separated from God. While it is capable of good, it is incapable of avoiding evil. It is who we are by nature, and it is who we remain if we do not allow God to intervene. We are descendants of Adam; we have inherited his fallen nature. As a result, we are separated from God. That is the old self.

When we lay that aside—like taking off an old coat and putting on a new one—we must leave behind the attitudes, habits, values, and actions that we had before we became a Christian. But the old self doesn't want to be left behind. So, aided and abetted by its devilish master, this deceitful self hangs around the house, enticing us to try it on again. This old self
—promises pleasure but delivers pain,
—promises satisfaction but delivers sorrow,
—promises a bright tomorrow but delivers a blighted future,
—promises good but delivers bad,
—promises right but delivers wrong,
—promises the truth but delivers a lie.
And it destroys . . . it always destroys.

Sin is like cocaine. It is addictive. It feels good at the moment, but in the end it destroys.

Think back over this past week. How did you spend your time? If you are at all typical, you spent it sleeping, working, driving to and from work, eating, listening to the news or reading the newspaper, watching your favorite television programs, doing household chores, running errands, driving the kids to Little League or Scouts, shopping, figuring bills and writing checks, going to church—and there are a multitude of things I didn't even mention.

My point? Where is God in all this? Does He only enter into the "going to church" part?

Our time and our minds are bombarded by the people we work with, the music on the radio, the images on television. This constant stream of information, stimulation, and occupation carries us in any number of directions and away from God. We row upstream toward Him on Sunday mornings, but the current is so powerful that often before the day is over we are floating downstream again, away from Him.

I used to preach against television and against rock 'n' roll and against country and western music. I would get people all stirred up, and many of them relinquished the tube or the music or something else that consumed them—for a while. Since they had nothing to replace it with, however, they eventually returned to it.

I don't preach against these things anymore. Instead, I ask people what they want out of life. When you ask most Christians this question, they will say, in some form or other: "a meaningful relationship with God, a meaningful relationship with my family and Christian friends, and a sense of purpose in what I do with my life." So then I ask them if they are willing to pay the price to get what they want.

We cannot have those things and still saturate our minds with every distraction this world offers. We must choose. Whatever we take in through our eyes and our ears feeds our minds, which in turn feeds our emotions and our souls. We are what we think. If we want to be different, then we must change our mental diet.

Most of us have been taught the black dog/white dog theory for years. This prevalent belief maintains that we have two natures—a righteous nature and an evil nature—and these two war against each other until we die. Sometimes the black dog wins, and sometimes the white dog wins.

On a certain level there is some truth to this. But overall, both practically and theologically, this schizophrenic identity causes big problems. If we believe that we are half bad, it is easier for us to act bad half of the time—at least. Plus, I don't believe Scripture teaches the "two-nature" theory. Look at Ephesians 4:24 as just one example: "Put on the new self, which in the likeness of God has been created in righteousness and holiness of the truth."

In his commentary on Ephesians, John MacArthur writes:

> Biblical terminology does not say that a Christian has two different natures. He has but one nature, the new nature in Christ. The old self dies and the new self lives; they do not coexist. . . . The Christian is a single new person, a totally new creation, not a spiritual schizophrenic. It is the filthy coat of remaining humanness in which the new creation

dwells that continues to hinder and contaminate his living. He is no longer the old man corrupted, but is now the new man created in righteousness and holiness, awaiting full salvation (Rom. 13:11) when he dies and is given a new body.[1]

Thus, when Satan's deadly suggestions tempt our susceptible flesh, our true, righteous "self" can say, "No, that isn't me. That is the power of darkness trying to deceive me in order to destroy me. I don't have to serve sin, and I choose not to." When we say that, we are strengthened not to sin.

This new self also throws up certain inner barriers to keep us away from sin. We call it our conscience. When we are tempted to do something we shouldn't, we encounter an internal barrier. If we knock it down and leap to the next level of involvement, we encounter another barrier. If we continue, it becomes easier and easier to break down the barriers, until finally our lives are irrevocably damaged or we are enslaved by the desires of the flesh.

Consider the dating process, for example. A boy and a girl (or a man and a woman) begin dating. First they hold hands. That is one barrier down. On the next date, they kiss. Another barrier down. A few dates later, they find themselves alone in the car and they get more physically involved. Realizing they have gone too far, they decide they will only hold hands and kiss occasionally. Yet rarely are couples able to return to a less intense level once the barriers of physical intimacy have been broken down. Once you break down one barrier, it becomes easier to break down the next one and the next one.

The same thing happens with alcohol. A kid begins drinking beer with his buddies in high school. In college he parties more heavily—going from beer to the hard stuff. Then, somewhere in his twenties, he realizes he's become dependent on alcohol. He's got a drinking problem! He decides he will stop altogether. Unfortunately it's not that easy. All the barriers are down.

If we see ourselves as two-headed monsters, both good and bad, it is easier to justify choosing bad alternatives. When we see ourselves as righteous spiritual beings, however, temporarily housed in bodies that feel the pull to sin, it is easier to say, "This pull is not from within me. This pull to sin is coming from without . . . from the power of sin in my flesh . . . from the efforts of the powers of darkness to pander to my fallen body." It is easier to say no.

To do this, we must first see ourselves as God sees us: as those who have been spiritually reborn—created in the image of God, in holiness and righteousness—despite being temporarily housed in sin-racked earth suits. Then we must cooperate with Him in the process of conforming our outer lifestyles to our inner holiness in Christ.

So, Paul says . . . put off the old self and put on the new.

> This I say therefore, and affirm together with the Lord, that you walk no longer just as the Gentiles also walk, in the futility of their mind, being darkened in their understanding, excluded from the life of God, because of the ignorance that is in them, because of the hardness of their heart; and they, having become callous, have given themselves over to sensuality, for the practice of every kind of impurity with greediness. But you did not learn Christ in this way, if indeed you have heard Him and have been taught in Him, just as truth is in Jesus, that, in reference to your former manner of life, you lay aside the old self, which is being corrupted in accordance with the lusts of deceit, and that you be renewed in the spirit of your mind, and put on the new self, which in the likeness of God has been created in righteousness and holiness of the truth.
>
> Ephesians 4:17–24

The Wayward Walk

Madison Avenue promises us "the good life." If we drive this car or drink that beverage or live in this home or use that investment company, we will enjoy the good life—and, by implication, be happy and fulfilled. Brainwashed into believing that the good life is something we can buy, we Americans have more gadgets, more toys, and more diversions than any other people on earth. Yet we have more trouble with anxiety, with fear, and with boredom.

The problem is: We worship the wrong god.

Man has always worshiped a variety of gods: Bacchus, the god of wine and pleasure; Venus, the goddess of love; Athena, the goddess of wisdom. Although their names have changed, the gods themselves haven't; we still worship them today. In addition, we have added Self, the god of individualism. The words of William E. Henley pulsate through our national consciousness:

> It matters not how straight the gate,
> How charged with punishment the scroll;
> I am the master of my fate,
> I am the captain of my soul.

That sounds noble and profound, but it is utter nonsense. When we attempt to captain the ship of the soul, we soon sail into dangerous waters.

Before long, we smash to pieces on the rocks of darkened understanding and moral corruption.

In his chilling novel, *The Lord of the Flies,* William Golding tells the story of a group of young schoolboys stranded, after a plane wreck, on a deserted island. Isolated, without the restraints of adults, culture, or civilization, the boys gradually turn into a pack of wild animals, reverting to primitive tribalism and ritual murder.

The few boys who resist this moral and social disintegration are hunted down by the others. One is knocked over a cliff. In a cruel and heartless scene, Ralph, the leader of the "good boys," is chased through the underbrush toward the seashore.

Terrified, certain of his impending death, Ralph breaks out onto the beach and falls at the feet of a naval officer from a rescue ship. As the hunting pack breaks out of the brush onto the beach, spears ready in frenzied pursuit of their kill, they are brought up short at the sight of the naval officers. The boys drop their crude weapons, and the wild, primitive tribe once again becomes a group of frightened, bewildered schoolchildren.

Reacting to all he has been through, Ralph breaks into tears for the first time. "With filthy body, matted hair, and unwiped nose, Ralph wept for the end of innocence, the darkness of man's heart, and the fall through the air of the true, wise friend called Piggy."[2]

The darkness of the human heart is like a sinister cloud that can spread from horizon to horizon in the human soul, blocking out the sun. Paul describes that darkness as the wayward walk of those who do not follow the Lord. Therefore, he exhorts believers to "walk no longer just as the Gentiles also walk" (4:17).

No doubt about it—the Gentiles in Ephesus were sinful. Ephesus was a leading city of commerce and culture in the Roman Empire, a key city in the central Mediterranean, and a seat of proconsular power from which the whole province of Asia could be influenced. It was also a stronghold of pagan religion, being the home of the temple of Diana, one of the seven wonders of the ancient world. Worship of Diana was a pagan cult associated with fertility rituals, orgiastic rites, and religious prostitution. Its influence made Ephesus a wicked place indeed. And since many of the Christians in the church at Ephesus came out of that evil background, Paul uses it as a contrast to the Christian walk.

"Don't live like that any longer!" he says. "It is futile. Their understanding is darkened. Because of their ignorance and the hardness of their heart, they are excluded from the life of God. Having become callous, they have devoted themselves to sensuality and the greedy practice of every kind of impurity" (4:17–19, paraphrase mine).

The mind set against God leads nowhere. Almost three thousand years ago, Solomon—the epitome of wisdom—said that he had pursued everything the world offered: fame, fortune, accomplishment, pleasure . . . everything. Nothing satisfied. It was all vanity—empty, purposeless, futile. The mind set against God is spiritually and morally bankrupt.

We have all seen the bumper sticker, "He who dies with the most toys wins." Yet I have never heard of anyone on his deathbed calling for his toys to comfort him. I have never heard of anyone saying, "Everything's getting dark now. Wide-screen TV and stereo VCR, come a little closer. Bring me my glitter-finished bass boat, my one-hundred-watt stereo with wrap-around speakers and digitally channeled woofers and tweeters. Now, where's my law degree and my Rolex watch? Where's my E. F. Hutton portfolio? Okay, everything's here. I can die now."

There are many parallels between the darkness cast by Ephesian society and the shadow drifting across our own national landscape. Spiritual and moral restraints are being cast off with horrifying consequences: homosexuality, AIDS, drugs, abortion, pornography, and crime. In education, in the legal and penal system, in government we are reaping the consequences of a darkened understanding. We have an economy in collapse, education in crisis, crime in epidemic proportions.

And even in the face of this, many in the culture want to rid our country of every vestige of religious influence. They have turned their backs on God to walk in their own futility of mind and darkened understanding.

In the beginning our nation functioned on Judeo-Christian principles. Then in the 1960s, God was proclaimed dead and the sexual revolution was born. The rise of drugs, crime, economic problems, government corruption, sexual disease, and loss of the work ethic can be traced back to that fundamental change in our national morality.

Like many in our nation, the Ephesians had turned their backs on God. As a result, their hearts were darkened by sin and their lives became morally corrupt, devoted to sensuality and every kind of impurity. They were dead in their trespasses and sins. That's why God hates sin . . . because it destroys His creation.

"Don't live that way," Paul says. "Please don't live that way. That is the old way. Christ is the new way. The old way is self-destructive. The new way is self-sustaining. Make the break. Now that you are in Christ, you can no longer be who you were."

Walking the Talk

Many people think sin is like Twinkies. Those gooey little goodies might not be good for us, but eaten in moderation they won't hurt either.

Well, I've got bad news for them. Sin is not like Twinkies. Sin is like cocaine. It doesn't take much to get hooked, and once we do . . . it destroys us.

But the good news is that we don't have to stay hooked, huddled in the darkness of sin.

We don't have to be lost . . . we can be saved.

We don't have to walk in darkness . . . we can walk in light.

We don't have to be confused . . . we can know truth.

We don't have to be consumed by doubt . . . we can be filled with faith.

We don't have to drown in despair . . . we can be rescued by hope.

We don't have to live in fear and hate . . . we can live in love.

God is not only willing to lead us out of the darkness, He is eager to do so . . . to lift us to higher ground, a lighter path, a greener pasture . . . no matter how long or how deep we have been in sin.

In her book, *Tramp for the Lord,* Corrie ten Boom wrote:

[After the war, I converted a] concentration camp to use as a home for displaced persons. . . . Often I would walk through the camp talking with the lonely, defeated people and trying to bring them hope and cheer.

One afternoon, I spotted an elderly woman huddled in the corner. . . . She was obviously new to the camp. . . . There she crouched, like a whipped child, her faded, worn dress pulled tightly around her frail, wasted body. . . . defeated by life itself.

I went to her, sat beside her on the floor, and asked who she was. I learned she had been a professor of music at the Dresden Conservatory before the war. . . .

"You were a professor of piano?" I asked excitedly. "I am a great lover of Germany's master musician, Johann Sebastian Bach."

The only piano in the area belonged to a minister in a nearby town, and he invited Corrie to make use of it. Unfortunately, the instrument was in sad shape. While it had survived the bombing during the war, it had been exposed to the weather. Strings were rusted, pedals broken off, and the keyboard was almost entirely without ivory. If it could play a note, it would be a miracle. But the woman looked up at Corrie and said, "What would you like me to play?"

> Then, to my own amazement, I heard myself saying, "Would you please play the 'Chromatic Phantasy' of Bach?"
> I was aghast. Why had I picked one of the most difficult of all piano pieces for this old woman to play on such a ruined instrument? Yet the moment I said it, I saw a light flicker behind her eyes and a slight, knowing smile played across her tired face. She nodded and, with great finesse, put her fingers on the broken keyboard.
> I could hardly believe my ears. From that damp, battered old piano flowed the beautiful music of Bach as her skilled fingers raced up and down the broken, chipped keys. . . .
> As we walked back . . . my companion had a new spring in her step. "It has been many years since I played the 'Chromatic Phantasy,'" she said. "Once I was a concert pianist and many of my pupils are now outstanding musicians. I had a beautiful home in Dresden that was destroyed by the bombs. I had to flee and was not able to take one thing with me."
> "Oh, no, you are wrong," I said. "You took with you your most prized possession."
> "And what was that?" she asked, shocked.
> "Your music. For that which is in your heart can never be taken from you."[3]

What a marvelous ray of light in a darkened world . . . *that which is in your heart can never be taken from you.*

Has something you loved been taken from you? Have you lost your job? Your sense of purpose? Are you having difficulty replacing some broken barriers? Are you afraid to take the risk . . . to make the full commitment? Is that old self still hanging around, trying to get your attention? Have you allowed yourself to fall back into some of your old ways?

God specializes in taking broken lives and making them whole
> in taking aimless lives and giving them direction,
> in taking meaningless lives and giving them purpose,
> in taking hateful lives and filling them with love,
> in taking sad lives and giving them joy,
> in taking harried lives and giving them peace.

As we walk the new way . . . in the light of Christ's love . . . what people see on the outside begins to look more like the transformed self on the inside.

Focus Questions

1. What is your greatest fear in giving yourself unreservedly to Christ? Do you think the fear is justified?

2. What activities are you engaging in that might be holding you back from a more complete walk with Christ?

3. We don't worship actual "gods" in American culture. What do we worship in their place?

13

What We Look Like When We Look Like Christ

(Ephesians 4:25–32)

In our pursuit of righteousness, we cannot be unrighteous. Being on our way home is no justification for tramping through a flower bed.

Source unknown

*W*hen we give Christ the freedom to rule our lives, He leaves a definite mark on our lifestyle. Old values, old attitudes, old habits give way to new values, new attitudes, new habits. We are no longer to live as the Gentiles live, Paul says. Then he gets specific . . . very specific . . . occasionally excruciatingly specific in detailing the implications of this in four key areas of our lives: honesty, anger, work, and attitude.

To Tell the Truth

Therefore, laying aside falsehood, speak truth, each one of you, with his neighbor, for we are members of one another.

Ephesians 4:25

One day a minister spotted a group of small boys out in the church parking lot gathered around an irresistibly cute puppy. They were making quite a commotion, so the minister walked over to them and asked, "Well, boys, what's going on here?"

"We found this puppy," said one of the boys, "and all of us want to keep it. So we're having a contest. The one who can tell the biggest lie wins the puppy."

"Shame on you boys!" said the minister. "I can't believe you would do such a thing. Deliberately telling lies. Why, when I was your age, I never told a lie."

The boys fidgeted and looked at each other nervously. Finally one boy said, "Okay, mister. You win the dog."

Lies. Big ones . . . little white ones . . . medium-sized gray ones . . . whoppers. There isn't one of us who hasn't stretched the truth or even told a barefaced lie. It's part of the fall . . . to lie.

Becoming a Christian does not mean becoming a robot who automatically obeys everything God commands. So if you have a problem with lying before you become a Christian, there is a good chance you will be tempted to lie after you become a Christian. If and when the temptation comes, you need the strength of the Holy Spirit to attack it, surround it, and conquer it, for the Bible is totally unambiguous about lying: *Lying alienates us from God, violates who we have become in Christ, and plays into the strategy of Satan.*

Few things are as essential to the character of God as truth. At the beginning of his epistle to Titus, Paul makes the astounding claim: "God . . . cannot lie" (Titus 1:2). God cannot lie!

Can God do anything in the world? No. He cannot lie. He can do anything that is consistent with His character, and lying is not consistent with His character.

The ninth commandment says: "You shall not bear false witness against your neighbor" (Exod. 20:16). In other words: Don't lie. Because to be a Christian means to be brought into fellowship with God, and to lie means to break fellowship with the One who cannot lie.

In his commentary on Ephesians, Martin Lloyd-Jones writes:

> Nothing is so characteristic of the Christian life as the fact that it belongs to the whole realm of truth. We describe what has happened to a man who has become a Christian by saying that he has seen the truth, or he has seen the light. That is what we claim for the Bible and the gospel. This, we say, is truth! and nothing else is truth. We thank God that we have been delivered out of the realm of the lie by which the world is governed. But we have been brought into the realm of truth, and we glory in it.

"God our Savior," Paul writes to Timothy, ". . . desires all men to be saved and to come to the knowledge of the truth" (1 Tim. 2:3–4). And in his first epistle, John argues repeatedly that the Christian lives in the realm of truth. The darkness is past; the light has come. Clearly, therefore, everything in our lives should indicate that, having arrived at a knowledge of the truth, we are now living in the truth and that lying is utterly incompatible with the realm to which we now belong.

Satan is a liar and wants to destroy us with his lies. He began by lying to Eve. He deceived her into thinking that God was not looking out for her best interest and that she would have to take things into her own hands.

Satan is still lying. He is still trying to deceive us into thinking that God is not looking out for our best interests and that if we want the best for ourselves, we must take things into our own hands.

Proverbs 6:16–17 says there are six things God hates, and lying is one of them. Commitment to the truth is imperative if we are to align ourselves with His nature. One of our purposes as God's children is to be conformed to the character and image of His Son. We are redeemed to reflect His character. When we lie, we abort this purpose and tarnish the reflection of His glory through us.

When we speak the truth, we deny Satan's lies. We align our lives with God, we reflect His glory, and we live in obedience to His commands.

God commands us to live and speak the truth. He commands us to tell the truth. Our consciences cannot be clear before Him, and our joy cannot be full if we fail to live truthful lives. If we abide in Him, John says, and His Word abides in us, then we will keep His commandments (John 15).

Finally, Paul appeals to our spiritual unity in the body of Christ. How can there be fellowship if there is not truth?

Trust makes fellowship possible—mutual trust, mutual reliance, a sense that because you can trust one another you can speak freely and openly. Without trust, fellowship is destroyed.

Do you want close fellowship between husband and wife?
You must speak truth to one another.

Do you want close fellowship between parent and child?
You must speak truth to one another.

Do you want close fellowship between brothers and sisters?
You must speak truth to one another.

Do you want close fellowship between friends?
You must speak truth to one another.

We are to put away falsehood; that much is clear. If we are to do this, however, we need to be aware of some of the ways we promote falsehood:

1. We fail to distinguish between facts and opinions. ("Jack Nicklaus is the greatest golfer ever to play the game!")
2. We exaggerate. ("He's always late." "She always nags me." "He never says thank you.")
3. We rationalize. ("I shouldn't get so angry, but then I'm Irish.")

A truthful person has integrity. A truthful person is trustworthy, dependable, reputable, and credible. So put away lying. Speak truth . . . for we are members with one another.

Attitude Adjustment, Eternity Style

Be angry, and yet do not sin; do not let the sun go down on your anger, and do not give the devil an opportunity.

Ephesians 4:26–27

"We all know that Alexander the Great conquered the world. But what few people know is that this mighty general could not conquer himself," writes Erwin Lutzer in his book *Managing Your Emotions.*

Cletus, a dear friend of Alexander's and a general in his army, became intoxicated and ridiculed the emperor in front of his men. Blinded by anger, quick as lightening, Alexander snatched a spear from the hand of a soldier and hurled it at Cletus. Though he had only intended to scare the drunken general, his aim was true and the spear took the life of his childhood friend.

Deep remorse followed his anger. Overcome with guilt, Alexander tried to take his own life with the same spear, but he was stopped by his men. For days he lay sick, calling for his friend, Cletus, chiding himself as a murderer.

Alexander the Great conquered many cities; he conquered many countries, but he failed to conquer his own spirit.[1]

Few of us vent our anger to this degree or with such terrible consequences. Yet we all face the same challenge: to be slow to anger. If you think that isn't a problem, ask yourself:

—Have I ever become angry in traffic and said something I really wouldn't want anyone to hear?
—Have I ever felt frustrated with my spouse and said something cruel or unkind in the heat of the moment?

—Have I ever felt exasperated with my children and exploded?

—Have I ever been fed up with a co-worker or a schoolmate or a neighbor and given him or her a piece of my mind?

This passage speaks to all of us. For when it comes to troublesome human emotions or shortcomings, anger tops the list.

In his book *Three Steps Forward, Two Steps Back,* Chuck Swindoll writes:

> American statesman, Thomas Jefferson, worked out a way to handle his anger. He included it in his "Rules of Living," which describes how he believed adult men and women should live. He wrote this: "When angry, count ten before you speak; if very angry, a hundred."
>
> Author Mark Twain, about seventy-five years later, revised Jefferson's words. He wrote: "When angry, count four. When very angry, swear."
>
> Those of us with a streak of honesty will have to say we've tried nearly everything from Jefferson's philosophy to Twain's, and we still are troubled with anger. It's a real problem. If you wrestle with a bad temper, you may be laughing on the outside, but crying on the inside. I don't know of anything more frustrating to deal with than anger. It has a way of disarming us, of robbing us of our testimonies. It injures our home lives and our relationships with co-workers."[2]

The Bible says a great deal about anger, and as we look at this specific passage in Ephesians, three things seem clear:

—anger may be legitimate,
> but
—anger must have safeguards
> because
—anger may lead to sin.

To distinguish proper anger, it might help to use the term "righteous indignation," which means getting angry at whatever makes God angry. Jesus was angry when the Father was maligned. God was angry when the Israelites reveled in idolatry and immorality. Both Father and Son were angered by injustice.

Throughout the Old Testament we read of the anger of God burning against the sins of the Israelites. In Psalms it says, "God is angry with the wicked every day" (Ps. 7:11 KJV). In the New Testament we see that Jesus got angry. John describes how He drove the moneychangers out of the temple and poured out their coins and overturned their tables. "Take these things away," He said, "stop making My Father's house a house of merchandise" (John 2:16). In righteous anger He cleansed the temple.

Improper anger, on the other hand, has no place, even temporarily, in the Christian life. This kind of anger is usually caused by jealousy, selfishness, and vindictiveness. Anger rooted in pride, self-centeredness, materialism, or any selfish motivation is wrong and leads us into sin. "Let all bitterness and wrath and anger . . . be put away from you," Paul writes, for these grieve the Holy Spirit (Eph. 4:31).

We're all familiar with the story of the prodigal son. But how many of us remember the faithful son who stayed at home and then blew his cork when his brother returned? "It isn't right. It isn't fair," he complained. Why? Because he was jealous of his brother, he got angry.

When we want something and someone or something else gets in our way, we get angry . . . whether it is a slow driver who keeps us from making the green light or a teacher who gives us an unfair grade or a boss who fails to give us a promotion. When things don't go our way, we get angry. In fact, selfishness is probably at the root of most unjustified anger.

"Do not let the sun go down on your anger," says Paul. In other words, don't hang on to anger or allow it to fester in your heart. Get rid of it before it takes root. Pray about it, commit the matter to the Lord, and sleep in His sovereignty. That's usually going to be easier, of course, when the anger involves those things that make God angry. When it's something personal, the anger is more difficult to give up at the end of the day. Pride can nurse anger for days—or even years.

Anger not only hurts others and destroys or interferes with relationships, it also hurts you.

When you get angry, acid pumps into your stomach and adrenaline pours into your bloodstream. Your muscles tense; your internal organs shut down. Your physical body takes a terrible beating when you get angry.

Anger can cost you your reputation. It can cost you friendships and relationships. It can cost you a job or a promotion. It can cost you happiness and satisfaction. Anger damages everything it touches. So

—face your anger as sin;

—confess every angry thought or action as soon as it happens;

—ask God to take away the anger;

—ask for forgiveness from anyone you offend or hurt in your anger;

—forgive others who hurt you;

—give up your rights and trust the Lord;

—memorize and meditate upon Scripture that speaks to your anger.

Let's face it: Most of us aren't exactly tied up in knots that often over righteous indignation. Most of our anger is selfish and inappropriate. Therefore, most of our anger is sin. Anger is one of the most common and destructive forces in human relationships, and if we as individuals, or as a church, are going to live satisfying lives, we must gain mastery over anger.

Consider just a few: "Cease from anger . . . forsake wrath. . . . Be not hasty in thy spirit to be angry: for anger resteth in the bosom of fools. . . . A hot-tempered man stirs up strife, But the slow to anger pacifies contention. . . . He who is slow to anger is better than the mighty, And he who rules his spirit, than he who captures a city. . . . But now you also, put them all aside: anger, wrath, malice, slander, and abusive speech from your mouth" (Ps. 37:8; Eccl. 7:9 KJV; Prov. 15:18; 16:32; Col. 3:8).

A Good Day's Work

Let him who steals steal no longer; but rather let him labor, performing with his own hands what is good, in order that he may have something to share with him who has need.

Ephesians 4:28

A man sent the IRS a check and a note that said, "A while back I failed to report some income to you, and I am having trouble sleeping. Here is a check for $500. If I still can't sleep, I'll send the rest."

Being a totally honest person is not easy. We may be honest one day and not another; we may be honest in one matter and not another. We may be honest at home but not at work. We may be honest at church and not when we travel. We may be honest when we are preparing our own bills but not when reporting our income.

But Christianity cannot be compartmentalized. We are to be like Jesus in every area of our life. And Jesus was totally honest—in all situations and at all times. That's our standard.

The eighth commandment says, "Thou shalt not steal." In many ways stealing—taking someone else's property—is the most obvious form of dishonesty. Yet stealing takes many forms. Interestingly enough, as far as I can ascertain, stealing is considered wrong in all civilizations. It is a timeless and universal value. No one wants their possessions taken from them. However, this command has far more subtle ramifications than swindling, burglary, or highway robbery. And when we look below the surface, there's something there for all of us.

Somehow today—perhaps accelerated by the greed mongers of high finance—there is a widespread attitude that theft is not inherently wrong. Okay, if you get caught, you have to pay. But if you don't get caught, more power to you. As a result, billions of dollars are drained out of the economy annually, contributing to inflationary pressure. Intentional overestimating, falsifying cost overruns, padding expense accounts, reporting more hours than were worked, failing to report income to the IRS, and countless other deceptions are accepted as the norm by many people. Yet it is all stealing, and it is all sin.

We can steal money, we can steal time, we can steal ideas (plagiarism). We can steal by not paying back a debt we have incurred. If we take credit for another person's work or ideas, we steal that person's honor and recognition. If we fail to give an honest day's work, we are stealing from our employer.

I remember Jim, one of my college classmates, telling me about his experience with factory work. The company he worked for made machine parts, and he was on "piece" work, which meant he was paid a certain amount of money per hour and in return was expected to produce a certain number of pieces each hour.

Before long he was able to turn out many more pieces per hour than he was expected to. However, he soon learned that that was not how the game was played. The other workers produced their hourly quota in fifteen minutes. Then they sat down and played cards for forty-five minutes. Then they worked for another fifteen minutes and played cards for another forty-five.

Jim was not a card player, so he worked for the entire hour and produced four times what the other workers produced. They were furious with him. They called in their supervisor who threatened to fire him if he didn't quit working. It had taken the union a long time to get the number of pieces required per hour down to that level, they told him, and if someone were to reveal how ridiculously low that level was, it would mess up their easy job.

Unfortunately, in this fallen world, work is often looked upon as something bad—or at least to be avoided. But work isn't bad. Work is as old as God—if we can put it in those somewhat finite terms. God works. His first great work was Creation itself. Before the Fall, He instituted work. Jesus worked as a carpenter, Paul made tents, Luke was a doctor, and David was a shepherd.

Since we are created in God's image, we are created with an innate desire to have purpose, to create, to be doing something . . . to work. Work is good. Work has purpose. Through our work we serve both God and other people.

Just think about breakfast. At breakfast you thank God for providing your bacon and eggs. But exactly how did He do that? Through the people at the grocery store, through the truckers who brought the products to the store, through the farmers who produced the products, and through the people who packaged the products. God uses a whole web of people and products to give us our breakfast. Multiply this many times, and you begin to realize the broad range of people and services required to meet just our everyday needs.

Wouldn't it change your perspective if you went to work each day recognizing that you are serving God by serving other people? Through your work God meets your needs and the needs of your family. Through your work you love and serve Christ. Ultimately, therefore, your boss is not your employer—God is. And Jesus is your silent partner, to whom you are accountable for your performance on the job.

Most of us have little difficulty seeing why missionaries or pastors must do their work God's way. Yet those same standards apply to all of us. No matter what our vocation, our calling, or our occupation, we are all in full-time Christian work. That means we must reflect God's image in the way we act day to day on the job, in the way we do our work, in the way we treat our co-workers, in the way we resolve conflict, in the way we react to stressful situations, in the way we handle misunderstandings.

Like the rest of our world, the workplace is an imperfect place. Not all will share our Christian values, which can sometimes place us in potentially compromising situations. We need discernment to know when it is okay to remain in our job, and when we may have to get out. Our commitment to Christ places demands and limitations on what we can and cannot do.

In his book, *Your Work Matters to God*, Doug Sherman suggests some of the dilemmas that could face a believer in the workplace: If you are a developer, would you allow a strip joint or a pornography shop to come into your shopping center? Would you work in a convenience store that sold pornographic material? He then goes on to differentiate between direct and indirect participation in evil.

In some ways, just by virtue of living within a fallen culture, we cannot avoid participating indirectly in evil. For example, we must pay taxes—render unto Caesar—yet some of our tax dollars may pay for things that as Christians we believe are wrong.

Where God holds us responsible is when we participate directly in evil. For example, if your boss asks you to falsify a tax form and you do, you are participating directly in evil—you are lying and stealing. You may find a creative way to avoid such participation, or you may be able to convince your boss to let you off the hook, or, if he pushes you to the wall, you may have to resign. Bottom line: You must do the right thing, according to God's standards, not the world's.

Sometimes it is not this clear, of course. Everything is not always black and white. The solution is to get as much information as possible and then ask the Holy Spirit to direct your conscience and decision.

If the church has failed to influence culture as it should, it may be because it has not equipped believers to make a connection between what they do at work all day and what God calls them to do—the work of God in the culture. Not just as Sunday school teachers, but as truck drivers, building contractors, construction workers, real estate agents, bank tellers, and homemakers.

We do not work just to make a living or to get by or to put our kids through school or to have personal fulfillment; we work so we will be able to help others. That includes the homeless in our own city, the starving souls in Somalia, and the continued advancement of the gospel both here and abroad.

By ourselves we cannot meet all the needs in the world, but we can be generous according to our means. In fact, one of the litmus tests of commitment and maturity is generosity—whether we live for others or solely for ourselves. Whether we have graduated from baby steps to walking by faith.

When we give as the Lord asks us, we express our trust in Him to meet our financial needs and we express our gratitude for what He has done for us. By our financial generosity to the kingdom we acknowledge that true reality lies in the next world, not in this one. That is the real purpose of giving: the allocation of our financial resources toward eternal things.

God doesn't want our gold; He wants our hearts. But sometimes the test of whether or not He has our hearts is our willingness to give Him our gold.

It's What's Inside That Counts

Let no unwholesome word proceed from your mouth, but only such a word as is good for edification according to the need of the moment, that it may give grace to those who hear. And do not grieve the Holy

Spirit of God, by whom you were sealed for the day of redemption. Let all bitterness and wrath and anger and clamor and slander be put away from you, along with all malice. And be kind to one another, tender-hearted, forgiving each other, just as God in Christ also has forgiven you.

Ephesians 4:29–32

If you bump a glass of water, water spills out. If you bump a glass of orange juice, orange juice spills out. If you bump a glass of battery acid, battery acid spills out. And if you bump a joyous heart, joy will spill out. Bump a patient heart, and patience will spill out. Bump a frustrated heart, and frustration will spill out. Bump an angry heart, and anger will spill out.

Often we say that we cannot know what is inside another person—what he is truly thinking or feeling—and to a degree that is true. Only God truly knows the heart. However, what spills out of our mouths is often a pretty good gauge of what is in our hearts.

If our hearts are under His control, so are our tongues. We tell the truth. Our speech is wholesome. We build others up with our words, rather than tear them down. Our words are constructive, encouraging, instructive, uplifting, and sometimes corrective . . . speaking the truth in love.

Our words are appropriate to the need of the moment. Sometimes they are humorous or lighthearted . . . sometimes they are deep and profound. When the situation is serious, we should be serious. When there is need for encouragement, we should encourage. We should discern the need of the moment, and speak to that need. This gives grace (strength) to those who hear.

Words have power!

The words of Hitler twisted men and women into human gargoyles.

The words of Winston Churchill galvanized the British nation into a magnificent force against seemingly insurmountable odds.

The words of Martin Luther King charged an entire nation with a sense of social justice.

The words of a parent can challenge a child to achieve beyond his or her ability.

The words of a parent can also crush a child's spirit.

Words hurt; words heal.

Words guide; words lead astray.

Words build up; words tear down.

The good man brings good things out of the good stored up in his heart, and the evil man brings evil things out of the evil stored up in his heart. For out of the overflow of his heart his mouth speaks.

Luke 6:45 NIV

Focus Questions

1. On a scale of 1 to 10, how big a problem for you are the three kinds of "acceptable dishonesty": (1) failing to distinguish between fact and opinion, (2) exaggeration, and (3) rationalizing?

2. How much of your anger is legitimate? How much is not?

3. If people were to judge your life solely on what they see of you at work, how would they evaluate your Christian life?

14

The Imitation of God

(Ephesians 5:1–3)

He who imitates evil always goes beyond the example that is set;
he who imitates what is good always falls short.

Francesco Guicciardini

*I*n his autobiography, Benjamin Franklin tells of wanting to convince the citizens of Philadelphia to light the streets at night as a protection against crime and a convenience for evening travel. When he failed to influence them by his words, Franklin bought an attractive lantern, polished the glass, and placed it on a long bracket that extended from the front of his house. Each evening at dusk, he lit the wick. Franklin's neighbors soon noticed the warm glow in front of his house. Passersby appreciated the light that helped them make their way over the cobblestone roadway. Soon others began placing lanterns in front of their own homes, until eventually the city recognized the need for having well-lighted streets.

"Example is always more effective than teaching," wrote Samuel Johnson. And Albert Schweitzer maintained, "Example is not the main thing in influencing others. It is the only thing."

More lightheartedly, but equally succinctly, Mark Twain concurred when he said, "There are few things harder to put up with than the annoyance of a good example."

Because of the power of example, the Christian life is more easily caught than taught, and we catch it by imitating the very One who was sent to earth to be our example: Jesus Christ.

The great task of the Christian life is to cooperate with the Lord in the process of bringing the actions of our outer life into conformity with the righteousness of our inner life. To do this, Paul says, we must imitate God.

God's Real Gift of Love

Therefore be imitators of God, as beloved children; and walk in love, just as Christ also loved you, and gave Himself up for us, an offering and a sacrifice to God as a fragrant aroma.

Ephesians 5:1–2

To imitate God, Paul says, is to live a life of love. Before we can do that, however, we must understand what love is.

Love is God's primary motivating attribute. "God is love," said the apostle John (1 John 4:16). And the primary characteristic of love is that it "gives."

"Walk in love, just as Christ also *loved* you, *and gave*" (Eph. 5:2, italics added). "Husbands, love your wives, just as Christ also *loved* the church *and gave*" (Eph. 5:25, italics added). And in John 3:16 we read, "For God *so loved* the world, *that He gave*," (italics added). Throughout the Scripture, we see love giving.

So if we are to imitate God, we must love. If we are to love, we must give ourselves to others.

The Myth of Romantic Love

This concept of love that gives is quite different from the understanding that most people have of love. Most of us have been deeply influenced by the notion that love is essentially "romantic." And no wonder. The popular media are saturated with a false idea of what it means to love, constantly confusing love with emotional bonding.

Now emotional bonding is one of the most powerful temporary phenomena on earth. When you bond emotionally to someone, you lose objectivity. You can't think about anything but that person. You don't want to do anything but be with that person. You think that your entire happiness in life depends on a relationship with that person. And you are certain that those who caution you about your relationship with that person have either turned against you or lost their sanity. They just don't understand.

People typically get married, or establish an intimate relationship, based on the power of emotional bonding. But emotional bonding does not last. It was not intended by God to last. Emotional bonding is a strong emotional adhesive designed to get two souls to stick together momentarily. Once stuck together by the outside agent of emotional bonding, the two souls are to begin to grow together and actually become one. After the honeymoon, so to speak, God intends the relationship to grow together in genuine love. He doesn't intend for it to be held together indefinitely by the power of unending breathless emotion.

Love can be defined as the steadfast direction of my will for the welfare of another person. Emotional bonding can be defined as an emotional attachment to another person, based on personal attraction.

The confusion between love and emotional bonding is promoted and reinforced by popular movies and music. Recently I was watching an old black-and-white movie made in the thirties, and in one sequence a woman was singing a song entitled, "How Do You Fall in Love?" After a verse of mindless drivel, she warbled the refrain, "Well, it just (boom, boom) happens!" Everyone in the film audience smiled with common understanding and nodded approval.

But love doesn't just (boom, boom) happen! You don't *fall* in love. You can fall into infatuation or emotional bonding, but you don't fall in love. You *decide* to love. With eyes wide open, you make a lifetime commitment to love someone else—to direct your will toward the welfare and benefit of that person. That is love. That is imitating God, because that is what He has done for us. If God's love toward us depended on His emotional attachment to us, we'd be in big trouble.

When I was young and dating my future wife, I believed that emotional bonding was actually love. So when Margie and I got married, essentially I married her because she made me feel good. And she married me because I made her feel good. We married each other so that we could make each other feel good the rest of our lives.

Shortly after our wedding, however, we stopped making each other feel good. Life came down to money in the bank (or lack, thereof), heavy work loads, a car, a house, and too little sleep. Pretty soon, neither one of us was feeling good. The first five years of our marriage were something neither one of us ever want to repeat. But fortunately we also had an unshakable commitment to our relationship. While there were many things we didn't know, the one thing we did know was that we wouldn't divorce.

Because of that commitment, and because we were so miserable with the relationship as it was that we were willing to do whatever we had to do to make it better, we were able to grow into a deeply satisfying relationship. Each year has gotten better. Each one. Without fail. But only because of deep commitment and hard work. Not because of the emotional bonding that we felt before we got married.

Love isn't raging hormones. Love isn't infatuation. Love isn't emotional bonding.

> Love is patient, love is kind, and is not jealous; love does not brag and is not arrogant, does not act unbecomingly; it does not seek its own, is not provoked, does not take into account a wrong suffered, does not rejoice in unrighteousness, but rejoices with the truth; bears all things, believes all things, hopes all things, endures all things. Love never fails.
>
> 1 Corinthians 13:4–8

If someone is doing nothing but "taking" in a relationship, that person isn't loving you. If you are dating someone who wants you to compromise your moral standards, that is not love. That is a hormone surge. It is purely biological. It has absolutely nothing to do with love. It's counterfeit. Don't confuse it with the real thing.

To imitate God, we must love . . . and love gives. Lasting relationships must be based on "giving" love. If they are based on anything else, they won't last.

Satan's Counterfeit

> But do not let immorality or any impurity or greed even be named among you, as is proper among saints.
>
> Ephesians 5:3

Wherever God has given something good, Satan stands ready to pervert it. In the place of love, he offers sex. In the place of commitment, he offers an easy way out. In the place of selflessness, he offers selfishness.

Ephesians was written to Christians; Paul makes that clear from the very outset. Yet he warns against immorality and impurity and greed.

Immorality

God hates sexual immorality. Not because He is a celestial prude and has decided to spoil our fun. He hates immorality because of what it does to us: It destroys us. God loves us. Immorality damages us. Therefore, God hates immorality.

With sexual immorality, Satan offers us a counterfeit of the love God intends for us. Satan offers perverted and permissive sex, which kills love and meaningful relationships. Certainly God wants us to have the delight and joy of *romantic* love in our marriages, but He also wants us to have the joy of the spiritual and physical oneness of the sexual relationship that only occurs between a husband and wife who have a *committed* love for each other.

Instead of giving us love, harmony, and sexual unity, immorality spirals us down into a meaningless life in which sexual union takes on all the significance of a good burp. Sexual purity, on the other hand, because it grows out of and reflects the very image of God, preserves the self-worth of man and woman and maintains the integrity essential to meaningful living.

God is no cosmic kill-joy. He is no providential prude. He just wants the best for us. His instructions and commands are for our own good, and we reject them at our own peril.

No meaningful relationship was ever founded on selfishness. No meaningful relationship was ever sustained by emotions alone. No meaningful relationship was ever improved by hormones.

Paul says we are to imitate God: We are to love others as Christ loved us—selflessly, sacrificially. Love based on anything else is no more lasting than a rainbow in the desert.

Greed

If immorality is the counterfeit of romantic love, greed is the counterfeit of "friendship" love. The foundation of "friendship love" is the Golden Rule: "Do unto others as you would have others do unto you." The opposite of the Golden Rule is greed: "Do unto others before they do unto you."

Human relationships cannot be sustained on that level, and before long civilized society reverts to the law of the jungle: the survival of the fittest. If we are to sustain "friendship" relationships, as well as preserve a climate in which democracy can survive, we must be willing to look out for the other person. This is why Paul warns us about greed.

Harvey Mackay, owner of a large business in Minneapolis, tells of a marvelous example of God's love being manifested in the business world.

> My friend Al, a public relations expert, used to do volunteer work for the Billy Graham Evangelistic Association, even though he was not a Christian. Then one day, Al was loudly and publicly fired from his job at the public relations firm. As a result, no other firm in town would touch him, so he started his own business. After three weeks of mostly twiddling his thumbs, "Arthur" from Billy Graham called Al and asked him if he could

do some work for BG. Al managed to find the time. When he had completed the project, Arthur asked Al to bring over his bill. Al thought that was kind of curious—most people expect you to mail it in—but he figured, well, they want to go over it with me. So Al nervously put together his statement very carefully, itemized everything, and went over.

Arthur barely glanced at it. He called his secretary in and said, "Will you see if we can cut Al's check right now?" They did, and Al was paid before he left the building. . . .

Three years later, Al's business had taken off; he was thriving. He had done a number of other big jobs for Billy Graham. Then, around Christmas time, Arthur called Al again. "Would you like to earn a little Christmas money?" Al was too busy himself, but said he could get someone else to do it. "No, that's okay," Arthur said. "Thanks anyway. I'm glad you're doing so well."

Al relates the story: "We talked for a little while more, just chit chat stuff, but when I hung up the phone, I started to shake, and then I started to cry. All those jobs I'd done before, all the business he had given me when I was sitting there by myself. It wasn't because I was such a great PR guy. There are many in town who could have done it better. They knew the territory a lot better then I did. But Arthur asked me because they knew I was hurting, and I needed the business. And then they called me again, just checking in, kind of, to see if I still needed help. Nobody I've ever done business with before has ever cared about me the way the Billy Graham organization did. And I'm Jewish."[1]

That's how "love that gives" can work itself out in the marketplace. Or in a hundred other ways in the home, in the family, in the neighborhood. Love gives. Not immorality and greed, but the steadfast direction of our will toward the benefit of another.

When Sir Ernest Shackleton, an Arctic explorer, was asked to describe his most terrible moment in the Arctic, he said it occurred one night when he and the other members of his expedition were huddled together in a barren hut, trying to sleep. They had divided up the last of their food rations. There was nothing more to divide.

Then, in the cold darkness, Sir Ernest heard a quiet movement. He turned and saw one of the men reach over and pick up the provision bag of the man beside him. Shackleton said he lived through an eternity of suspense in the next few moments. He would have trusted his life to this man. Was he now turning out to be a thief who would steal his comrade's last morsel of food?

Then Shackleton saw the man open his own provision bag, take out his last biscuit, and place it in the bag of his sleeping friend. Shackleton said, "I felt I had witnessed a secret moment between that man and God."

That's what we must be like. Men and women who will love one another in such a way, openly or in secret, that we are raised above the level of mere mortals to become more like our Creator. That is truly the imitation of God.

Focus Questions

1. What personal pain have you experienced or witnessed in others because emotional bonding was confused with love?

2. Immorality is Satan's perversion of a legitimate gift of God. Why do you think so many people get involved in immorality even though it causes so much pain?

3. Greed is Satan's perversion of the Golden Rule. Do you think it is possible to operate according to the Golden Rule in a world of greed? Explain.

15

People with Purpose
(Ephesians 5:3–17)

God has one destined end for mankind—holiness. His aim is
the production of saints. God is not an eternal blessing-machine
for men. He did not come to save men out of pity. He came to
save men because He had created them to be holy.

Oswald Chambers

*G*eneral Chuck Yeager was the first man to break the sound barrier, Mach 1, flying the experimental X-1, which was little more than a rocket with a seatbelt. As the first man to fly faster than the speed of sound, Yeager was "the hero who defined a certain quality that all the hotshot fly-boys of the postwar era aimed to achieve: the right stuff."

In his autobiography, *Yeager,* the "greatest test pilot of them all" recounts that historic moment and his subsequent test-flying adventures. During the testing of the X-1, Yeager says, there were many times when he had the opportunity to flout the laws of physics, but he knew if he did he would pay the penalty. So while he always pushed the edge of the envelope, he also stayed within certain bounds. "The secret of my success," he says, "is that I always managed to live to fly another day."[1]

The physical world is governed by intrinsic laws that determine what we can and cannot do. When we obey them, we benefit; when we disobey them, we're in trouble. We don't see these laws as being good or bad; we see them as true. They just are, and we work within them. They order the universe, and in that way they order our lives.

Just as there are physical laws that govern the physical universe, so there are spiritual laws that govern our spiritual lives. In Ephesians, Paul posts God's warning signs. He tells us about these spiritual laws and warns of the danger of ignoring these laws.

143

Warnings are rooted in compassion. If we didn't care, we wouldn't put up signs at railroad crossings. If we didn't care, we wouldn't put poison labels on lethal substances. If we didn't care, we wouldn't pass laws requiring seat belts. If God didn't love us, He would not warn us of the peril that awaits those who disregard His laws.

Stop, Look, and Listen

> Therefore be imitators of God, as beloved children; and walk in love, just as Christ also loved you, and gave Himself up for us, an offering and a sacrifice to God as a fragrant aroma. *But* do not let immorality or any impurity or greed even be named among you, as is proper among saints. . . . For this you know with certainty, that no immoral or impure person or covetous man, who is an idolater, has an inheritance in the kingdom of Christ and God.
>
> Ephesians 5:1–3, 5, italics added

Chuck Yeager knew that if he ignored the laws of physics, he could pay with his life. And when we ignore the laws of God, there is a price to pay.

This doesn't mean that if a Christian does these things, he will lose his salvation. What it does mean is that if a person lives a life that is characterized by these things, he has no confidence from Scripture that he is a Christian. "Therefore, if anyone is in Christ, he is a new creation; the old has gone, the new has come" (2 Cor. 5:17 NIV).

If nothing becomes new in a person's life after he or she supposedly accepts Christ, it is a sign that either the person did not really understand what it means to become a Christian or that person was not sincere in his or her confession. No one has a biblical basis to say he is a Christian if it has made no difference in his life.

If a person's life is characterized by immorality, impurity, greed, filthiness, silly talk, and course jesting, Paul says, he has no inheritance in the kingdom of God. "The wrath of God comes upon the sons of disobedience" (Eph. 5:6). For the non-Christian this means separation from God and the horrors of hell for eternity.

If a Christian stumbles into immorality or begins living in rebellion, he is taking part in the sins of the sons of disobedience (5:7). The child of God is spared separation from God and the horrors of hell because his salvation is secure in Christ. Jesus paid the price for our sin, and we do not have to bear it again. But that does not mean we cannot suffer the judgment of

God. Just as loving earthly parents chasten their children in an effort to get them to correct their self-destructive behavior, so the loving hand of the Lord chastens us. He does not want us participating in immorality, impurity, greed, filthy talk, foolish talk, and coarse jesting directly *or* vicariously. In a world where these things can come into our homes by way of television, assaulting us and our children visually and audibly, this becomes a real challenge.

Twenty years ago, most of the church threw off legalism: the philosophy that the Christian life is measured purely by the things we don't do. Unfortunately, in reaction, many boomeranged all the way over to profound indiscrimination in their enjoyment of that which had previously been denied them. As a result, today there appears to be little difference between the habits of many Christians and average non-Christians.

Literature, the only widespread media available before the electronic age, once centered on wholesome stories with moral values. In the last century, however, there has been an astonishing degeneration of themes and values presented in both print and electronic media. Today the focus is on the personalities and activities of anti-heroes, immoral relationships, criminals, deranged people, and horror figures. There is a preoccupation with sex, violence, and death, as well as deviation from traditional Judeo-Christian values and activities. Western media have become a cesspool of pathology and sin.

Noble, sacrificial love is mocked; lust is fueled and applauded. Wrong has become right, good has become bad, perverted has become normal.

Nevertheless, the church in America turns on the same TV programs, listens to the same music, goes to the same movies, and reads the same books as the world.

The late Francis Schaeffer chronicled this decline of Western civilization in his book, *How Should We Then Live?* showing the direct correlation between perversion in art and the denial of a personal God to whom we are accountable. Without God, Schaeffer said, media and art turn ugly.

In careless disregard for what we let into our minds, we participate in the sins of the sons of disobedience vicariously as we entertain and divert ourselves to death. Movies, music, television, major network programming, MTV, HBO, Cinemax, books, and magazines create a hotbed of voyeurism as those who might never do such things take pleasure in watching them.

Sadly, when parents partake in these sins vicariously, they not only pay the price themselves, but also visit their sins on their children, who go beyond their parents and become involved in these things directly.

Society is being ravaged by moral disintegration. Runaway crime, unwed mothers, broken homes, runaway children, economic collapse, breakdown in our schools and education system, corruption in business and government, drug abuse, homosexuality, AIDS, and the occult.

If we participate in the sins of the sons of disobedience, we will participate in the judgment, and we can already see this happening. The church is being ravaged right along with the rest of society. Divorce, alcoholism, and child abuse are nearly as prevalent in the church as in the world. In the workplace, many Christians are no more ethical and honest than non-Christians. Our teenagers are in an alarming state of either active or passive rebellion against Christian principles. And abortion has become a serious problem on Christian college campuses.

Why? Because members of the church do not have a relationship with Christ that is meaningful enough to give them the strength to withstand the pull of the world. You cannot move away from God without getting closer to evil. As a result, we are coming under the judgment of God, just as the world is.

Simply put: We are not a holy people, and we are paying the price personally and are passing the pain on to our children.

So God is issuing a warning. Not because He doesn't love us, but because He does. Not because He wants to keep us down, but because He wants to lift us up. Not because He wants to limit us, but because He wants to elevate us. God is on our side.

Bondage to the value system of the world can be broken. We can break out. We can be free. God will bless us, lead us, and empower us. It will not be easy, but there are five things we must do if we are to break the world's hold on us:

1. We must agree that we are experiencing the judgment of God as a church because we are partaking in the sins of the sons of disobedience.

2. We must commit ourselves to break out of bondage of our sinful culture.

3. We must put away anything that falls into the category of the sins of the sons of disobedience, directly or vicariously.

4. We must join one another, take strength from one another, help one another, hold one another up. We must bear one another's burdens and thus fulfill the law of Christ.

5. We must call upon God to give us strength and dedicate ourselves to prayer and following Him.

William Barclay, the great biblical scholar of an earlier generation, said, "The aim of reconciliation (to God) is holiness. Christ carried out His sacrificial work of reconciliation in order to present us to God, holy, unblemished and irreproachable."

God warns us: Do not partake in the sins of the sons of disobedience. But the warning is rooted in compassion. Yes, God's glory is tarnished if we do. Yes, our influence in other's lives is damaged if we do. But also, we lose. We begin to destroy ourselves. That's God's compassion. Because He made us, He knows that sin will destroy us. And He doesn't want that.

He wants us to walk in love, not in sin. The price of liberty is eternal vigilance.

Spiritual Vigilance

My brother, who was a lieutenant in the army infantry in Vietnam, was wounded when one of his men stepped on a land mine. Land mines have been a fact of life in every war. An army will even mine the perimeter of its own camp as protection from infiltration or advance by the enemy. Soldiers then have to memorize the paths through these cleverly concealed and deadly devices.

Walking through a known mine field takes total concentration. One slip of the memory and you're dead. And when you enter an area the enemy may have mined, you walk *very* carefully.

The Christian life is not a playground; it's a battlefield. And that battlefield is filled with dangerous spiritual land mines. So the Christian walk requires total concentration.

In the beginning of chapter 5, Paul exhorted us to be imitators of God and walk in love. Because great dangers exist on the battlefield of our spiritual lives and because the dangers are so devastating, he says:

> Be careful how you walk, not as unwise men, but as wise, making the most of your time, because the days are evil. So then do not be foolish, but understand what the will of the Lord is.
>
> Ephesians 5:15–17

The Smart Walk

"Don't be a fool," Paul says.

Do you think you will find happiness by getting a lot of money? Don't be a fool.

Do you think you will find happiness by buying that house you want so badly?

Don't be a fool.

Do you think you will find happiness if you can just date that good-looking guy or girl?

Don't be a fool.

Do you think you will find happiness if you can just land that job?

Don't be a fool.

Do you think you will find happiness by drinking or using drugs?

Don't be a fool.

Do you think you will find happiness by throwing off all authority and doing only what you want?

Don't be a fool.

Do you think you will find happiness by manipulating others, by being dishonest, and by trying to control others by controlling the truth?

Don't be a fool.

Do you think you will find happiness if you can just get accepted by a certain group of people?

Don't be a fool.

The apostle's words echo what Solomon said three thousand years ago. None of this brings happiness. None of it brings lasting meaning. It is all like trying to capture a moonbeam. It is all a lie. There is only one thing that satisfies, and that is loving God and fulfilling His commandments. Everything else is a vain attempt.

Don't be like some mindless lemming rushing off the bank into the ocean to your doom, just because everyone around you is jumping in. Be smart. Don't be a fool.

The Effective Walk

In this finite world, time is life. If you fiddle around with time, you are fiddling around with life. If you waste time, you waste life. If you misuse time, you misuse life. If you control time, you control life. If you use time wisely and effectively, you use life wisely and effectively. Time is life. What you do with one, you do with the other.

If we are going to live wisely, walking carefully through the battlefield of the spiritual life, we must be effective. We must use our time wisely.

Too many of us float through life like a cork moving downstream, just bobbing along with the stream of events. Instead of working our way upstream, we take the easy way—moving with every current of life. Moving against the current is harder, but it is infinitely more rewarding.

To do it, however, we must control time. We must use it wisely, making time flow in the direction of our priorities.

In his book *Growing Strong in the Seasons of Life,* Chuck Swindoll writes:

> Allow me to introduce a professional thief.
>
> Chances are you'd never pick this slick little guy out of a crowd, but . . . he can pick any lock in your office. Once inside, his winsome ways will captivate your attentions. . . . Master of clever logic that he is, the bandit will rearrange the facts just enough to gain your sympathies. . . . Too late, you'll see through his ruse and give him grudging credit as the shrewdest of all thieves. Some never come to such a realization at all. They stroll to their graves arm-in-arm with the very robber who has stolen away their lives.
>
> His name? Procrastination. His specialty? Stealing time and incentive. Like the proverbial packrat, he makes off with priceless valuables, leaving cheap substitutes in their place: excuses, rationalizations, empty promises, embarrassment, and guilt.[2]

Other professional thieves are "wrong priorities, carelessness, and never saying no." They all steal your time. Therefore, they steal your life. They keep you from pursuing the best God has for you.

Wisdom is knowledge effectively applied to life's problems. So after Paul tells us that we need to live wisely, he gets more specific: "Make the most of your time," he says, "because the days are evil."

We cannot buy back time. Once it's gone, it's gone. So we must make the most of it while we have it. This is not merely an exhortation to use time effectively. We can use our time effectively in the pursuit of worthless things. Thus, Paul qualifies his warning by saying that we must make the most of our time in the pursuit of things that counter the evil days in which we live. The things that advance the kingdom of God.

Being wise means making the most of our time by looking for opportunities to use our resources to advance the kingdom and to understand the will of God.

The Discerning Walk

This may come as a shock and disappointment to you, but God's will for your life is not to make you rich and famous. God's will for your life is not to give you a life of ease. God's will for your life is not to have you floating along on a bed of roses or on a cloud of ease and luxury.

God's will for your life is to make you like Jesus. And He feels perfectly free to use anything at His disposal to accomplish that purpose.

When Paul says that we are to understand the will of God, he is not talking about what college we should go to, or who we should marry, or what job we should accept. He means we are to understand the moral will of God for our lives . . . which is in direct contrast to anything immoral or impure or greedy or filthy or silly or coarse. We are to walk in the light. That is God's will. And to ignore it is foolish.

Have you ever asked yourself what you want out of life? Usually we do this at three different stages.

The first stage is when we are young, enthusiastic, and optimistic . . . when we feel invincible and immortal. "What do I want out of life?" we ask ourselves, and the sky's the limit.

The second stage is middle age, when the vision and enthusiasm of youth have been refined into a more limited sense of the possible. We redefine, reorganize, and tackle realistic objectives.

The third stage comes in the autumn of life when we say, "I only have a little more time left. What will I do to invest each day with meaning?"

If we are willing to look realistically at our limitations, we can have much of what we want . . . if we are willing to pay the price. But we must be very careful how we define these things, or we will climb the ladder of success only to find it is leaning against the wrong wall.

There is nothing wrong with setting goals and experiencing some degree of satisfaction in meeting them, with having specific measurable accomplishments, but we must not link our happiness to them. We can work for them, but we must be willing to take them or leave them, as the will of God allows.

And remember, the effective pursuit of life's goals can only be achieved with the effective control of time. If we do not, we will find our time flowing into the areas of least importance. If we do not control our time, there are a hundred people who are willing to control it for us.

To this end, I suggest that you write out your life goals on a three-by-five card. Put a Scripture passage beside each goal so that you are sure you can justify the goal biblically. Review these goals every morning. Then spend at least fifteen minutes prioritizing the use of your time for that day according to your goals. Make sure that you can justify the use of all of your time. Then each evening, review the goals and evaluate whether or not you used your time wisely. Don't just float through life, letting life happen to you.

You don't have to break the sound barrier. You don't have to leap tall buildings with a single bound, be faster than a speeding bullet, stronger than a locomotive, and talk directly with God. But you must seize the initiative. Take control, by the leading of the Lord, so that your time flows in the direction of eternal priorities.

Focus Questions

1. Are you suffering pain right now because you disregarded God's instructions? Repentance is the first step in addressing this kind of pain. Are you willing? What practical steps might you need to take to deal with the issue?

2. Analyze your values, motives, and actions. Then consider Solomon's conclusions about life. He said that money, pleasure, wisdom, accomplishments, and fame do not satisfy; the only thing that satisfies is to fear God and keep His commandments. What evidence is there in your life that you believe Solomon?

3. What eternal priorities would you need to use to give your life direction and purpose? What is the first step to take in the pursuit of each priority?

Part 3

===

Love

God wants us to have love. We must be careful not to settle for sex.

16

The Fountain of Love

(Ephesians 5:18)

When I have learned to love God better than my earthly dearest, I shall love my earthly dearest better than I do now.

C. S. Lewis

*I*t is said that the Eskimos have forty-seven words in their language for the word we know as "snow." For those living in warmer regions, if it's white and cold, it's snow. But for the Eskimo, understanding the various words for "snow" can make a difference between life and death.

For example, they might have a word like "fliff-fluff," which means the light, fluffy, powdery kind of snow that floats softly to earth and gently covers everything with a pristine twelve-inch blanket of dazzling white—perfect for photographs and Christmas cards. Or they might have a word like "screamin-freezer," which means the bitter kind of storm-driven, horizontal, freeze-your-eyebrows-off stuff that howls for days and buries everything under a suffocating avalanche of white death.

Now, let's say you are a missionary to the Eskimos, newly arrived, so you speak only English. You have been spending the afternoon with an Eskimo family. The igloo is cozy and warm, and through a translator you've been able to communicate with these new friends. When it's time to leave and you don your Eddie Bauer gear, Father Eskimo says, "It is going to fliff-fluff." You don't understand, so you lean over to your translator and ask, "What did he say?" The translator replies, "He says it's going to snow."

"I'm not afraid of a little snow," you think, so you head for home. As you walk, light, fluffy, powdery flakes begin drifting to earth, blanketing the ground in a foot of dazzling white. "Oh, this is lovely!" you say. "It's like walking home through a Currier and Ives scene."

A week later you are visiting in the home of another local family, and as you get ready to leave the Eskimo says, "It is going to screamin-freezer."

You've learned a number of words already, but this is a new one. "What did he say?" you ask. And your translator buddy replies, "He says it's going to snow."

Ah, snow! That delightful, light, fluffy, powdery stuff. How nice it will be to walk home in that pristine glory again. So you leave. Suddenly, up comes this sixty-mile-an-hour wind and snow so heavy you can't see your eyelashes. Bitter-cold ice pellets sting your eyelids as you lean forward into the blast, making what seems like inch-by-inch progress. You get home just seconds before your eyebrows fall off, and you think, "Why didn't that guy tell us the weather was going to be so terrible?"

He did, of course, but the translator missed the nuances of his language. So while the word "snow" was accurate, it was woefully inadequate.

That happens occasionally in the Bible. Most of the time, I believe, the English translation of the Scriptures enables us to understand the Word of God. But once in a while, because of the limitations of the English language, we stub our toe on a misunderstanding and fall headlong into mental mud. One good example of this is the word "love." In the Greek language in which the New Testament Scriptures were written, there are three primary words for love. One is *eros,* which means physical love. Another is *philos,* meaning emotional, friendship love. And the third is *agape,* meaning spiritual love. So when the English Bible says "love," we don't know whether it means physical love, emotional love, or spiritual love. The result is a breakdown in our understanding of one of the most important teachings in all the Bible.

Another good example is found in Ephesians 5:18, when Paul commands that we be filled with the Spirit. There are two words in Greek which mean "to be filled." One is *plerao* and the other is *pimplemi,* and they mean two significantly different things. So when the Bible tells us that we should be filled with the Spirit, we need to understand whether it means we should be "plerao-ed" with the Spirit or "pimplemi-ed" with the Spirit. To that end, we must dig back through the original meaning to be sure we understand everything that is at stake.

Paul has just exhorted us to understand the will of God. Then, in what seems to be a rather disjointed comment, he says, "Do not get drunk with wine . . . but be filled with the Spirit." Why does he mention drunkenness in this context? A number of reasons could be suggested, but the strongest, I think, is cultural.

Ephesus was a polytheistic city, and one of the gods they worshiped was Bacchus, the god of wine and drunken revelry. The pagans believed they could get in touch with Bacchus by getting drunk. As a result, drunken debauchery was common and widespread in Ephesus at the time

Paul wrote. So when the apostle said, "Don't get drunk with wine, but be filled with the Holy Spirit—that's how you commune with God," everyone knew what he meant.

Traditional Interpretation

While this cultural context provides a background for understanding, the nuances of the language itself still leave room for more than one interpretation. Generally there are two understandings for "being filled with the Spirit."

First is the charismatic meaning, in which being filled with the Spirit manifested itself in speaking in tongues. This view teaches that everyone should manifest the characteristics that were evident on the day of Pentecost when everyone spoke in tongues. The problem with this interpretation is that the word "to be filled" in Ephesians 5:18 is not the same word used in Acts. For reasons we are going to see in a minute, this interpretation is difficult to attach to this verse.

In passing, I should mention that it is not my intent in this book—nor is it in keeping with its purpose—to deal with the subject of charismatic manifestations in general, nor of speaking in tongues in particular. All I am attempting to do is suggest that that is not the intent of the command in Ephesians 5:18.

A second major interpretation is "the victorious Christian life." This position, which I was taught in the early days of my Christian walk and in much of my formal theological training, maintains that the filling of the Spirit is God's empowering for victorious Christian living and service, but that it is not related to speaking in tongues. Certain conditions must be met, and when you meet these conditions you are filled with the Spirit; then you are ready, on the spot, to live the Christian life on a more victorious level and you become empowered for service. These conditions are that (1) you must confess sin and put away any sins that you are harboring in your life, (2) ask to be filled, and (3) believe by faith that God will fill you if you ask Him.

I will never forget the first time I heard a speaker cite these conditions for being filled. I had been a Christian for about a year, and I was sitting in a large church in Daytona Beach, Florida, during my spring break from college. The meeting was sponsored by one of the many Christian organizations engaging in beach evangelism during the annual migration of thousands of students from northern states to Florida for spring break.

The speaker was trying to get us all filled with the Spirit before we hit the beaches to do personal evangelism. After listing these conditions, he said,

"All right, all of you who believe you are filled, stand up." Hundreds of students stood up. I didn't. In fact, as far as I could tell, I was the only one who didn't stand. I'm sure they all thought I was a spiritual derelict.

Staying seated that day was one of the hardest things I have ever done. But my mind rebelled at what I was being taught. *This is impossible,* I thought. *I'm a goner. I can't get more spiritual until I get filled with the Spirit, but I can't get filled with the Spirit until I get more spiritual.* I was caught between a rock and a hard place—between two impossibilities. But I didn't believe that was the answer. And thus began my ten-year search for what it truly means to be filled with the Spirit.

Before I explain my understanding of this passage, however, I want to explain in greater detail why I think the first two options are not accurate.

First, throughout the book of Acts the word used for "filled" is *pimplemi.* The results of being "pimplemi-ed" with the Spirit are dramatic: tongues, prophecies, or powerful messages preached spontaneously. Meanwhile, the verb *plerao* occurs only twice in the New Testament, and it does not have extraordinary events connected with it.

Second, we do not find *pimplemi* after Acts 19, which means that the purpose of the dramatic manifestations appeared to be the validating of the new message of salvation by grace through faith in the risen Lord. This happened to Jews in Acts 2 and to Gentiles several times in the rest of Acts—Acts 19 being the last time it is mentioned.

Third, the verb always used with *pimplemi* suggests that the filling did not last long (aorist tense in Greek) and that the people being filled did not have control over the filling (passive voice in Greek). God sovereignly filled them for a certain period of time.

Finally, the dramatic events surrounding *pimplemi* are designed to accomplish a certain task, while the purpose of *plerao* is to cause a person to be filled with joy or the Spirit as a continuous state. The former is task-oriented; the latter is person-oriented.

Because people have confused the use of the two different words, they have taken the miraculous manifestations which occurred with *pimplemi* and generalized them to try to fit *plerao* in Ephesians 5:18, not realizing that they aren't even dealing with the same word.

The Fullness of Christ

Thus, I believe that when Paul encourages us to be filled with the Spirit, he is encouraging us to allow ourselves to be controlled by the fullness of Christ in our lives.

In Ephesians 5:19–6:6 the results of being filled with the Spirit are:

speaking in psalms,

singing,

giving thanks,

and a harmony of relationships between husbands and wives, parents and children, masters and slaves.

In Colossians 3:16–22 we see the same results:

teaching with psalms,

singing,

thankfulness,

and harmony between husbands and wives, parents and children, masters and slaves.

However, the results in Colossians are produced not by being filled with the Spirit, but by "let[ting] the word of Christ richly dwell within you." Being filled with the Spirit and letting the Word of Christ dwell within you produce exactly the same results. Therefore, they must be understood to be essentially the same thing.

In Acts 13:52 we find the only other occurrence of the verb form of *plerao,* where we read, "And the disciples were continually filled with joy and with the Holy Spirit." Just as the disciples were filled with and controlled by joy, so we are to allow ourselves to be filled with and controlled by the Spirit. We do this by allowing the Word of Christ to dwell within us.

As the Word dwells within us, we come to understand the will of God. The Holy Spirit applies God's truth to our hearts, and as we yield to it, allowing ourselves to be controlled by it, we experience the fruit of the Spirit: love, joy, peace . . . And gradually, more and more over time, we are filled with the Spirit in a non-sensational manner that is just as miraculous as any dramatic manifestation.

So this is what it means to be filled with the Spirit. It means to allow the Word of Christ to dwell within us—yielding ourselves to it so that over time we begin to experience the fruit of the Spirit in our lives and live up to the fullness of Christ.

We are not controlled by wine; we are controlled by the Holy Spirit. Not in a passive sense, whereby the Holy Spirit just takes over, but in an active sense. The Holy Spirit lets us know what we should do, and we do it. Not like a hand controlling the functioning of a glove, but like a speed-limit sign controlling how fast we drive. We are controlled by it in the sense that we have yielded to its authority.

This solves the catch-22 situation I felt that day at spring break—of needing to be filled with the Spirit so we could be more spiritual, but needing to be more spiritual so we could be filled with the Spirit. It is also accurate with the text.

Paul then goes on to explain what happens when we are filled with the Spirit:

> We speak to one another in psalms and hymns and spiritual songs (we minister to one another in truth).

> We sing and make melody in our heart to the Lord (we have joy).

> We give thanks for all things in the name of our Lord Jesus Christ to God the Father (we are grateful).

> We are subject to one another in the fear of Christ (we have a servant's heart).

These four things—mutual ministry, joy, gratitude, and a servant's heart—characterize a life which has allowed the Word of Christ to dwell in it and which is being filled with the Spirit. We cannot get these things from the world (by being filled with wine). We get them only by being filled with the Spirit. This world cannot satisfy our deepest longings. Earth can't fill a heavenly vacuum.

How often we look for fulfillment in the wrong places. Deceived by the enemy and by our own natural inclinations, we pursue things that will never satisfy.

Corrie ten Boom, a Dutch Christian who was imprisoned in a German concentration camp during World War II for helping and hiding Jews in the Netherlands, wrote in her marvelous book, *Tramp for the Lord:*

> The war was over. Even before I left the concentration camp, I knew I would be busy helping those who had lost their way. Now I found myself starting just such a work in Bloemendaal [Holland]. It was more than a home for the homeless; it was a refuge for those who had lost their way spiritually as well as physically.

> Yet, because I had lived so close to death, looking it in the face day after day, I often felt like a stranger among my own people—many of whom looked upon money, honor of men, and success as the important issues of life. Standing in front of a crematorium, knowing that any day could be your last day, gives one a different perspective on life. The words of an old German motto kept flashing in my mind:

"What I spent, I had; what I saved, I lost; what I gave, I have."

How well I understood the feeling of the artist who painted the picture of the corpse of a once wealthy man and entitled it, *Sic transit gloria mundi*—So passes the glory of this world. The material things of this world no longer excited me—nor would they ever again.[1]

The lesson Corrie learned is the lesson Paul is trying to teach us in this passage. Don't look for things in the wrong places.

Corrie is saying, "Don't look for meaning in the passing things of this world."

Paul is saying, "Don't look for communion with God in wine. That is nothing but drunkenness. Don't let wine or work or pleasure or money fill your life. Rather, be filled with the Holy Spirit."

Focus Questions

1. If the results of "letting the Word of Christ richly dwell within you" (Col. 3:16) are the same as "being filled with the Spirit" (Eph. 5:18), what does that tell you about the role of Scripture in our being filled with the Holy Spirit?

2. There are four characteristics of being filled with the Spirit. Two have to do with music: (1) speaking to one another in psalms, hymns, and spiritual songs, and (2) singing and making melody in your heart to the Lord. How could we fulfill these two characteristics today?

3. Gratitude to the Lord and a spirit of deference to each other are two other characteristics of being filled with the Holy Spirit. How might we pursue these?

17

Singing in the Rain
(Ephesians 5:19–21)

The spirit-filled saint is a song-filled saint. Animals can't sing.
Neither can pews or pulpits or Bibles or buildings. Only you.
And your melody is broadcast right into heaven—live—where
God's antenna is always receptive . . . where the soothing
strains of your song are always appreciated. . . . Never mind
how beautiful or pitiful you may sound. Sing loud enough to
drown out those defeating thoughts that normally clamor for
attention. Release yourself from that cage of introspective reluc-
tance. SING OUT! You are not auditioning for the choir, you
are making melody with your heart.

Chuck Swindoll

*I*n the previous chapter we saw that the command to be filled with the Spirit
in Ephesians 5:18 is not a command to speak in tongues or to prophesy or
to call down fire from heaven. The first consequence of the Spirit-filled life
is simply a heart that sings . . . a heart that cries out to minister to
others . . . a heart filled with joy . . . a heart that serves. While that may
not seem as dramatic as some ecstatic spiritual experience or mountain-
moving phenomenon, it is just as miraculous.

The human heart cannot be changed by man. But let God get hold of
it, and see what happens.

First of all, the Spirit-filled heart ministers to others.

Mutual Ministry

. . . speaking to one another in psalms and hymns and spiritual
songs . . .

Ephesians 5:19

Christians are not rugged individualists. We do not stand alone. We are not islands. Nor are we to erect barriers between ourselves and others, daring them to cross. As part of the body of Christ, we need others, and others need us.

Each of us has been gifted to minister to others, and each of us is responsible to minister to others. Some of us, of course, have been called by God to labor vocationally in ministry. But God intends all of us to minister when opportunity arises—in our workplaces, in our neighborhoods, in our families, and in our society. Realizing that we have this personal responsibility and then having a heart to help others is a mark of being filled with the Holy Spirit.

The totality of all believers—all true Christians—is called the body of Christ. The human body is a picture of that spiritual body. By observing how the human body functions, we gain insight on how the spiritual body should function.

For example, consider the cooperation of the entire body involved when a toddler takes his first steps:

> If we traced all the body signals involved in walking, we would find in that grinning, perilously balanced toddler a machine of unfathomable complexity. Over one hundred million sense cells in each eye compose a picture of the table he is walking toward. Stretch receptors in the neck relate the attitude of his head to the trunk and maintain appropriate muscle tension. Joint receptors fire off messages that report the angles of limb bones. The sense organs inside the ear inform the brain of the direction of gravity and the body's balance. Pressure from the ground on each toe triggers messages about the type of surface on which he is walking. . . . A casual glance down to avoid a toy on the carpet will cause all these sense organs to shift dramatically; the image of the ground moves rapidly across the retina, but the inner ear and stretch receptors assure the brain the body is not falling. Any movement of the head alters the body's center of gravity, affecting the tension in each of the limb muscles. The toddler's body crackles with millions of messages informing his brain and giving directions to perform the extraordinary feat of walking.[1]

When seen up close, in detail, the physical act of walking is a stupefying miracle. When seen up close, in detail, the spiritual act of "walking together" is an equally stupefying miracle. It requires millions of individual beings, contaminated by the impulse to act independently, to reject that impulse and subordinate themselves to the leading of Jesus, the Head, and move in concert with His will, rather than millions of individual wills. The miracle of spiritual unity is no less awesome than the miracle of physical unity.

Lone rangers are not filled with the Spirit. Human islands are not filled with the Spirit. Caustic and abrasive people who tend to drive others away are not filled with the Spirit.

Those who are filled with the Holy Spirit sense the importance of mutual ministry; they understand that they are part of a larger whole, and they see the need for unity with the Head and the body of which they are a part.

And out of that sense of wholeness the Spirit-filled heart finds joy.

Inner Joy

> . . . singing and making melody with your heart to the Lord . . .
> Ephesians 5:19

You need not have a beautiful voice to have a beautiful heart. Yet when the Holy Spirit invades your heart, inner joy expresses itself in inner song.

And this inner joy does not depend on circumstances; it survives in spite of the circumstances.

In his book *Winning Over Pain, Fear, and Worry,* John Haggai tells how his son suffered severe physical trauma at birth because the doctor, a respected obstetrician, was intoxicated at the time.

> During the first year of the little lad's life, eight doctors said he could not possibly survive. For the first two years of his life, my wife had to feed him every three hours with a Brecht feeder. It took a half hour to prepare for the feeding and it took another half hour to clean up and put him back to bed. Not once during that time did she ever get out of the house for any diversion whatsoever. Never did she get more than two hours sleep at one time.
>
> My wife, Christine, had once been acclaimed by some of the nation's leading musicians as one of the outstanding contemporary female vocalists in America. From the time she was thirteen she had been popular as a singer—and constantly in the public eye. Hers was the experience of receiving and rejecting some fancy offers with even fancier incomes to marry an aspiring Baptist pastor with no church to pastor!

Then, after five years of marriage, the tragedy struck! . . . She was now marooned within the walls of our home. Her beautiful voice no longer enraptured public audiences.[2]

Although John Edmund, Jr., was paralyzed, able to sit in his wheelchair only with the assistance of full-length body braces, his parents rejoiced to have him with them for over twenty years—and rejoiced that he committed his heart and life to Jesus Christ and evidenced genuine concern for the things of the Lord.

I attribute his commitment to Jesus Christ and his wonderful disposition to the sparkling radiance of an emotionally mature, Christ-centered mother who has mastered the discipline of living one day at a time. Never have I—nor has anyone else—heard a word of complaint from her.[3]

Ah, God's mercy. Sometimes it is so severe. Yet the Spirit-filled life is a life of joy, surviving not because of the circumstances, but in spite of them.

I believe that some people, like Christine Haggai, are gifted to respond to music more than others. But everyone who is filled with the Spirit will enjoy and appreciate the music of the soul that lifts his or her heart to God.

And out of that joy the Spirit-filled heart gives thanks.

Giving Thanks

. . . always giving thanks for all things in the name of our Lord Jesus Christ to God, even the Father.

Ephesians 5:20

When we trace the word "thanksgiving" through the Bible—both the Old and New Testaments—we get a sense of God's attitude to gratitude. Consider just a few passages:

For in the days of David and Asaph, in ancient times, there were leaders of the singers, songs of praise and hymns of thanksgiving to God.

Nehemiah 12:46

I will praise the name of God with song,
And shall magnify Him with thanksgiving.

Psalm 69:30

Let us come before His presence with thanksgiving;
Let us shout joyfully to Him with psalms.

Psalm 95:2

Enter His gates with thanksgiving,
And His courts with praise.
Give thanks to Him; bless His name.

Psalm 100:4

Blessing and glory and wisdom and thanksgiving and honor and power
and might, be to our God forever and ever. Amen.

Revelation 7:12

With this kind of emphasis, it's little wonder that the third manifestation of the filling of the Spirit is a grateful heart.

Having 20/20 spiritual sight, the Spirit-filled heart is thankful.

If we understood how perilously our lives hang in the balance as we go about our daily living . . . if we understood how powerful the spiritual warfare is around us . . . if we understood how fortunate we are to have food on the table and a roof over our head . . . if we grasped how dependent we are on the common grace of God and the goodness of others for our basic necessities in life . . . we would be grateful people. Grateful for what we do have, rather than ungrateful for what we don't have.

And finally, the heart that ministers to others, beating with joy and thanksgiving, is truly the heart of a servant.

Servant Heart

and be subject to one another . . .

Ephesians 5:21

Anyone who knows anything about chickens knows that there is a pecking order in the barnyard. There is Top Chicken, who can peck anyone in the coop without fear of reprisal. And there is Bottom Chicken, who can't peck anybody in the coop without reprisal. All the other chickens are aligned in a hierarchy of power between these two.

If a kernel of corn falls between any two chickens, the one with a higher pecking order gets the kernel. If there is any question as to which is which, a fracas breaks out—anywhere from a skirmish to all-out war. When the fight is over, the winner establishes or reestablishes dominance over the other, and the hierarchy adjusts itself accordingly from top to bottom.

The same order can be observed in the great Corporate Chicken Coop, the human workplace. There is a Top Human and a Bottom Human; and in between all the others are aligned in a hierarchy of power . . . a great human pecking order.

If an opportunity for advancement falls between two humans, a fracas breaks out—anywhere from a little skirmish to all-out war. This can mean anything from dirty looks to actual murder, whereby humans establish dominance over other humans, and the hierarchy is established.

Just as chickens constantly jockey for position in the barnyard pecking order, so humans constantly jockey for power in the workplace. It is only natural.

As Christians, however, we are not to participate in this great posturing for position. We are not to follow our natural inclinations; we are to act supernaturally.

This is exactly what occurred when James and John, two brothers who were Christ's disciples, began jockeying for position in the coming kingdom (Mark 10:35–45). "Master," they said, "when your kingdom comes, let one of us sit on your right hand and the other on your left." They wanted to be top chickens in the kingdom of God.

"Men, you have it all wrong," Jesus replied. "That's the way the world acts. They love to lord it over others. But things are entirely different in my kingdom. In my kingdom, if you want to be great, you must become a servant to everyone else."

What a shock. In heaven, the pecking order is reversed. The first shall be last and the last shall be first. Those who humble themselves, God exalts. Those who exalt themselves, God humbles.

"For even the Son of Man did not come to be served, but to serve, and to give His life a ransom for many" (Mark 10:45).

The Lifetime Achievement Award

A vine produces a squash in six weeks. A great oak takes a hundred years. And a Spirit-filled Christian produces the fruits of ministry, joy, thankfulness, and servanthood. These manifestations of the Spirit will not come on you suddenly with great force. They will come slowly, even imperceptibly at times. But in the end they will endure.

Paul's command to be filled with the Spirit does not mean we have to speak in tongues or prophesy or call down fire from heaven. Instead, we minister to others, we find joy in our heart, we discover gratitude in our soul, and we serve others as Jesus did when He was here.

Come to think of it, isn't that as miraculous as any fire from heaven?

Focus Questions

1. Mutual ministry is one characteristic of being filled with the Holy Spirit. What is your ministry to other Christians? What ministry are you receiving from other Christians? Do you have significant relationships with other Christians that offer you sufficient encouragement to face life's trials?

2. What do you do to encourage the role of music in your Christian walk?

3. Do you struggle with any "pecking order" problems in life? What is the answer to relieving the strain of pecking order issues?

18

Making Love Come Alive
(Ephesians 5:22–6:9)

Anything can make us look; only love can make us see.
Archibald MacLeish

*I*f you look at a map of the world in Australia, it will look quite different from the map you are used to in the United States. Australia is top and center. Down below are China, North America, and Europe. It is upside down to us, but not to the Australians. It is all a matter of perspective.

The same is true of God's eternal perspective. Up seems down, right seems wrong, good seems bad, and truth seems false. Why? Because we are looking at the map upside down, from our earthly perspective. From our perspective, God's perspective seems full of paradoxes and contradictions.

Nowhere is this more evident than in the area of human relationships. Certainly in my own life I have had this burned deeply into my heart and mind.

I grew up in a large family of modest means in rural Indiana. I was a skinny kid, and my nose and ears stuck out too far. These and a number of other factors combined to give me a nagging sense of inferiority. To earn significance in the eyes of others, I became an overachiever.

This continued through high school and intensified in college. I was in sports, student government, yearbook staff, dance band, marching band, stage band, school plays, Young Republicans . . . the list went on and on.

I began college at Indiana University, aiming for a degree in motivational research and business and planning to go into advertising and become at least rich—and perhaps famous. Then I became a Christian and that no longer seemed a worthy goal—so I began plotting my life of success in the ministry. This seminary . . . that degree . . . a first job teaching at a prestigious college . . . I was almost as selfish and carnal in my plans for the ministry as I had been in planning to get rich and famous, never realizing that I was pursuing these things because of an inner sense of insecurity and inferiority. I thought I was just highly motivated.

A key ingredient in my equation for bringing myself security and recognition was to have a model wife. Margie fit the bill. She was attractive, pleasant to be with, and had a bubbly personality. Everybody liked her—and I loved her. So I married her.

Then we moved to Dallas so I could continue my seminary studies, and there my scheme began to unravel. This bubbly little cherub began having long and dark bouts of depression, and to ease her inner pain she began to eat and to gain weight. Before long, she wasn't fitting the picture.

This threatened me, so I devised a plan to fix her. When she was unhappy, I told her to cheer up. When she ate, I told her to stop eating. When she gained weight, I told her to lose it. When she acted unpleasant, I told her to shape up. And I meant it. I had a lot at stake here. I was committed to the relationship, and the thought of divorce never once crossed my mind, but I began to have some major regrets about having gotten married in the first place. It wasn't that I didn't want to be married to Margie; it was that I wanted to be married to who I thought she was before we got married. Now she seemed like someone else.

Margie had had a difficult childhood, but I didn't know that. She was living with emotional scars and struggling to find meaning and purpose in her own life. She didn't understand that her emotional struggles in the present were rooted in the difficulties of her past—and I certainly didn't. All I knew was that she was attacking the very core of my own insecurities.

So I bullied her emotionally. Oh, I was always pretty civil about it. I didn't yell at her. I just withdrew my affection, which left her totally alone and doubled her emotional struggle. Along with all this, she was having difficulty coping with her job, where the pressures of the working conditions were such that even twenty-year employees were quitting. My response was, "Margie, the Lord wants you to learn some spiritual lessons, and if you don't learn them there at work, you'll just have to learn them somewhere else."

I kept the pressure on relentlessly. Then one night when I came home from work, the house was dark. Margie's car was outside, but the lights were not on—which was strange, since it was dark outside. When I got inside and turned on a light, I heard sobbing coming from the bedroom. It was Margie, in bed crying.

"Sweetheart, what's wrong?" I said.

"I don't know," she said. "I can't quit crying."

I was scared. So I went to the phone and called one of my seminary professors and explained the situation to him. He was in bed himself with a temperature of 103, but he said, "Bring her right over."

We went over and talked a while, probing for the source of the problem. We still didn't understand the underlying cause, the difficult childhood, but the one issue we were able to focus on was that Margie hated her job.

"I don't think this is the whole thing," my professor said, "but I think you need to let her quit work."

"Prof, we can't make it if she quits work," I said.

"Buddy, you're not going to make it if she doesn't," was his reply. Then he talked straight to me about loving my wife as Christ loved the church and gave Himself up for her.

At that moment my life flashed in front of me. I saw that everything I had ever wanted in life since becoming a Christian depended on having a wife at my side, and that by trying to force Margie to conform to my expectations I had driven her to the brink of a nervous breakdown. I was standing at a fork in the road, and I would either have to chuck my dreams or I would have to chuck Margie. By the grace of God, in a quick, silent moment, I gave up everything I had ever wanted. And I said to God, "I give up everything else, and I now dedicate myself to one primary thing in life: giving myself to Margie's well-being."

It is no overstatement to say that that was a major turning point in my life. Though only a few months away from graduation, I volunteered to quit seminary and get a job, so that Margie could quit hers. "No," she said. "Don't quit yet. If I know I can quit work, I think I can hang on long enough for you to at least graduate, and then we can decide what to do."

That was many years ago. Since that time, I have never let a decision come between me and what was best for Margie. Not that I've always been a model husband. But with the Lord's help I've held to that commitment to love Margie unconditionally and to put her interests before my own.

Through Margie's difficulties, God changed me. And through a changed me, the stage was set for the Lord to begin to change Margie. Although imperfect, my demonstrations of unconditional love helped her to believe in God's unconditional love for her, and healing began.

Through the years and the grace of God, Margie and I have developed a wonderful, warm, and satisfying relationship and a solid marriage. She is truly my best friend.

But I want to stress three things:

1. Sticking to the commitment I made that night to God and Margie is one of the hardest things I have ever done—because the good things that have resulted didn't happen overnight; they have taken years.

2. God can take a difficult relationship and bring healing and make it the kind of relationship He wants it to be.

3. Making a relationship work can only be done God's way. In the end, nothing else will work. It is God's way or nothing.

When I say that we may be called upon to do some difficult and painful things, I want you to know I understand something of the difficulty and pain. I want you to know that when I challenge your being to its very core, I'm challenging myself, too—as I've been challenged in the past. And I want you to know that though the path may be rough and the woods may be dark, there is a way out. There is hope.

The Secret Is Submission

Be subject to one another in the fear of Christ.
                                                    Ephesians 5:21

The key to all significant relationships is the fourth mark of being filled with the Holy Spirit (the spirit-filled heart), which we spoke of in the last chapter. It is the servant heart. It is being subject to one another, caring for another more than you care for yourself, putting someone else first. When we don't do this, relationships wither and die. Thus, when it comes to the success of the significant relationships in our lives, mutual submission is the secret.

Although we relate to people on a daily basis and in many capacities, there are basically three types of relationships central to our lives: the relationship between husband and wife, the relationship between parent and child, and the relationship between employer and employee (tantamount to the master and servant in Scripture).

While we will look at each of these separately, in detail, in the following chapters, I'd like first to deal generally with the matter of mutual submission.

Submission. Just the word can be a red flag for many on every part of the spectrum. Yet it defines an attitude that was at the very heart of Jesus' character, an attitude that took Him to the cross.

The word submission comes from the Greek word *hupotasso*, which means "to place under." The chickens fight for their pecking order; we are to submit to that order. To submit, to subordinate. It is a word that today's so-ciety finds unpleasant, even reprehensible. In fact, our very country was founded by people who wouldn't submit. We are the rugged individualists of the world—and consequently, we don't submit very well to anyone. (I told you this wasn't going to be easy!)

Consequently, submission is not an easy word to talk about. But if you'll stick with me, I believe you will discover that it is not odious but es-sential, and you will embrace the absolute necessity of building the word and what it portends into the very fabric of both home and society.

The principle of mutual submission maintains that relationships are not fifty-fifty—no relationship ever is. Rather, relationships are reciprocal and re-sponsive; we are responsive to the authority of others and we are responsive to the needs of others. The husband is to be submissive to the needs of the wife, while the wife is to be submissive to the authority of the husband. Par-ents are to be submissive to the needs of their children, while the children are to be submissive to the authority of their parents. The employer is to be sub-missive to the needs of the employee, while the employee is to be submissive to the authority of the employer.

Many see submission as somehow "giving in." In reality, submission is *giving*. The old self, of course, only wants to take. The old self "gets" by "tak-ing." The old self gains personal satisfaction (at least to the degree that he can experience that) at the expense of others. In other words, the old self is "self-ish," taking from others whatever it wants, leaving them victimized . . . used . . . empty.

But the new self, the Spirit-filled heart, cannot find purpose and fulfill-ment in using others.

And ultimately, of course, neither can the old self. Grabbing and grasp-ing individualism is a dead-end street, leading to the disintegration of rela-tionships—which should be the reflection of eternal relationships. And before long, the very thing we hoped for most has vanished.

When we submit to each other, in Christ, however, we give rather than take. And then we begin "getting" what we all long for in relationships: re-spect, friendship, intimacy, camaraderie, caring, closeness—which all spells love.

Focus Questions

1. Describe a husband/wife relationship that you admire. What characteris-tics of that relationship model "mutual submission"?

2. Why do you think submission is such an odious concept in today's society?

3. What are some of the difficulties that arise in a relationship when one partner is not willing to practice mutual submission? (This will also be explored more fully in a later chapter.)

19

The Character of a
Godly Wife

(Ephesians 5:22–24, 33)

Submission! How I hated that word. When it flashed into my mind, all I could conjure up was a nonentity, a nothing sort of yes-woman. I didn't want to be only a reflection of another person.

Yet here I was faced with the no-nonsense command of God, "Wives, be subject to your own husbands, as to the Lord" (Ephesians 5:22). I had argued with God and with everyone else that this verse could not mean what it looked like on the surface; that it was surely a cultural statement that had meaning only for Bible times.

My next attempt was to reconstruct the verse to read, "Wives, submit yourselves unto your husbands as to the Lord WHEN THEY ARE ACTING LIKE THE LORD." But I knew it didn't mean that.

As I searched the Word that fifth year of our marriage, I had to conclude that this verse meant I was to submit myself to Jack in the same free and "nothing-held-back" way that I wanted to submit to Jesus Christ.

Up to that point I had felt that marriage was a 50/50 proposition, and if Jack would give his 50%, I would give mine. However, it seemed that frequently we would fight to determine whose turn it was to give that 50%. I had yet to learn that a happy biblical marriage is one that is a 100% proposition with each partner willing to give 100%.

Carol Mayhall in Marriage Takes More Than Love

*W*e are living in a day in which there is a crisis of authority, and it is easy to understand why. Those in authority have abused their power, causing us to have difficulty accepting anyone's authority without question.

Presidents have lied to us, government leaders have been dishonest, unethical, and immoral. Corporate executives have defrauded our companies.

Banking officials have misused and stolen billions of dollars of our invest-
ments. Military officials have abused power. Politicians have abused power.
Nationally recognized religious leaders have abused power. Educators have
abused power. Doctors have abused power. Journalists have abused power.

This abuse of power and crisis of authority have filtered into every level
and area of society. Nowhere is it more evident—and more destructive—
than at the very foundation of society: the home. Here, where the fundamental building blocks of society are produced, we have men who won't lead,
women who won't follow, children who won't obey, and parents who won't
nurture. We all want it "our way" because "we're worth it." As a result, our
families are in chaos and our homes are in disarray.

"Family values" is a term bandied about on every hand—often by
people who haven't the foggiest idea of what they're talking about. But our
families are in jeopardy and our values are up for grabs—and our nation is in
dire straits. Why? Because the family is the building block of society, and the
family is in big trouble.

Standing out starkly against this ominous backdrop, the Bible still
speaks—and it still speaks truth. It still speaks words which, if followed, will
bring order, truth, and harmony to life. If we will just assume our God-given
role, the home can be full of peace, joy, and harmony.

Why Submit?

> Wives, be subject to your own husbands, as to the Lord. For the husband
> is the head of the wife, as Christ also is the head of the church, He Him-
> self being the Savior of the body. But as the church is subject to Christ,
> so also the wives ought to be to their husbands in everything.
>
> Ephesians 5:22–24

First of all, let's get one thing straight: Submission does not mean inferiority—not in any way. A wife is to be in submission to her husband. A
husband is to be in submission to Christ. Christ is in submission to God the
Father. So unless you are prepared to impute inferiority to Christ for being
in submission to God the Father, you cannot impute any inferiority to the
wife for being in submission to her husband.

Submission is not about worth or intelligence or talent; it is simply a
structure which God has established . . . and of which He is a part.

Nor does submission mean that wives must submit to their husbands in
every respect as though they were obeying the Lord. That is going too far.

The submission of every Christian to the Lord is absolute. We are not exhorted to submit in that way to another person. Husbands are imperfect, and if their authority were to be absolute, it could put a wife in the position of having to disobey God to obey her husband.

What does submission mean, then? To understand, we need to look at the higher reality.

Every major spiritual truth of God is pictured in His creation by a physical truth. For example: death and resurrection are pictured by sleep and by the four seasons; the relationship between us and our heavenly Father is pictured by the relationship between us and our earthly father; spiritual reproduction and spiritual growth are pictured by physical reproduction and physical growth. In the same way, the relationship between Christ and the church is pictured by the relationship between husband and wife.

When a husband and wife fail to picture the relationship between Christ and the church, they strike at the heart of the great spiritual truth. Even though they may have their children at the church every time the doors are open, if their relationship at home is one of conflict, bickering, and animosity—two people living in the same home but not truly one—then the reality their children see gives lie to the spiritual truth.

In other words, we don't submit to each other for our own sakes; we submit because it is an expression of our submission to the Lord. We are doing it for Him.

A Christian husband and wife who do not model spiritual truth contribute to the possibility that their children will reject spiritual truth.

The role of submission, then, is to picture to the world, and especially to one's children, the relationship between Christ and the church and to make that a positive picture so that our children will want to be related to Christ and be part of His church.

Children do not recognize this symbolism, of course. All they know is whether or not they have a happy home, and whether the life of their parents is attractive to them. If it is, they will want to serve the same God their parents do. If it is not, they won't.

How Do We Submit?

We must abandon forever the idea that this passage teaches that a husband has the freedom to exercise some kind of military authority over his wife. Using His own willingness to wash His disciples' feet as an illustration, Jesus taught them that authority was for the purpose of service, not as an opportunity to set themselves over others. The greatest should be like the least, He said, and the one who rules like one who serves (Luke 22:24–27).

Now this does not mean that Christ has no authority—certainly He does. Nor did it mean that the disciples had no authority; they regularly exercised certain authority. What the example of Jesus does teach us is that He does not crush us or impose His will in a way that denies our humanity or dignity or initiative. And Paul calls husbands to imitate the Lord, not by setting aside authority but by serving the needs of their wives.

Husbands must learn that form of sacrificial leadership which fosters the growth of others. Wives must learn that form of active submission which is not demeaning but joyfully upbuilding.

And we must abandon the idea that there is no difference between husbands and wives in God's eyes . . . that there is no need for wives to be submissive to husbands. There is. There are no fifty-fifty marriages in God's eyes. There is a clear and unambiguous standard of authority and submission.

As a wife, you are to submit to your husband. You are not to usurp his authority and turn your home into a matriarchal preserve. You are to respect your husband because God is going to lead you and guide you through him. God is going to work in your life through him. God wants you to change, to become more like Christ, and He has almost certainly given your husband some characteristic which will cause you to rebel or cause you to become more like Christ.

You must submit to your husband because God has commanded you, for by submitting to your husband you are submitting to God.

However, this submission is mutual. A husband and wife are to be mutually submissive to one another. Not mutually submissive in authority, for if everyone is responsible, no one is responsible. The wife is to be submissive to the authority of her husband, and the husband is to be submissive to his wife in love (more about this in detail in the next chapter). The husband gives spiritual leadership in the home, and the wife is to play a supportive role in that process. As husband and wife live a life of love and submission with one another, the results will be peace, love, and joy.

That is the standard God has for us. To live together in love. When we do that, chafing under words like authority and submit become unnecessary.

The Snags in Submission

God's goal for the home is not a power struggle in which the husband lords it over his wife and the wife chafes against her husband's power. God's goal is harmony—a spiritual oneness characterized by love, peace, and joy. In an ideal relationship, husband and wife, having become a spiritual unit before God, function in a practical consensus, living in a relationship of sensitivity to each other.

Now, life being what it is and people being who they are, there are bound to be some circumstances or situations in which a husband and wife do not agree, yet time does not allow them to delay a decision. It might play itself out, philosophically, as Dr. James Hurley has indicated in his book *Man and Woman in Biblical Perspective:*

> Husband: Not because I am inherently wiser or more righteous, nor because I am right (although I believe I am or I would not stand firm), but because it is finally my responsibility before God, we will take the course which I believe right. If I am being sinfully stubborn, may God forgive me and give me the grace to yield to you.

> Wife: Not because I believe you are wiser in this matter (I don't), or more righteous, nor because I accept that you are right (because I don't or I would not oppose you), but because I am a servant of God who has called me to honor your headship, I willingly yield to your decision. If I am wrong, may God show me. If you are wrong, may He give you grace to acknowledge it and to change.[1]

With this kind of attitude, God can lead a husband and a wife into the fullness of the marriage He intends them to have.

The Passive or Neglectful Relationship

A passive relationship is one in which the husband does not assume leadership in the home. He sees his role as breadwinner: he goes to work to earn money to provide for the family. His wife's responsibility is to keep the house, raise the kids, direct the social life, and, in essence, do everything at home. At home, his primary concern is peace. He works hard all day, and when he comes home he doesn't want to be disturbed.

He has little knowledge or understanding or inclination to have an intimate relationship either with his wife or with his children. He moves in his orbit and the wife and children move in their orbit. He may be perfectly happy being married and having a family, but his role is a passive one. In more advanced cases, the passive husband may not even attend any of the children's or family functions; he isn't home much and when he is, he is consumed by his own interests or lives in front of the TV. In less advanced cases, he may be a fairly model husband in public, but he gives his wife and kids little emotional connection.

Sometimes this kind of husband is more than passive; he is neglectful. He may be inconsistent about going to work and earning money. He may spend money for a new car when the home needs new appliances, not a new car; he may spend money for a bass boat when the kids need clothing or when the rent is not paid. He may have no interest in spiritual things and may even be antagonistic to them.

Sometimes this problem is rooted in the fact that a Christian woman was not careful enough about marrying a spiritually motivated man. In other cases, the wife has matured as a Christian after the marriage while her husband has not. In either case, the emotional pain can be significant.

There are three basic principles that govern the passive or neglectful relationship: attitude, adaptability, acceptance: "let the wife see to it that she respect her husband" (Eph. 5:33).

Attitude

Paul wrote to husbands and wives in the church, calling both partners to consider and imitate the pattern of Christ and His church. Peter wrote to a suffering church about the meaning of Christian life under oppressive governments, oppressive slave masters, and oppressive husbands (see 1 Pet. 3:1–7), described by Dr. Hurley.

> Before them Peter holds the example of Christ, who did not retaliate and made no threats, but instead entrusted himself to him who judges justly. The behavior which Peter urged was not justified by its effect on husbands only. It was rather presented as "of great worth in God's sight," as the way of "women who put their hope in God," and as "what is right."
>
> The suffering wife of an unbeliever is called by God, even in her painful situation, faithfully to demonstrate the obedient love of the church for Christ by her submissive love for her husband . . . and her willing suffering love for her husband not only shows the church's love for Christ but also shows the willing suffering and love of Christ for his church (1 Pet. 2:21–25). It is not an easy calling which Peter lays before the Christian wife of an unbeliever.[2]

When it comes to "attitude," a wife's first line of defense is to check her attitude and be sure she is living out the principles of 1 Peter. If she is, there is some hope that things might change. If she is not, there is little hope.

A woman in this situation should ask the Lord to work first in her life. If it is a great emotional struggle, form a support group of other wives who can help each other to be faithful in the midst of the struggle. Even if the marriage relationship does not change, it is "of great worth in God's sight" when women display a godly attitude and put their hope in Him.

Adaptability

The wife of a passive or neglectful husband must assume responsibility and exercise creativity in finding solutions to problems, but always with a loving attitude. Lack of respect for her husband or failure to honor his position in their home and relationship, even if he is not acting honorably, leads only to deeper problems.

First, he is not motivated to change. In fact, he usually digs in stubbornly to prove he is a "man." And second, children are taught to disrespect their father. Daughters, by implication, are taught to disrespect their husbands, and sons may be encouraged toward homosexuality because they resent the matriarchal leadership.

Now, please understand, I am not saying that a wife cannot exercise any leadership whatsoever in the home. What I am saying is that when a wife exercises leadership with an attitude of disrespect for her husband, it creates these problems. If you have respect and love for your husband and are clearly serving the Lord by honoring him, this message will come through loud and clear to your children and you will make a significant, positive impression on their lives.

If, on the other hand, your husband is not acting honorably and you approach things with the attitude, "Listen kids, ignore this jerk. He isn't a man now, and he never will be. Do what I tell you," it will wreak havoc in your children's lives.

But if you display the attitude, "Well, your father may not be doing all that he should, but that doesn't mean that we can't do all we can. Let's love him and help him however we can, and honor the Lord by honoring him." That is a subtle but a very real difference.

You can even honor your husband when you are put in a position of having to disobey him, if your attitude clearly indicates that you are disobeying out of a higher calling to be faithful to Christ, rather than because you think he is a jerk.

Attitude cannot be camouflaged. What we think is revealed by what we do and say. And it just may be that the Lord cannot begin His work in your husband until you have responded to the work He wants to do in your life.

Acceptance

After you have done all you can to bring godly and creative change to your marriage relationship, you must accept circumstances as they are.

As Dr. James Dobson reminds us in his book, *What Wives Wish Their Husbands Knew About Women:*

> Some . . . men . . . will never be able to understand the feminine needs I have described. Their emotional structure makes it impossible for them to comprehend the feelings and frustrations of another—particularly those occurring in the opposite sex. . . . They have never been required to "give," and have no idea how it is done. What, then, is to be the reaction of their wives? What would you do if your husband lacked the insight to be what you need him to be?
>
> My advice is that you change that which can be altered, explain that which can be understood, teach that which can be learned, revise that which can be improved, resolve that which can be settled, and negotiate that which is open to compromise. Create the best marriage possible from the raw materials brought by two imperfect human beings with two distinctly unique personalities. But for all the rough edges which can never be smoothed and the faults which can never be eradicated, try to develop the best possible perspective and determine in your mind to accept reality exactly as it is. The first principle of mental health is to accept that which cannot be changed. You could easily go to pieces over the adverse circumstances beyond your control, but you can resolve to withstand them. You can WILL to hang tough, or you can yield to cowardice.[3]

Acceptance does not mean putting on a falsely happy face and pretending that everything is okay. It is okay to desire involvement from your husband and to hurt when he is passive and neglectful. Acceptance means that while you do not deny the pain that comes with the disappointment of legitimate desires, you allow your pain to drive you to God, rather than to retaliate or withdraw.

The Abusive Relationship

There is no doubt that abusive relationships exist—and that they exist in the church. There are four kinds of abuse: alcohol/chemical, emotional, physical, and sexual. All four can be devastating—even life-threatening. For a woman faced with this reality, the question naturally arises: Must I be submissive to my husband in all things?

The answer is no. A wife does not have to accept unquestioningly everything her husband does, nor must she obey everything he commands or desires.

The answer to this question has potential applications to every husband/wife relationship, but it is particularly urgent in the abusive relationship.

Throughout Scripture there is ample evidence that God's law is the highest law, most succinctly stated in Acts 5:29: "We must obey God rather than men." Obedience to God supersedes everything else on earth.

Therefore, if a husband commands his wife to do something immoral, she is not obligated to do so; in fact, she had better not. If he asks her to swap partners after a party or to watch or participate in something sexually immoral, she should not do so. If he asks her to rob a bank or hurt someone, she should not do so.

Often our choices are not so clear-cut, of course, and require thoughtfulness and wisdom in determining how to respond. Nevertheless, this principle of higher law must always be applied.

Living in submission does not mean a wife must accept unquestioningly everything her husband does.

In fact, there are times when disobedience can be the most effective form of submission. For example, a drunken husband beats his wife or children, then demands that his wife tell no one. He threatens further reprisals if she does. By complying, she merely assists her husband in his own destructive behavior. By telling the truth to someone who can help her . . . sometimes even by leaving him temporarily if the circumstances call for it . . . in an earnest and loving attempt to encourage change in his life and to preserve the marriage and family, she shows the greatest respect for him and their relationship.

When a woman is chaste and respectful, gentle and quiet, humble in spirit, and desirous of the Lord's best in her life and in the marriage relationship, she honors her husband and loves him most completely. This is the true spirit of submission.

The Bible gives general principles which we are to follow. In some cases, however, when the people involved are living in flagrant violation of other biblical principles, the principles begin to collide and great wisdom must be used to sort out the truth.

If a husband is beating his wife in a fit of temper, it is not wrong for her to leave and tell someone who can protect her. It is merely a matter of self-protection, which the Bible gives us freedom to do.

Nor should a wife stay with a husband, knowing that he may kill her or one of their children. Should she contribute to a murder in order to be submissive? No.

Can a wife leave if there are no children and she is the only one being beaten? Yes.

Should a wife sit by and let her husband teach the children to be dishonest, unkind, and immoral? No. She should try to counter such teachings.

Whether or not a wife sins in these or similar situations depends on the attitudes and motives with which she takes action.

Sadly, many wives stay in an abusive situation because their self-image says, "It's my fault. If I were a better person, he wouldn't treat me this way," and they try to figure out how to change themselves so their husbands will treat them better. This is noble but faulty thinking. There is no excuse, period, for a husband's abusing his wife or children. None. Whatever the circumstances, it cannot be excused. And a wife need not stay in an abusive situation. (Please note that I am not talking about divorce. That is an enormous matter which we cannot even get into here. I am merely talking about removing yourself from a dangerous environment.)

Whether we are in a normal marriage relationship or in a frustrating, neglectful, or abusive one, however, the bottom line is that we are living for the Lord, not for this world. And God has promised to give grace sufficient for all our needs.

In the end, all spouses must come to the point where they say, "Lord, it doesn't matter what this life does to me, I will follow You." If you are willing to be brought to that point, God can give you a rich life in spite of your pain. If you are not willing to make that commitment, your life will never be rich and full, no matter what your circumstances or how hard you try.

God has not promised us an easy life, but He has promised to give us peace and joy and love no matter how tough things get.

G. K. Chesterton once said: "Christianity has not been tried and found wanting. It has been found difficult and not been tried."

Submission is probably one of the most difficult teachings in all the Bible, particularly because of the times in which we live. But now is the time, by the grace of God, when we must rise to the challenge.

Focus Questions

1. Why do women often find the concept of submission difficult to accept?

2. How well does the average husband understand his role of being submissive to the needs of his wife?

3. How much has the breakdown in the understanding of mutual submission contributed to the feminist movement?

20

The Character of a Godly Husband

(Ephesians 5:25–33)

What causes us to carve our names or initials on our school desks or on park benches or tree trunks? . . . We want our identity to be remembered, our love immortalized. We want to leave a message to the next generation: . . . "Remember. We two were so much in love."

Luci Shaw

Conflict in husband/wife relationships is as old as Adam and Eve. I suppose, since a relationship by its very definition requires at least two, a certain amount of conflict is inevitable. As Billy Graham is fond of saying, if two people agree on absolutely everything, one of them isn't necessary!

We've all smiled at the story of the meeting between Winston Churchill and Nancy Astor. When she visited Blenheim Palace, the ancestral home of the Churchill family, Lady Astor began expounding on the subject of women's rights, an issue that was to take her into the House of Commons as the first woman member of Parliament. Churchill opposed her on this and other causes that she held dear. In some exasperation, Lady Astor finally said, "Winston, if I were married to you, I'd put poison in your coffee." Churchill responded, "And if you were my wife, I would drink it."

While we may have fun joking about the foibles of married couples, and while there is certainly nothing wrong with laughing at ourselves at times, the marriage relationship is no laughing matter. In fact, the quality of a married person's life is usually measured by his or her marriage. If they have a good marriage, they will say they have a good life. If they have a bad marriage, they will say they have a bad life.

In the end, however, a good marriage or a bad marriage usually boils down to one thing: attitude.

Recently I was reading about England in 1840, when Queen Victoria married Prince Albert. Shortly after the wedding, they quarreled, and Albert stalked out of the room and locked himself in his private apartments. Victoria followed him and hammered furiously on the door. "Who's there?" came his voice from the other side of the door. "The queen of England, and she demands to be admitted." There was no response, and the door remained locked. Victoria hammered at the door again. "Who's there?" The reply was still, "The queen of England." No response. More fruitless and furious knocking was followed by a pause. Then there was a gentle tap. "Who's there?" And when the queen replied, "Your wife, Albert," the prince opened the door.

Attitude! If two people have the right attitude toward their marriage and each other, there is nothing, by the grace of God, they cannot work out. And the underlying attitude of the husband must be love.

The Standard of Love

Husbands, love your wives, just as Christ also loved the church and gave Himself up for her.

Ephesians 5:25

"Husbands, love your wives." Simple, huh? Well, yes and no.

Your initial response is probably, "Of course I love my wife." But then comes the qualifier, "Love your wives . . . just as Christ loved the church." Whoa. Now that's a whole other matter. To that you say, "How did Christ love the church?" And the Bible says, "He gave Himself up for her."

Now notice that it does not say Christ gave *of* Himself. It says, "He gave *Himself.*"

How did Christ love the church?

By giving.

Christ's attitude toward the church—His bride—was one of total sacrifice. He

gave His time . . . the church was His number one priority;
gave His presence . . . He didn't send memos; He sent Himself;
gave His truth . . . to set us free;
gave His love . . . to meet our needs;
gave His prayers . . . to the Father for us;
gave His forgiveness . . . for our restoration;

gave His leadership . . . for our direction;

gave His inheritance . . . sharing with us His wealth and power.

Ultimately, of course, He gave His life.

All that Christ had and all that He was, He directed to the welfare of His bride, the church.

Husband, if you love your wife as Christ loved the church, you must focus your entire life on her welfare and the welfare of your relationship with her. You must

give your time . . . she is your number one priority;

give your presence . . . both your physical and emotional presence;

give truth . . . take spiritual leadership in the home, making sure your wife and family are learning the truth;

give your love . . . to meet her needs;

give your prayers . . . to the Father for her tender care;

give your forgiveness . . . to restore the relationship;

give your leadership . . . for the home and family;

give your inheritance . . . sharing all that is yours with her.

Often we think a husband loves his wife when he provides for her by bringing home a paycheck and buying the material things she needs. That is part of love, certainly, but it falls pitifully short of the standard Christ set in His love for the church. If that is as far as you have gotten as a husband, you barely have your big toe inside the door of biblical love.

The Consequences of Love

So husbands ought also to love their own wives as their own bodies. He who loves his own wife loves himself; for no one ever hated his own flesh, but nourishes and cherishes it, just as Christ also does the church.

Ephesians 5:28–29

While the relationship of Christ and the church transcends the picture represented by the relationship of husband and wife, we can say that when the husband loves, nourishes, and cherishes his wife, he becomes all she ever wanted in a husband. Then—barring any major complications such as the wife's not being a Christian or wanting nothing to do with any of this—the wife responds to this, becoming all the husband ever wanted in a wife.

This is not an overnight sensation, and it is not a perfect process. But it is a reality. I have seen it in other marriages, and I have experienced it in my own.

Margie and I put our best feet forward and on that basis married each other. But after the wedding, we each had to bring along our other feet. They were not as good as the ones we put forward before the wedding, and there were some adjustments we had to make. There were some things I wished weren't true about her. And, though I found it hard to believe at first, there were some things she wished weren't true about me.

We were in a dilemma, because we didn't want to live that way the rest of our lives and we were committed to the relationship. We did not consider divorce an option.

Dame Sybil Thorndike was married to Sir Lewis Casson. Both were distinguished British actors and frequently toured together. After Sir Lewis's death, Dame Sybil was asked about their long and happy marriage. "Did you ever think of divorce?" was one of the questions. "Divorce?" she said. "Never! But murder, often!"

Margie and I never considered divorce either (the murder part, well . . . !) But we were both miserable. So either both of us had to change simultaneously, or else one of us had to start. And I knew who that had to be.

Let there be no mistake about it: While we cannot minimize the importance of a wife's chaste and respectful attitude and gentle and quiet spirit as a catalyst for change, God's priority in change is the husband. If the husband is a Christian and listens to the Word, the Lord places the welfare of the relationship squarely on his shoulders first. When he becomes "Christ" to her, she can more easily become "the church" to him.

What Paul says about the husband/wife relationship goes beyond what could ever be true of our earthly relationships; it can only be true of Christ and the church. And this, he says, is a great mystery . . . speaking of the relationship between Christ and the church.

But he says, "Even though what I have said goes beyond earthly husband/wife relationships, there is truth here for you, and that truth is that a husband must love his wife, and the wife must respect her husband."

The Maintenance of Love

In his book *What Wives Wish Their Husbands Knew About Women,* James Dobson says that the greatest problem women face is low self-esteem (according to a survey of thousands of women). They have difficulty feeling good about themselves . . . feeling that they have worth and dignity as human beings.

If that is the greatest felt need for wives, then that becomes the number one priority for husbands . . . to find ways of communicating their wives' worth and dignity, building their self-esteem.

Dobson goes on to say:

> If women felt genuinely respected in their role as wives and mothers, they would not need to abandon it for something better. If they felt equal with men in personal worth, they would not need to be equivalent to men in responsibility. If they could only bask in the dignity and status granted them by the Creator, then their femininity would be valued as their greatest asset, rather than scorned as an old garment to be discarded. Without question, the future of a nation depends on how it sees its women, and I hope we will teach our little girls to be glad they were chosen by God for the special pleasures of womanhood.[1]

After the problem of self-esteem, the most pressing problems for women, especially those with young children, are fatigue and time pressures.

Husbands, you must be alert to the demands placed upon your wife and be sure you are helping her in that area, not hurting her.

How can you hurt her? By being sloppy yourself, by being passive, by being negligent.

If you were to use one word to describe Margie in this area, you would use "tidy." If you were to use one word for me in this area, the word would be "informal." Margie and I have separate closets—and one glance shows the dramatic difference between us. Margie's closet looks like a closet in a model home. There is a place for everything, and everything is in its place. All of her shoes are lined up neatly, with an equal amount of space between each pair. The sleeves of her blouses hang in rank and file, as though on parade.

Now, my closet is pretty tidy, too, because Margie oversees it—but there are tell-tale signs that mark it as *my* closet. For example, I never hang up my pajamas. I sort of "gather them up" and lump them on the top shelf of my closet—always in the same place, but not hung up and not folded. Same with my bathrobe. I don't hang up my casual slacks that I put on after work either, and sometimes my shoes are out of order. I've even been known, in haste, to drop one pair of shoes on top of another. And without Margie's constant oversight, I fear my closet would deteriorate further and the differences would be even more obvious.

I'm not a slob. I'm just preoccupied. I like the way Margie keeps the house, but I have to work at my goal of not making her job harder. Just think about the practical implications of that. It means you . . .

Pick up after yourself, especially in the living room. That's the most vulnerable room in the house for a woman, because it is the most public. Don't leave the bathroom sink a disaster. When most men leave the house in the morning, the bathroom sink looks like the Spanish Armada was destroyed in it. Help her with the dishes. And bathe the kids and read to them and help get them to bed. Make her job easier, not harder.

In his book *Letters to Philip,* Charlie Shedd writes:

> Do you realize, my dear boy, what a tremendous undertaking it is to serve a good meal? Planning, buying, preparing, cooking, setting the table, dishing up, and then the whole messy business in reverse when it's over. In fact, one good meal is such an accomplishment that for you to sit there, devour it, and then hurry on back to your TV game without ever saying a good word must be a mortal sin. Of course, I'm not God and I don't know the answer to the old argument about whether there are major and minor evils. But I've had to get up a few meals from beginning to end, and if there IS a difference then neglecting to compliment the wife on a good dinner must be a very major error.[2]

Along with the practical help, give your wife the encouragement she needs. What are her life goals, and how can you help her reach them? What are her longings, hopes, and aspirations? Encourage and aid her in achieving her potential as a human being before God.

Jack Mayhall writes in *Marriage Takes More Than Love:*

> When a husband begins to compliment his wife, there is a side benefit other than letting her know you appreciate her. Many wives have told me that, as their husbands compliment them, the children have begun to pick up the habit. They hear Dad compliment Mom, and so little four-year-old junior begins to do the same thing. So when Mom comes home from the beauty parlor, he says, "Gee, Mom, you look great." Then after dinner, "Mom, that was a terrific meal." That makes Mom's day. But it is Dad who must set the pace.[3]

Encourage your wife. Certainly a relationship takes hard work, and there may be times when you may have to confront her about an attitude or a habit or an action. But when confrontation is done in love and in balance with all these other things, even that can be encouraging, because she will know that you are doing it because you want to help her become all that she can be.

Honor your wife—which means, for one thing, you never, never embarrass her in public. Never make a negative statement to her or about her in public. Remember the old adage: If you can't say something nice, don't say anything at all.

Find out if she has any major emotional hurdles to overcome, and work with her to overcome them. Did you know that today some estimates report that one out of every four girls is sexually abused by the age of eighteen? This is truly one of the tragic statistics of our day. And a woman who has been sexually abused often has extra struggles dealing with those devastating scars. The same is true of other kinds of abuse—physical, emotional, alcohol, or chemical.

If you seem to have extra problems in your marriage, it is possible that there are some scars from the past at the root of the problems, without your ever realizing it. In fact, many women do not even remember these traumatic events until they get into counseling for other, seemingly unrelated, problems.

And finally, even as you love your wife, make her feel loved. Every woman needs three things to feel loved. Oh, you may love her and she may know you love her, but if you don't do these three things, she will not feel loved:

—eye contact
—physical contact
—focused attention

Memorize 1 Corinthians 13:4–8 and make it your life passage for your wife and family.

> Love is patient, love is kind, and is not jealous; love does not brag and is not arrogant, does not act unbecomingly; it does not seek its own, is not provoked, does not take into account a wrong suffered, does not rejoice in unrighteousness, but rejoices with the truth; bears all things, believes all things, hopes all things, endures all things. Love never fails.

I'm serious about this. This passage gets a grip on you more fully if you memorize it . . . make it your own.

Husbands, we have a long way to go—evidenced by the two women who were overheard talking about the beautiful diamond one of them was wearing.

> Woman #1: What a stunning stone. I have never seen one so large or so beautiful.

Woman #2: Yes, it's the Klopman diamond, one of the largest and most valuable in the world. But it comes with a curse, you know.

Woman #1: A curse? Why I had no idea. What is the curse?

Woman #2: Mr. Klopman.

Husbands, God has placed the primary responsibility for the welfare of your wife and family squarely on your shoulders. He has commanded you to love your wife as Christ loved the church and gave Himself for her—a tall order.

Your wife's responsibility is to respect you and love you and submit to your authority, but this becomes very difficult when you fail to honor her and love her and submit to her needs.

Focus Questions

1. How well does the typical husband understand his responsibility to love his wife as Christ loved the church?

2. What is the major reason husbands fail in this area?

3. How could the church help men do a better job in this area?

21

The Character of a
Godly Family

(Ephesians 6:1–4)

*God is not saying, "Bring up a child as YOU see him." Instead,
He says, "If you want your training to be godly and wise, observe your child, be sensitive and alert, so as to discover HIS
way, and adapt your training accordingly.*

Chuck Swindoll

*T*he family is in serious trouble today. Just the statistics make your head
swim, your heart palpitate, and your knees weak, let alone the real-life situations we see all around us. Yet no matter how bleak things look, the situation is not hopeless.

One of the late, great senators from the state of Michigan once said, "In
my first term in Congress, I wanted to save the world. In my second term, I
wanted to save the United States. In my third term, I wanted to save Michigan. Now, at the end of my fourth term, if I can just save those sand dunes
on Lake Michigan, I'll be a happy man."

We may not be able to do anything about the family nationwide, but
we can do something within our own sphere of influence. We may not be
able to save the world, but we can save the sand dunes. And if we save
enough sand dunes, we will have an impact on the world.

This is where the principle of mutual submission comes in, for it is not
just for the husband/wife relationship; it is for the family relationship as well.
Mutual submission establishes a reciprocal relationship of being responsive to
authority, and being responsive to needs. When it comes to the family, parents are to be submissive to the needs of their children, and children are to
be submissive to the authority of their parents.

Properly seen, parent/child relationships are an outgrowth of being filled with the Spirit. Spirit-filled Christians are to be subject to one another. As a parent, that means you will be submissive to the needs of your child. As a child, it means you will be submissive to the authority of your parents. This mutual submission involves obedience on the part of the child and nurturing on the part of the parent.

Children, Obey Your Parents

Children, obey your parents in the Lord, for this is right. Honor your father and mother (which is the first commandment with a promise), that it may be well with you, and that you may live long on the earth.

Ephesians 6:1–3

Paul offers three reasons why children should obey their parents:
—by doing so you are obeying God;
—it is the right thing to do;
—it has its reward.

By obeying their parents, children are obeying God. If children are filled with the Holy Spirit, which means they are allowing the Holy Spirit to be the dominant influence in their lives, then it will manifest itself in an attitude of mutual submission. Because the Lord has instructed such obedience, to disobey parents is to disobey these instructions, which is to disobey the Lord. To obey these instructions is to obey the Lord. (Please note: We are not talking here about a child-abuse situation, which lies outside the scope of this book. We are talking about the desired biblical pattern in a normal parent-child situation.)

"For this," says Paul, "is right." In this day of relativity and "values clarification," what a straightforward, unembellished statement that is. Do it, he says, simply because it is right.

Attitudes, habits, and values are passed from one generation to the next through the family. If the family breaks down, society breaks down. Therefore, children must obey their parents.

And because it is right, God has promised some good results when we obey. In fact, Paul says, it's the first commandment that comes with a promise: Obey and honor your parents and you will live long and prosper.

Now that's not an absolute guarantee. For example, we all know of obedient children who died young and of disobedient ones who lived to a ripe old age. Nevertheless, as a general rule, children who follow the sound teachings of godly parents will tend to live long and well-ordered lives. Children who disregard the teachings of godly parents tend to live disobedient and destructive lives.

Children are to do more than obey, however; they are to honor their parents. You can obey without honoring. To honor your parents means to uphold their worth and authority by doing those things that will cause them to be well regarded in the eyes of the public. It also means that you affirm them and love them.

Now, I know this is difficult if you do not have a good emotional relationship with your parents. My father and I had a good relationship on the surface, but when I was growing up, he never talked to me about anything deeper than news, weather, or sports. I never remember my father hugging me or telling me he loved me. He let me know in other ways that he did, and I never doubted it. But he never told me. As a result, an invisible barrier built up, so that when I became an adult I could not talk with my father about things I thought and felt deeply. I had a fierce admiration for my father as a man, but I could not talk with him about personal things. So, from a distance, I wrote him letters and told him things I couldn't tell him in person. And I would look for opportunities to buy things for him for his birthday and Christmas that I thought he might especially like. In other words, I looked for indirect ways to show him I loved him and respected him—to love and affirm him.

So children who do not have the kind of personal relationship with their parents that allows them to love and honor them directly, must find ways to do it indirectly.

When you honor your parents, you also love and care for them in their old age. This means that you do not neglect them and let them live out their days as though you had never been their child. You may not be able to live in the same town with them, but you will find ways to honor them.

Parents, Nurture Your Children

Do not provoke your children to anger; but bring them up in the discipline and instruction of the Lord.

Ephesians 6:4

A similar passage in Colossians says, "Do not exasperate your children, that they may not lose heart" (3:21). Both "anger" and "exasperate" come from the same root word.

How do we anger and exasperate our children? There are many ways.

1. Parents can overprotect their children, doing everything for them and never allowing them to gain any degree of independence.

2. Parents can overdiscipline or be overly restrictive about where their children can go and what they can do. These parents never trust their children to do things on their own, and they continually question their children's judgment.

3. Parents can expect more from their children than they can ever deliver. For these perfectionistic parents, the child's performance is never good enough.

4. Parents can expect too little of their children and discourage their decisions and dreams, never approving, affirming, or encouraging.

5. Parents can fail to sacrifice for their children, making the children feel like an intrusion.

6. Parents can emotionally, verbally, or physically abuse their children.

In *Ten Mistakes Parents Make with Teenagers,* Jay Kessler offers further warning about mistakes parents make that anger or exasperate their children and damage the parent/child relationship.

Mistake #1—Failure to be a consistent model.
   "Do as I say, not as I do."

Mistake #2—Failure to admit when you are wrong.
   "I'm the adult. I am right."

Mistake #3—Failure to give honest answers to honest questions.
   "Because I said so, that's why."

Mistake #4—Failure to let your teenager develop a personal identity.
   "You want to be what?"

Mistake #5—Failure to major on the majors and minor on the minors.
   "This room's a pigsty!"

Mistake #6—Failure to communicate approval and acceptance.
   "Can't you do anything right?"

Mistake #7—Failure to approve your teenager's friends without making any attempt to get to know them.
   "Where did you find him?"

Mistake #8—Failure to give your teenager the right to fail.
"You did what?"

Mistake #9—Failure to discuss the uncomfortable.
"Can we talk about something else?"

Mistake #10—Failure to take time.
"I'm kind of busy right now. Could you come back later?"[1]

In Hebrew culture, you were a child until you were an adult. There was no such thing as an adolescent. So a child was anyone still under the "training up" process. During all those years parents were to train up their children properly, instructing and disciplining them in the things of the Lord and not provoking them to anger.

In every child God places in our arms, there is a bent, a set of characteristics already established. The bent is fixed and determined before the child is given over to our care. The child is not, in fact, a pliable piece of clay. The initial molding has already been made in the womb. And the parents who want to train this child correctly will discover that bent.

A balance of discipline and love sets the stage for a child's success in every other area. If a child gets too much discipline and not enough love, he is likely to be angry and rebellious. He will tend to think too little of himself. If a child gets too much love and not enough discipline, he is likely to be selfish, self-centered, and demanding. He will tend to think too much of himself.

A child must feel loved, and there are three things a child needs to feel loved:
—eye contact
—physical contact
—focused attention

If children do not get adequate amounts of each of these, they will not feel loved, regardless of how much you may actually love them.

Children tend to feel insecure, inferior, and inadequate. Their feelings in these areas are linked to the three great coins of human worth—as the world measures it: the gold coin of beauty, the silver coin of intelligence, and the bronze coin of talent. Failure to possess the gold coin of beauty makes you feel insecure. Failure to possess the silver coin of intelligence makes you feel inferior. Failure to possess the bronze coin of talent makes you feel inadequate.

It is the task of parents to make children feel that their worth is inherent: based on the image of God within, their value in Christ (assuming they are Christians), and their value simply as your children. Period. No other reason.

Children tend to get their sense of significance and worth from the world around them. They are constantly reading the feedback and gravitating toward that which gives them the greatest sense of belonging and worth. If children do not get that sense of belonging and worth from their parents, they will get it from the next best thing—usually, their peer group.

If parents are involved enough in the lives of their children, giving them a sense of belonging and significance, the children's attitudes toward their friends will be determined by their parents. They will choose their friends based on their relationship with their parents. If they do not have that degree of involvement with their parents, then their attitude toward their parents will be determined by their peers.

This kind of involvement in our children's lives requires a great deal of time—more, I am convinced, than most parents are willing to spend. It means getting under the skin of the child and finding out what he or she is like. It means adjusting your world to nurture and cultivate your children to help them reach their absolute potential as individuals.

This is totally contrary to the parenting model most of us instinctively embrace: that is, the husband works, the wife keeps house and/or works outside the home, the children go to school. Then when they graduate, they will go out and become like us.

Parenting demands time. It demands emotional involvement. It demands working your job around your family, not working your family around your job.

Henry Brandt has said it as well as anyone:

> In our restaurant business, we trained our waiters and waitresses to be busy. When not waiting on customers, they were to be completing other assignments: refilling supplies, dusting, straightening up.
>
> Picture this situation. A waitress is dusting when a customer comes in. If she forgets her main reasons for being there, she might consider the customer an interruption, instead of her primary responsibility.
>
> A lifeguard may be sitting up in his lifeguard chair, comfortable and getting a nice tan. If a swimmer suddenly needs his help, the lifeguard shouldn't consider this some sort of interruption. These swimmers are his primary responsibility.

Parents need to consider children as their primary responsibility . . . not as interruptions.

Parents have needs too, no doubt about it, and life must be kept balanced in other areas. But children are not an interruption. They are a primary responsibility, and if we sacrifice them for the sake of our job or our hobby or the church, we will have a serious problem on our hands.

The Family

The family is not suffering today because people don't want good families; the desire to have happy and healthy families is as great as it ever was. The family is suffering today because people are not contributing to the family in ways that make it become what they want it to be. They want strong families, but then act in ways that weaken the family.

Yet, just because most families are floundering does not mean it is impossible to have a healthy family. The biblical principles still work. The promises of God are still good. The social forces which ravage the family can be held in check; they can be deflected. But, strong, healthy, happy families do not just happen. They are the result of hard work.

When Professor Nick Stinnett, chairman of the Department of Human Development and the Family at the University of Nebraska, studied more than three thousand families to determine what makes families strong, he discovered six main qualities in strong families:

—strong families are committed to the family;
—strong families spend time together;
—strong families have good family communication;
—strong families express appreciation to each other;
—strong families have a spiritual commitment;
—strong families are able to solve problems in a crisis.

How are families able to do all those things? Well, for that answer we need to turn to the Scripture.

In Ephesians we see some of the very factors that contribute to a healthy home. At the heart of healthy family relationships is mutual submission: husbands to the needs of their wives, wives to the authority of their husbands, parents to the needs of their children, and children to the authority of their parents. Children are to obey and honor their parents, and parents are not to provoke their children to anger, but are to bring them up in the training and instruction of the Lord.

Each Christian family is responsible to pass on the baton of commitment to Christ to the next generation by bringing them up in the training and instruction of the Lord. An Old Testament passage, Deuteronomy 6:6, 9, gives some of the best information in all the Bible on passing on the baton.

> These words, which I am commanding you today, shall be on your heart; and you shall teach them diligently to your sons and shall talk of them when you sit in your house and when you walk by the way and when you lie down and when you rise up. . . . And you shall write them on the doorposts of your house and on your gates.

You cannot impart what you do not possess, so do not expect your children to have a devotion to God unless you do. Do not expect them to walk with God unless you do. Do not expect Christ to make a difference in your children's lives unless He is making a difference in yours. It is no small thing to say you believe in God; it must be written on your heart, not merely in your head.

During childhood and early adulthood, your children are likely to have less of a walk with the Lord than you do. If your walk is weak, theirs will likely be nonexistent. If your walk is strong, theirs will likely be moderate. Then, when they move into adulthood and choose their values for themselves, your modeling will determine whether Christ will be at the center of their lives. When it comes to commitment to Christ, if you want your kids to be snow, you are going to have to be a blizzard. And not just religious activity, pious platitudes, or somber faces. It has to be genuine. Not perfect, but sincere.

"You shall know the truth, and the truth shall set you free," said Jesus (John 8:32). If you do not know the truth, you are in bondage to ignorance.

In this context, the issue is scriptural truth. "These words, which I am commanding you today shall be on your heart; and you shall teach them diligently to your sons." Our children must know the Scriptures. They must know the words of God.

If our children are to be free from bondage to ignorance, they must know truth. In order to know truth, they must be taught it. That is one of the reasons you take your children to church. But if you are depending on the Sunday school and church and youth group to solve all your problems, you have misplaced hopes. The home is the dominant influence in a child's life. A church will reinforce truth if it is upheld at home. If it is not, the truth will be drowned in a sea of contradiction.

If a child learns at church that he should live a pure life, and then at home you watch sex, violence, and vulgarity on television, your child will grow up thinking that sex, violence, and vulgarity are not all that bad— while at the same time having the impression that the church is a social dinosaur, an irrelevant relic from the past. Mom and Dad go, but it doesn't have anything to do with real life.

If a child learns at church that she should be honest, and then at home sees you being dishonest, padding your expense accounts, or manipulating tax figures or having your child tell someone who has called on the telephone that you are not home, these realities contradict the teachings she has received on Sunday morning.

You reveal your value system to the world, and ingrain it in your children, by what you have in your home and the way you treat what you have in your home.

What pictures do you have on the wall? What books do you have on the bookshelf? What magazines do you subscribe to? What television programs do you watch? What music do you listen to? What do you talk about? What recreation do you engage in? What do you laugh at? Do you laugh? Do you affirm and encourage one another? Do you have fun together? Do you ever have people into the home and talk about spiritual things?

All these things combine to create an environment in the home, and it is not neutral. It makes an impact on your child's world view, on his value system, on what is important to him and not important to him.

What messages are you sending to your child? Is your home environment contributing to a spiritual breakdown, or are you passing the spiritual baton to your child's generation?

Inevitably, some of you are sitting there saying, "If that is the standard, I've already blown it. What do I do?"

First of all, you must accept the fact that God forgives and restores. This is an imperfect world, and we are imperfect people. So when we have blown anything, which we invariably do, the only thing we can do is go to the Lord, confess, ask His forgiveness and restoration to fellowship and His help in doing better in the future.

Next, you must accept the fact that you cannot turn back the clock and change history. You cannot go back; you can only go forward. If you allow yourself to get buried with guilt, it will not help anything in the past and will only impede progress in the future. There may be a time of grieving and remorse, and there may be inescapable flashbacks of sadness, but overall you must move forward in hope. Determine that you will let God use your experiences to make things better in the future.

Finally, if you have blown it with your child—and what parent hasn't?—there may be some practical things you can do, but the bottom line is that you must go to your child and ask him to forgive you. Admit that you are struggling and learning, but that by God's grace you are trying. If you care and if you try, you stand a good chance of keeping your child on your team.

Kids don't expect parents to be perfect. They just expect them to be real. They don't demand flawlessness. They just want their parents' love and direction. There is no danger in asking a child for forgiveness because if you have blown it, the child knows it. Refusing to admit it only confirms in the child's mind that you are unaware or unwilling to set things straight.

How do we pass the baton? By having a real Christian experience ourselves. By instructing our children in truth. By using everyday life to help our children understand how that truth is lived out. And to cultivate an environment which encourages, not discourages, spiritual growth.

In one of his many journeys "on the road," television correspondent Charles Kuralt made a Thanksgiving visit to the home of Alex and Mary Chandler in Mississippi.

> A long road took nine children out of the cotton fields, out of poverty, out of Mississippi. But roads go both ways, and this Thanksgiving weekend, they all returned. . . . One after another, and from every corner of America, the cars turned into the yard. With much cheering and much hugging, the nine children of Alex and Mary Chandler were coming home for their parents' fiftieth wedding anniversary. . . .
>
> All nine children had memories of a sharecropper's cabin and nothing to wear and nothing to eat. All nine are college graduates.
>
> [There is] Gloria Chandler Coleman, master of arts, University of Missouri, a teacher in Kansas City. . . . Cooking the meal in the kitchen of the new house the children built for their parents four years ago is Bessie Chandler Beasley, BA Tuskegee, MA Central Michigan, dietitian at a veteran's hospital, married to a Ph.D. And helping out, Princess Chandler Norman, MA Indiana University, a schoolteacher in Gary, Indiana.
>
> Alex Chandler remembers the time when he had a horse and a cow and tried to buy a mule and couldn't make the payments and lost the mule, the horse, and the cow. And about that time, Cleveland, the first son, decided he wanted to go to college.

ALEX CHANDLER: We didn't have any money. And we went to town; he wanted to catch the bus to go on up there. And so we went to town and borrowed two dollars and a half from her niece, and bought him a bus ticket. And when he got there, that's all he had.

From that beginning he became Dr. Cleveland Chandler. He is chairman of the economics department at Howard University. How did they do it, starting on one of the poorest farms in the poorest part of the poorest state in America?

PRINCESS CHANDLER NORMAN: We worked. . . .

NORMAN: Yes, picked cotton, and pulled corn, stripped millet, dug potatoes.

They all left. Luther left for the University of Omaha and went on to become the Public Service Employment Manager for Kansas City. He helped his younger brother, James come to Omaha University, too, and go on to graduate work at Yale. And in his turn, James helped Herman, who graduated from Morgan State and is a technical manager in Dallas. And they helped themselves. Fortson, a Baptist minister in Pueblo, Colorado, wanted to go to Morehouse College. . . .

So, helping themselves and helping one another, they all went away. And now, fifty years after life began for the Chandler family in a one-room shack in a cotton field, now, just as they were sitting down in the new house to the ham and turkey and sweet potatoes and cornbread and collard greens and two kinds of pie and three kinds of cake, now Donald arrived—the youngest—who had driven with his family all the way down from Minneapolis. And now the Chandlers were all together again.

ALEX CHANDLER (*saying grace*): Our Father in heaven, we come at this moment, giving thee thanks for thou hast been so good and so kind. We want to thank you, oh God, for this, for your love and for your son. Thank you that you have provided for all of us through all these years. (*Mr. Chandler begins weeping.*)

Remembering all those years of sharecropping and going hungry and working for a white man for fifty cents a day and worrying about his children's future, remembering all that Alex Chandler almost didn't get through this blessing.

ALEX (*continuing grace*): In Jesus' name, amen.

And neither did the others. (Family members wiping tears away)

The Chandler family started with as near nothing as any family in America ever did. And so their Thanksgiving weekend might have been more thankful than most.

"I'll Fly Away" . . . is Mr. Chandler's favorite [hymn]. His nine children flew away and made places for themselves in this country; and this weekend, came home again. There probably are no lessons in any of this, but I know that in the future, whenever I hear that the family is a dying institution, I'll think of them. Whenever I hear anything in America is impossible, I'll think of them.[2]

Charles Kuralt said there was probably no lesson to be learned. He was wrong. There is a lesson: This kind of dynamic family life doesn't just happen; it is a result of a dynamic faith these parents passed down to nine children. First, they modeled it. Second, they taught it, formally. Third, they taught it informally. Fourth, they cultivated an environment in which their children could thrive.

Focus Questions

1. In your home, what encourages spiritual development in your children?

2. What discourages it?

3. What is the single most important step you could take to encourage the parent/child relationships in your family?

22

How Would You Work If Jesus Were Your Boss?

(Ephesians 6:5–8)

The true foundation of Europe's magnificent cathedrals was not stone, but the understanding that work was a collaboration with God. That was why the builders stationed angels at the heights; they knew God saw what they were doing and cared.

Chuck Colson

*I*n the fairytale "Snow White and the Seven Dwarfs," the seven little fellows go marching off to work each morning singing, "Hi ho, hi ho, it's off to work we go," with a spring in their step and a lilt in their voice. You'd have a spring in your step too if you were going to the same job they were going to: they owned a diamond mine. According to the Disney comic book I read as a child, their mine was a cavelike tunnel with golf-ball sized diamonds, already cut and faceted, sticking halfway out of the sides of the shaft. What a job!

But most of us are not bouncing jauntily off to a diamond mine every morning. Instead, we chug off soberly with a bumper sticker that says, "I owe, I owe, it's off to work I go."

In fact, for many people work is drudgery, a meaningless necessity. With little connection between their workplace and the rest of their life, their life slogan is TGIF. Even Paul Harvey begins his Friday broadcasts with, "Good Morning America . . . it's Friday!"

Because work is such a large portion of our lives, however, and because it can sometimes be such a challenge, it is important for us to understand what the Bible says about work. Work is not a curse. God Himself works. And He intends for us to work and to find meaning in our work.

So how should the Christian view work? How should the Christian act and perform at work? Is it all right to enjoy your work? If the Christian becomes truly committed, should he quit his job and go into full-time ministry? Is it possible to be a truly Christian business or professional person? Is it possible to be a truly Christian union member?

The Bible does have answers for our questions about work, and this passage in Ephesians introduces some of those answers.

Specifically, we are looking at Ephesians 6:5–8, but these verses refer back to 5:21 where we are commanded to be subject to one another in the fear of Christ. Paul then goes on to cite the specific types of relationships this encompasses: husband/wife, parent/child, master/slave. We serve Christ, he says, by serving each other, by being submissive to authority and submissive to needs.

In applying the principle of this passage to the culture of his day, Paul directed it specifically to slaves and masters; today these principles apply to employers and employees.

In the ancient Roman Empire, there were 60 million slaves; in fact, one-third of the Roman Empire was made up of slaves. Roman citizens had slaves to do everything for them. Some slaves were professionals: doctors, lawyers, teachers, musicians. But most were menial laborers, considered little more than human tools. They had no rights. Their lot in life was to serve their masters.

Nevertheless, the Bible does not explicitly forbid slavery. The Bible is not a book of political philosophy; it is a book that causes men to look to God. And while Christianity may eventually bring about political reform in the kingdoms of this world, it is not first and foremost a tool for political reform. It is, first and foremost, a message of salvation to save people out of this world, for Jesus' kingdom is not of this world.

However, while the Bible does not explicitly forbid slavery, the overall teaching of Scripture does. If we "do unto others as we would have others do unto us," we will not enslave them. If we love our neighbors as ourselves, by what stretch of the imagination can we subject them to a life of servitude? If we would not like to be a slave, we should not enslave another.

And Christianity eventually did kill slavery. It killed it with love and respect and honor and dignity. When the message of Christ began to be preached and fully accepted around the world, slavery began to disappear.

That was God's strategy: to use the message of Christ to further the kingdom of Christ, not to further kingdoms on earth. By instructing slaves to be obedient to their masters, the message of salvation by grace through faith in Christ was the message that was heard. It was not mixed with political motives. It was pure love—and had within it the power of God.

Jesus on the Job

> Slaves, be obedient to those who are your masters according to the flesh, with fear and trembling, in the sincerity of your heart, as to Christ; not by way of eyeservice, as men-pleasers, but as slaves of Christ, doing the will of God from the heart. With good will render service, as to the Lord, and not to men, knowing that whatever good thing each one does, this he will receive back from the Lord, whether slave or free.
>
> Ephesians 6:5–8

Today, when we think about taking these words literally, we are taken aback. How can this be? Yet no amount of examination removes any ink or alters any letters. What you see is what you get. It appears to say what it appears to say. "By returning only good for evil," it says, "you convince the world that Jesus is real, and by living as He lived, you show the world who He was. They see you, and they meet God."

This is exactly what Jesus meant when He said, "Let your light so shine before men, that they may see your good works, and glorify your Father who is in heaven" (Matt. 5:16 KJV).

Today, we do this by taking Jesus on the job. When we do, we take three things to the workplace with us: obedience, sincerity, and diligence.

"Be obedient to those who are your masters," Paul says. As long as our employers do not ask us to do something dishonest or immoral, we are to be obedient. Should they ask us to do something that violates the law of God, of course, we must obey God rather than man (Acts 5:29). But we must also be prepared to suffer the consequences, which could mean we lose our jobs.

However, Paul is not calling us to a fist-clenching, teeth-gritting, eye-squinting kind of subjugation. He is not asking for obedience from our hands while rebellion is in our hearts. He calls us to be obedient "in the sincerity of your heart . . . as slaves of Christ, doing the will of God from the heart." In other words, we serve Christ by serving our employers, so we are obedient because we are serving Christ. Not with gritted teeth, but with a sincere desire to respect and obey.

"All well and good," you may say, "but I work for an ill-tempered, shortsighted, small-talented, card-carrying member of the hairy unwashed and mentally unfocused. How can I obey him?"

What you must do is look beyond him. In a sense, he is incidental. You are Christ's slave, not his. However, during this chapter in your life he has been placed there for you to serve. It is Christ standing behind him that you must be concerned about. There is something God wants to do in your life, and as long as you work for him, you serve Christ by serving him.

We must have the mindset that we are working for the Lord, and that the Lord Himself is going to inspect our work. We work for God, not for men. Knowing that God will inspect our work, we are to be diligent.

Of course, we are not slaves, and one freedom we have is to change jobs. But as long as we have a given job, we are to serve Christ there. God sees our struggle with unreasonable employers. He sees, and He rewards. Our sincere, obedient, diligent service to an unreasonable employer on this earth—or any employer for that matter—will be rewarded with glory in heaven.

Lessons from Life

Somehow, many people think that work is a curse on mankind as a result of the Fall. Actually, it's quite the opposite. God Himself worked during Creation. "And by the seventh day God completed His *work* which He had done; and He rested on the seventh day from all His *work* which He had done" (Gen 2:2, italics mine). God created work, and by working we become colaborers with Him in extending His creation. God intended man and woman to inhabit and subdue the earth. Thus, our work has meaning and eternal significance.

Our work also serves others. When we produce a product or a service, we provide for the needs and interests of others; when we earn money, we provide for our families and can give charitably to help those beyond our immediate family.

By doing all this, ultimately we are serving God through our work. No matter what kind of work we are doing, if we believe it is a vocation which God has provided for us, it is significant. We are in God's will, doing what God wants us to do, and serving God by serving our employers.

Some believe that God is more pleased with people if they are missionaries or pastors. That is not true. God is pleased when we are doing what He has given us to do, whether that means working on an assembly line or preaching to thousands.

This does not mean it is wrong to change jobs at times. This passage was written to slaves, who did not have the option of mobility. We do.

And God can use that to guide us into different avenues of service or vocation.

We must, however, ask ourselves why we are changing jobs and if that is the best alternative. Some people bounce around from job to job because "the boss doesn't treat me right" . . . when the real problem is with them. Because they have personality and character weaknesses that cause the problems, every time they change jobs, they take the problems with them—and it happens all over again. So always ask, Is the problem with the job, the boss, the other employees—or is the problem me?

Even though the problem may be within you, however, there are times when the circumstances get overwhelming and you must change jobs just to survive, even as you are working on the problem. But you are still responsible to obey your employer as long as you are employed by him.

When we work for unpleasant people, we must learn to look past them, to see Christ (Col. 3:22–25). It's somewhat like going to war: the battle may be unpleasant, but your duty is to obey and please your commander-in-chief (1 Tim. 6:1–2).

When we respect our employers, when we are honest and cooperative, the doctrine of Christianity is supported. When we do not respect our employers, the doctrine of Christianity is undermined. If we are bad employees, in the eyes of our employers it casts a shadow over Christianity. If we are "well-pleasing" employees, we adorn the Gospel, helping people believe it is true because of the way we act (Titus 2:9–10).

Suffering for Christ in the workplace is no different than suffering for Christ on the mission field or in a country hostile to the gospel. When people suffer for doing right in those circumstances, we consider them heroes. Why, then, do we not consider people heroes when they suffer for Christ in the workplace? It is the same thing (1 Pet. 2:18–25). In fact, the workplace is the main arena where most of us have that opportunity—to give ourselves to the great cause of attracting people to Christ through the way we live.

When we refuse to retaliate against those who treat us poorly in the workplace, we win a hearing for the cause of Christ. We adorn the gospel with our actions and our attitudes.

If we see ourselves as missionaries first and workers second, then any suffering merely creates an opportunity to manifest Christ and, at some point, to share the gospel.

> The point of our lives in this world is not comfort, security, or even happiness, but training; not fulfillment but preparation. It's a lousy home,

but it's a fine gymnasium. We misunderstand where we are if we believe in earthly utopias. The universe is a soul-making machine, a
womb, an egg. Jesus didn't make it into a rose garden when he came,
though he could have. Rather, he wore the thorns from this world's
gardens. If we believe that, we will expect sufferings rather than resent
them as a scandal.

The point of this life is to become the person God can love perfectly, to satisfy his thirst to love. God doesn't want perfect perfor-
mances, but loving persons. "Being" counts more than "doing," the
singer more than the song. We learn by the mistakes we make and the
sufferings they bring.

We had better stop looking for alternatives, for escape hatches, for
this is our hatchery.[1]

Standing Above the Workplace Crowd

Have you ever wondered how Jesus would fry hamburgers or pump
gas? Have you ever wondered how He would go about selling stocks or life
insurance? Have you ever wondered how He would program computers or
teach a class or run a bank or manage a company?

You should. Because if we are to serve Christ in our work, then we must
do our work as He would if He had our job. Certainly we don't have His
personality or gifts or abilities—or His divinity. Nevertheless, in principle we
are to operate the way He would.

Remember, Jesus wasn't always an itinerant preacher. Until He was
thirty, He was a carpenter. And reflecting on what we know about Him, I
think at least three things would characterize His work.

First, He would be morally distinctive. He wouldn't swear or tell dirty
jokes or backstab or gossip; He wouldn't elevate Himself at the expense of
another. Second, He would do the best possible job He could with the talent, training, and tools available. He wouldn't put veneer over particle board
and sell it as solid wood. Third, He would treat those who did business with
Him with dignity and respect. He wouldn't yell or sneer or talk disrespect-
fully behind their backs. "I can't believe that old biddy. She comes in here
every week complaining about that kitchen table I made her." Words like
that would never pass his lips.

If that is how Jesus would have worked as a carpenter—morally, excel-
lently, and respectfully—and if we are going to work the way He would,
then we must do the same.

In his book *Your Work Matters to God* Doug Sherman says we are in the
midst of a "moral mudslide." The moral and ethical base on which our nation

was founded has begun to crack and crumble and is in danger of toppling the house. Nowhere is it more evident than in the workplace.

A recent Gallup Poll found that 80 percent of the executives polled had driven while drunk, 78 percent had used the company telephone for personal use, 35 percent overstated deductions on tax forms, 74 percent had taken home work supplies. The inescapable fact is that leaders set the moral and ethical tone for the organizations they run.

Small wonder, then, that employee theft is one of the greatest threats to business, reaching perhaps $50 billion a year. Time theft (late arrivals, early departures, prolonged breaks) costs perhaps $150 billion a year, triple the cost of merchandise theft. This equals $1,000 for every man, woman, and child in America.

Reader's Digest recently ran an article on automobile repair shops. When 226 garages were randomly selected to repair a car with only a missing sparkplug wire, 74 percent (167) repaired something not broken or did nothing and charged up to $500.

Lying has become a way of life in the workplace, and sexual immorality is epidemic—in spite of the AIDS crisis. Dr. Barbara Gutek, professor of psychology at Claremont Graduate School and author of *Sex and the Workplace,* reports that 80 percent of workers report some kind of "social-sexual" experience and as many as 35 percent have such an experience each week. She explains, "I have found sex at work a problem for up to half of all workers."

This disintegration in morals and ethics in the workplace is one reason America is in economic crisis today. There is a sin-tax on immoral behavior. Loss of productivity, theft, cost overruns, the cost of paying for worker absenteeism, alcohol and drug abuse, and health-care costs because of AIDS threaten to destroy our economy.

The most tragic thing in all of this is that the Christian community has had virtually no impact on these problems.

In fact, when it comes to lying, stealing, absenteeism, and time theft, Gallup has found no difference between the churched and the unchurched. Christians tend to have religion on Sunday and live like everyone else the rest of the week. But we don't have that option. If the Bible says on Sunday that we must not lie, then on Monday we must not lie. If the Bible says on Sunday that we must not act immorally, then on Monday we must not act immorally. If the Bible says on Sunday that we must be fair in all our dealings, then on Monday we must be fair in all our dealings. We cannot divide our religious life from our work life. If we are to be truly Christian in our lifestyle, we must be the same on Monday as we are on Sunday.

If you write up a contract and knowingly take advantage of a person, you are lying to that person and stealing from that person. If you have some-one punch in for you when you come to work late, or if you leave early and have someone punch out for you, you are stealing from your employer. If you witness to others on company time when you are supposed to be working, you are stealing from your employer—and the same holds true for having Bible studies or prayer on company time. From the world's point of view the Christian is stealing from his employer just as surely as if he quit work early or took too long a coffee break.

We must take a stand and live for Christ in the workplace, no matter what the cost.

We may have some limitations in our specific circumstances. We may not have an adequate budget or the right tools or properly trained help. We may not be as talented or as smart or as well-trained as someone else who might do our job. But we must have a passion for excellence in what we do and the confidence before God that we have done the best we could with what we have.

Shelby Carter, in his book *Ten Greatest Salespersons,* wrote:

> When our family had just moved into our new home—the whole gang, our six children and two dogs—it was the first day in the house and everything was in an uproar. The kids all poured into the family room, and the TV didn't work. I got out the Yellow Pages and called for a repairman, and he came right out. Well, after he re-paired the set, he asked me to come over and look at it. I stepped over the kids, our German shepherd, the books and instead of hand-ing me a bill, as I expected, he took out a bottle of Windex spray and cleaned the glass. That impressed me, because he showed me how proud he was of his work and the product he served. From that day on, when-ever we needed our TV fixed, I've said to my wife, "Honey, call the Windex guy."

Excellence is a game of inches. Often there is very little difference be-tween that which is excellent and that which is not—but that little difference makes all the difference.

If you do your work with excellence, people will notice. And if they know you are a Christian and that your commitment to excellence is rooted in your faith, they will see your good work and glorify your Father in heaven.

In *A Passion for Excellence,* Tom Peters writes: "At Disneyland and Disneyworld, every person who comes onto the property is called a guest. Moreover, should you ever write the word *Disney,* heaven help you if you don't capitalize it."

If you have genuine respect for the dignity and worth of other people, you will find ways of communicating it. And if you want to stand out in the workplace and represent the God you serve, you must treat people with dignity and respect.

Bruce Olson had been ministering among the Motilone Indians in the jungles along the Columbian/Venezuelan border for twenty-eight years when, in October 1988, he was captured by Communist revolutionaries.

The pro-Castro Communists wanted Bruce to use his influence to recruit the Indians to their cause. When he refused, they held him hostage and tortured him to try to get him to change his mind. In the boredom laced with terror, Bruce began to look for ways to show the love of Christ to his captors. As the days passed, even while the terrorists were trying to break down Bruce's resistance, he noticed that some of the guerrillas had malaria and others had symptoms of hepatitis.

> I knew their poor sanitation habits were contributing to the spread of the hepatitis virus. The guerrillas seemed to spit constantly, contaminating the ground and eventually the water and food. I mentioned the problem to one of the camp officers, and like magic, the spitting stopped.
>
> I taught the cooks how to prepare delicious sauces out of smoked palm grubs, made bread for the whole camp three times a week, and wrote flowery love letters for illiterate young guerrillas to send to their girlfriends. We each had a strategy: they wanted to enter my life, and I wanted to enter theirs. I was the one making the headway.[2]

As time passed, the guerrilla leaders used every conceivable trick to break Bruce psychologically. During this time, he continued to treat them kindly and helped them every way he could. Then, during a bout of diverticulitis, he needed a blood transfusion. Immediately a fight broke out among the guerrillas over who would have the honor of giving their blood to him. A young man who had become a Christian was chosen. Bruce's life was having an impact on the hardest of hearts.

Finally, after long months as a hostage, Bruce learned that his execution had been ordered. His executioners, eighteen of them with submachine guns, lined up. *There will not be much left of me,* Bruce thought, *but at least it will be quick.*

"Take aim," the leader ordered. Several of the men wept silently as they trained their weapons on him.

"Fire!"

Shots rang out, but Bruce felt nothing. The men in the firing squad looked at me with amazement, then examined their rifles.

"These are blanks!" one of them shouted.

It had been one final attempt to break him, but it hadn't worked.

The next morning he was released.

Because Bruce Olson had no personal agenda, he was able to manifest the love of Christ wherever the love of Christ took him. And everyone noticed. The kingdom of Christ was advanced, and God was glorified.

In our workplace we will never come close to the kind of suffering Bruce Olson was called upon to experience. But we are called to make a difference. If we lay down our personal agenda and determine that we are going to respond as Christ would if He were in our shoes, people will notice.

Honesty, excellence, and respect must be the marks of the Christian in the marketplace. We must stand out in bold relief against the unethical and immoral backdrop of our culture. We must stand head and shoulders above the crowd. We must shine as lights in the darkness.

Focus Questions

1. What can you do to be a more effective witness for Christ on your job?

2. What could the church do to help Christians be more distinctive in the workplace?

3. Who impresses you most in the workplace? Why?

23

How Would You "Boss" If Jesus Were Your Employee?

(Ephesians 6:9)

Treat a man as he appears to be, and you make him worse. But treat a man as if he already were what he potentially could be, and you make him what he should be.

Goethe

*I*n his introduction to *A Passion for Excellence,* Tom Peters writes:

> In the late sixties American management was touted by many, at home and abroad, as the primary asset that America could export to the world. And then came reality: OPEC, the Japanese, social and political unrest, and a changing work force. The vaunted American management mystique quickly turned out to be largely just that—mystique. The battering American business took in the seventies and early eighties has humbled virtually every American manager.
>
> Out of the failures of our organizations, as evidenced by faulty microchips and tanks that can't handle dust, by declining SAT scores and garbage lying about, has emerged the beginning of a fundamental reexamination of managing per se. [We must] attack the MBA-numbers-only mentality of American managers. [Today, the reawakening] puts the knock on mindless systems analysis and begins the examination of a misplaced emphasis on paper rather than on people.
>
> A revolution is brewing. What kind of revolution? In large measure, it is in fact a "back to basics" revolution. The two most important basics are pride in one's organization and enthusiasm for its work. Management, with its attendant images—cop, referee, devil's advocate, dispassionate analyst, naysayer, pronouncer—connotes controlling and arranging and demeaning and reducing. "Leadership" connotes unleashing

energy, building, freeing, and growing. American organizations have been overmanaged and underled.[1]

The revolution really gets back to people. In America we have developed a leadership style that does not preserve the dignity of people, and thus it is doomed to failure. Love is still the most powerful force in the world, even in the workplace. Nothing works long without love.

While the Bible is not a handy guide to corporate empowerment, it does contain truth that is helpful in management and leadership. If lived out, biblical truth will show us how to lead others in a way that preserves their dignity, which will, in turn, provide the base for social and economic strength. More and more, biblical principles—the truth of Scripture—is becoming undeniable in the marketplace.

This section of Ephesians, both directly and indirectly, deals with the marketplace. Directly, it refers to masters and slaves, appropriate to the specific culture and day in which it was written. But in principle it speaks to employees and employers and, even more broadly, to anyone involved in the business pecking order.

The umbrella principle, of course, traces back to Ephesians 5:18, where Paul writes, "be filled with the Spirit," and to part of the outworking of that filling, being subject to one another in our personal relationships: husbands and wives, parents and children, masters and slaves.

Specifically, Paul says, slaves are to be submissive to the authority of their masters, and masters are to be submissive to the needs of their slaves. Since we are no longer masters and slaves, we must look to the principle behind the passage to see what meaning it has for us today. When we do this, we find three principles that are to guide our actions today.

The Master Serves Christ

And, masters, do the same things to them, and give up threatening, knowing that both their Master and yours is in heaven, and there is no partiality with Him.

Ephesians 6:9

Doing "the same thing" most likely refers to "doing the will of God from the heart" in verse 6. In the marketplace, this might read, "Employers, do the will of God in your business."

In a recent article in the *Wall Street Journal* entitled "Christian-Based Firms Find Following Principles Pays," reporter Roger Ricklefs wrote:

It doesn't look like a way to get rich. An elevator contractor passes out potholders with spiritual slogans to customers and suppliers. A fast-food chain is barred from shopping malls because it won't open on Sundays. A motel operator forgoes a 20% increase in earnings because it won't serve alcohol.

These are "Christian-based" companies that explicitly try to run their businesses according to Biblical principles. Thousands of such companies are defying the conventional wisdom about the follow of mixing business and religion. And now, a study shows that their approach can pay off.

In the study conducted by management scholar Nabil A. Ibrahim, a group of 152 Christian-based companies grew significantly faster, by every criterion examined, than other companies in their fields. The study provides statistical support for the idea that ethics in business can be made to pay.

Thus, for moral, ethical, and even economic reasons, the employer should serve Christ.

The Master Serves the Servant

Doing "the same thing" also includes "with good will render service, as to the Lord, and not to men" in verse 7, which in the workplace might be translated, "Employers, treat your employees with good will, as to the Lord, and not to men."

A parallel passage in Colossians 4:1 reads, "Masters, grant to your slaves justice and fairness," which might be translated, "Treat your employees justly and fairly."

In an interview in the October 1983 issue of *Northwest Orient Magazine,* Andre Soltner of Lutece in New York, one of the world's premier restaurants, put it this way:

> I am more than thirty years a chef. I know what I am doing and each day I do my absolute best. I cook for you from my heart, with love. It must be the same with service. The waiter must serve with love. Otherwise, the food is nothing. Do you see? Many times, I will leave my kitchen and go to the tables to take the orders myself. It starts right then and there. That feeling the customer must have is relaxation. If not, then his evening is ruined. Mine, too, by the way. How can he love, if he's not relaxed? People ask me all the time what secrets I have. I tell them there is nothing mysterious about Lutece. I put love in my cooking and love in the serving. That is all.

Or, consider these words from Vince Lombardi, generally considered the best professional football coach ever, speaking to an American Management Association group shortly before his death:

> Mental toughness is humility, simplicity, Spartanism. And one other, love. I don't necessarily have to like my associates, but as a man I must love them. Love is loyalty. Love is teamwork. Love respects the dignity of the individual. Heartpower is the strength of your corporation.

You don't have to be a Christian to understand the importance of treating people who work for you with dignity and respect. But when you are a Christian, these concepts become even more vital. Those in authority must have an attitude of servanthood toward those who report to them.

The Master Brings Out the Best in Others

How has your life changed since Jesus came into your heart? I can tell you how mine has changed. B.C.—before Christ—I was a moral and social schizophrenic. Part of the time I acted nice and kind and good and moral, and part of the time I acted ugly and unkind and bad and immoral. But when Jesus came into my life, He started taking the bad away and replacing it with good. How? By expecting the best from me.

Jesus expects the best from those who believe in Him and, as a result, He brings out the best in them. Now certainly my life is not without its struggles, not without its weaknesses, not without its setbacks. But looking back over the long haul, Jesus has made such a difference. He is bringing out the best in me, and He will do the same for you. That's His specialty.

Joe Aldrich illustrates it this way in his book *Life-style Evangelism:*

> There is a legend which recounts the return of Jesus to glory after His time on earth. Even in heaven He bore the marks of His earthly pilgrimage with its cruel cross and shameful death. The angel Gabriel approached Him and said, "Master, you must have suffered terribly for men down there."
>
> "I did," He said.
>
> "And," continued Gabriel, "do they know all about how you loved them and what you did for them?"
>
> "Oh, no," said Jesus, "not yet. Right now only a handful of people in Palestine know."

Gabriel was perplexed. "Then what have you done," he asked, "to let everyone know about your love for them?"

Jesus said, "I've asked Peter, James, John, and a few more friends to tell other people about Me. Those who are told will in turn tell still other people about Me, and My story will be spread to the farthest reaches of the globe. Ultimately, all of mankind will have heard about My life and what I have done."

Gabriel frowned and looked rather skeptical. He knew well what poor stuff men were made of. "Yes," he said, "but what if Peter, James, and John grow weary? What if the people who come after them forget? What if way down in the twentieth century, people just don't tell others about you? Haven't you made any other plans?

Jesus answered, "I haven't made any other plans. I'm counting on them."[2]

Jesus expects the best from us, and we must expect the best from others.

In his book, *Bringing Out the Best in People,* Alan Loy McGinnis says, "I talked once to a woman with vast experience in politics who had observed the great and the near great. She said, 'Do you know what separates achievers from the masses? I once thought it was drive, intelligence, connections. But the longer I've watched people, the more I've discovered that, paradoxically, it is an ability to fail that makes for lasting success.'"

And when asked for the ingredients of good management, Charles Knight, CEO of Emerson Electric, said boldly, "You need the ability to fail. I'm amazed at the number of organizations that set up an environment where they do not permit people to be wrong. You cannot innovate unless you are willing to accept some mistakes."

Jesus created an environment where failure was not fatal—Peter being the most memorable and blatant example.

In the Garden of Gethsemane, Peter boasted, "Lord, if all these other chickens desert you, I won't. You can count on me."

Jesus replied, "Peter, before the rooster crows three times, you will have denied me three times."

As Jesus predicted it, so it happened. After the rooster crowed the third time, the Bible says, Peter went out and wept bitterly. He had failed. He had denied that he ever knew Jesus. How low could one man fall? How flagrantly could one person fail?

Yet a few days later, after His death and resurrection, Jesus was eating breakfast with Peter on the shores of Galilee in perfect fellowship and harmony. And Peter went on to become Jesus' apostle to the Jews and one of the great leaders of the early church. His failure was neither fatal nor final.

We crush people by never allowing them to make mistakes. Worse yet, if they do succeed and we won't recognize it, if we find something wrong with it or say it could have been done better, we destroy their initiative, their confidence, and their self-image.

If we want to bring out the best in people, we must allow for failure and we must reward success.

We must also model success.

When Lee Iacocca first became chairman of the board at Chrysler, the auto industry was in a slump and Chrysler was on the skids. The company's very survival was at stake. Sometime later, Iacocca addressed an insurance convention on the subject, "So You Think You've Got Troubles!" His stirring speech lasted sixty minutes, frequently interrupted by applause, as he related how Chrysler had cut their white-collar staff from forty thousand to twenty thousand, were producing more cars, and were finally making a modest profit again. It was a rags-to-riches story on a corporate scale.

Those in the audience reported how energized they were afterward. Whether they were corporate executives or not, Mr. Iacocca sent them out ready to attack their work with renewed zest and dedication.

When Harry Truman was asked how he could account for his success in politics, he pointed to several pictures of family ancestors and said gruffly, "I come from good stock, and I've got a lot to live up to."

There is something powerful about a good example. Leaders must model what they want to happen in other people's lives. When Jesus chose His twelve disciples, He called them "to be with Him"—life on life. Jesus understood the impact of modeling.

In 1 Corinthians 11:1, Paul writes, "Be imitators of me, just as I also am of Christ."

In Hebrews 13:7, we read: "Remember those who led you, who spoke the word of God to you; and considering the outcome of their way of life, imitate their faith."

And in 1 Thessalonians 1:5–7 Paul says, "Our gospel did not come to you in word only, but also in power and in the Holy Spirit and with full conviction; just as you know what kind of men we proved to be among you for your sake. You also became imitators of us and of the Lord, having received the word in much tribulation with the joy of the Holy Spirit, so that you became an example to all the believers in Macedonia and in Achaia."

Imitators become imitated.

If we want to bring out the best in people, we must model the behavior we want to see in others.

Bringing out the best in people is typified in a story told by Tom Peters in *A Passion for Excellence,* and it is taken from a speech given to the Armed Forces Staff College by a former commander of the U.S. Army's blood-and-guts 101st Airborne, the late Lieutenant General Melvin Zais:

> The one piece of advice which I believe will contribute more to making you a better leader and commander, will provide you with greater happiness and self-esteem and at the same time advance your career more than any other advice which I can provide you. And it doesn't call for a special personality, and it doesn't call for any certain chemistry. Any one of you can do it. And that advice is that you must care. . . .
>
> How do you know if you care? Well, for one thing, if you care, you listen to your junior officers and your soldiers. . . .
>
> To care, you must listen. Really listen. . . .
>
> You care if you go in the mess hall, and I don't mean go in with white gloves and rub dishes and pots and pans and find dust. You care if you go in the mess hall and you notice that the scrambled eggs are in a puddle of water and twenty pounds of toast has been done in advance and it's all lying there hard and cold, and the bacon is lying there dripping in the grease and the cooks got all their work done way ahead of time, and the cold pots of coffee are sitting on the tables getting even colder. If that really bothers you, if it really gripes you, if you want to tear up those cooks, you care.
>
> And . . . you really need to like soldiers. . . . and you have to understand that they're as lousy as you let them be, and as good as you make them be. You just have to really like them and feel good about being with them.[3]

What this world needs, desperately, is more leaders who care, more leaders who listen, more leaders who really like those they lead, more leaders who want to bring out the best in others. What this world needs is more leaders who will create an environment where failure is not fatal and who will, themselves, model the behavior they expect from others.

Focus Questions

1. Do you struggle with submission to authority at work? What do you think Ephesians 6:5–8 means in your job?

2. Do you have people working under you? If one of them were Jesus, would it change the way you treat that person?

3. What evidence is there to suggest that one of your major goals at work is to try to bring out the best in other people?

Part 4

Power

God wants us to have power. We must be careful not to settle for clout.

24

Spiritual Power
(Ephesians 6:10–12)

*Do you really want to see divine power at work? Then discard
your human notions of power and look at the way Christ lived
and died.*

Edmund A. Steimle

*F*or over two hundred years, Benedict Arnold has been cussed and discussed as an unfaithful American. Why? Because he attempted to smuggle
a diagram of the fort at West Point on the Hudson River to the British. The
cannons on the walls at West Point guarded all ship traffic moving up and
down the Hudson River. If the British could take the fort and silence those
cannons, they could sail shiploads of redcoats up the Hudson River and attack the American forces from the rear. It could be a turning point in the
War of Independence.

Benedict Arnold was meeting with a British officer, John Andre, to turn
over the plans when they were discovered. Arnold fled to the British side and
became one of their finest officers. But succeeding generations of Americans
have never forgiven him for his act of treason, and his name has entered our
language as a synonym for "traitor."

"Why would Arnold do such a thing?" countless history students have
asked. "What possessed one of the finest generals in the American army to
defect?" Well, let me tell you the rest of the story.

As one theory has it, at heart Benedict Arnold was not a traitor. He was
a committed and loyal American patriot. New light has been shed on the reasoning behind his treasonous act by the recent discovery of letters between
Arnold and Benjamin Franklin.

The American colonies had asked the French for help in their battle
with the British. The French, glad to oblige, sent troops and troops and

more troops across the Atlantic. At one time, there were more French troops fighting than there were American troops.

General Arnold became deeply suspicious of the French motives. Why would the French be so willing to spend such massive amounts of their own blood on behalf of the Americans? Was their plan perhaps to help the Americans defeat the British and then make America a French colony instead? And thus he reasoned in his letters to Benjamin Franklin.

The colonies could not defeat the British without French help. However, they would pay a price for that help: France would make them a French colony. So either way, Arnold wrote, America was going to be a colony of some other country—either British or French. And if that were the case, the former was preferable. If they remained a British colony, they would be ruled more or less benevolently and might eventually be given their freedom. If they became a French colony, they would be ruled by tyrants and never given freedom. Therefore, Arnold argued, the American colonies should sue for peace with England.

Franklin, who was ambassador to France at the time, agreed with Arnold's opinions. Nevertheless, he said, "I believe, in the sovereignty of God, it will somehow work out," and strongly opposed any overtures for peace with the British.

Well, Benedict Arnold was not content to entrust so much to the sovereignty of God. As far as he was concerned, the way to preserve the great dream of freedom was to help the British win. Therefore, in an act of what Arnold would have described as great patriotism, he attempted to turn the diagram of West Point over to the British. When that failed, he joined the British, not to defeat the colonies, but, as he saw it, to defeat the French and drive them off American soil.

Interestingly enough, shortly after the British were defeated, the French Revolution broke out and the French soldiers were called home. If it weren't for that, we might be "par-lee-vooing Franc-ee" right now. The French intention was thwarted by a greater scheme, and Franklin's hunch about the sovereignty of God proved true.

Warfare is not just armies on two sides of a line drawn in the sand having at it. Warfare is not just blood and guts. Warfare is also diplomacy, espionage, negotiations, and maneuvering behind the scenes—which at times can have a greater impact on the outcome than the fighting on the battlefront. Because, after all, what's really at stake is power.

Power is one of the greatest motivating forces in the world. History is marked by men and women who lusted for power, from the pharaohs of

Egypt to the Persian, Greek, and Roman conquerors to the political leaders of modern times. Much of this power has been misused and much has been used for great good.

Everyone wants power. Some want a little and some want a lot, but all of us want power. We may not want to rule over others, but we want to control our own lives. We want to be able to impose our will on a situation, whether it is our job, our bank account, our children, or just our dishwasher or lawnmower. Sometimes we have all the power we want and sometimes we do not; sometimes we use our power wisely and sometimes we use it foolishly. All told, however, much of life revolves around our search for and our use of power.

This desire for power is not wrong in and of itself. God has created us for great power. In heaven, He will give us more power than anyone on earth has ever had; there we will rule the universe with Christ. For now, however, God does not necessarily offer us the power to control the external affairs of life. Often He asks us to trust Him in many of those areas. But one area in which He extends to us all the power we need—an area in which we desperately need power—is the area of spiritual warfare. For here, too, power is really what's at stake: the powers of darkness pitting themselves against the power of light.

We are engaged in a titanic spiritual battle against the forces of darkness, and although these spiritual forces have great impact in our daily lives, it is often very subtle. Unless we are well instructed in the Scriptures and walking closely with the Lord, we can fall victim to the powers of darkness without realizing it.

This seems like strange talk in our nuts-and-bolts world. We are not used to thinking about invisible foes and celestial combat. Yet if we are not careful, we will be duped into thinking we are battling people and circumstances, when all the time things are being orchestrated by a mastermind behind the scenes. The evil mastermind of darkness is intelligent and powerful. If we try to pretend he is not there, or if we try to do battle with him in our own intelligence and strength, we are doomed to failure.

The Source of Our Strength

Be strong in the Lord, and in the strength of His might.
Ephesians 6:10

You cannot control a flood with a flamethrower. Flames have absolutely no effect on a wall of water. You cannot douse a forest fire with floodlights.

Bright lights have no effect on fire. And you cannot fight supernatural battles with natural strength. Natural power has no effect whatsoever on spiritual things.

If we could ever get that through our heads, it would change the way we do things. Instead of relying on hard work and creativity and shrewdness and politics and money, we would rely on prayer and Scripture and godliness and spiritual unity and sensitivity to the Lord.

Our power, our strength, is not in ourselves. It is in the Lord.

It's not that we shouldn't use hard work and creativity and shrewdness and politics and money. It's just that we can't rely on them. Our strength, our power, does not lie within ourselves.

This is a terribly difficult thing for us to accept. We may be very strong physically, and so we are used to relying on our physical strength to accomplish what needs accomplishing in our lives. Or we may be very skilled business executives, or very talented artists, or shrewd negotiators, and we rely on these talents to make our way through the world. So it is difficult for us to lay down those abilities at the foot of the cross, admit that we are powerless, and say, "Lord Jesus, help me." But until we come to that point, we are thoroughly duped . . . and we will be thoroughly defeated.

God does the work of God,
Man does the work of man.

Man cannot do the work of God,
And God will not do the work of man.

For the life of us, however, we cannot get this straight. We insist on trying to do the work of God while neglecting the work of man. Then we wonder why things aren't going so well.

Spiritual warfare is a work that has to be done God's way. Man cannot engage in spiritual warfare. Only God can. So the work of man is to learn how to rely on God—and God alone—in the spiritual war.

The strength of the believer is the strength of the Lord. So the first thing we learn about spiritual warfare is that we must rely on the strength of God.

The Weapons of War

Put on the full armor of God, that you may be able to stand firm against the schemes of the devil.

Ephesians 6:11

If it is true that we are in a spiritual battle . . . that our struggle in life is not against flesh and blood but against an invisible but very real foe . . . then it is also true that our weapons of war cannot be lead and steel. Rather, they must be spiritual weapons. And Ephesians 6 describes one of those weapons: the armor of God.

Of course, armor is a figure of speech. There is no steel-gray, mesh armor. This is merely a metaphor for the spiritual resources He provides for our protection, power, and effectiveness in the spiritual warfare against the forces of darkness: truth, righteousness, the gospel of peace, faith, salvation, and the Word of God. Those are the spiritual weapons for the good guys.

But this passage also tells us about the weapons of the bad guys: that is, "the schemes of the devil."

The word "schemes" in the Greek is *methodia,* from which we get the English word "method." This implies craftiness, cunning, and deception—all of which describe Satan's schemes.

Satan's name in Hebrew is *Abaddon* and in Greek is *Apollyon;* both mean "destroyer" (Rev. 9:11). He is also called "the serpent of old who is called the devil and Satan, who deceives the whole world" (Rev. 12:9). Satan is a deceiver and a destroyer; he deceives in order to destroy.

In the very beginning, in the Garden of Eden, Satan deceived Adam and Eve into rebelling against God. His purpose? To destroy them. Thousands of years later, Satan attempted to deceive Jesus into departing from the will of God (Matthew 4). His goal? To destroy Him and God's plan of redemption. He appears as "an angel of light" to deceive us, in order to destroy us (2 Cor. 11:14).

How does Satan deceive us? By taking that which is
—bad and making it look good
—false and making it look true
—wrong and making it look right
—ugly and making it look beautiful
—hurtful and making it look helpful
—painful and making it look pleasant

In every confusing, conniving, deceptive way possible, Satan attempts to mislead us with his schemes. In Matthew 24:24 we read that "false Christs and false prophets will arise and will show great signs and wonders, so as to mislead, if possible, even the elect." That is how great his powers of deception and destruction are.

By appealing to the lust of the flesh, the lust of the eyes, and the pride of life, he makes bad look good, false look true, wrong look right, ugly look beautiful, hurtful look helpful, and painful look pleasant (1 John 2:15–16).

So you can see that by ourselves, we are no match for Satan's spiritual weapons. We need the armor of God.

The powers of darkness encompass a hierarchy of evil spiritual beings who do the bidding of their master, Satan. Difficult though it is for us to think in these terms, we must be aware that there is a spirit world surrounding us of which we are not aware. And these forces of darkness are locked in mortal combat with the forces of light. Spiritual warfare is a reality!

If we do not prepare for this spiritual battle, we may be the next casualty. "Be on the alert," Peter writes. "Your adversary, the devil, prowls about like a roaring lion, seeking someone to devour" (1 Pet. 5:8). And Paul warns, he "disguises himself as an angel of light" (2 Cor. 11:14). Jesus asserted that Satan is "the father of lies" (John 8:44). He can make poison taste like candy. He is the master illusionist.

Every day we are engaged in spiritual warfare, and we cannot succeed in our own strength. As soldiers of the cross we need the strength, the power—the armor—of the Lord.

Satan's Methods of Deception

> For our struggle is not against flesh and blood, but against the rulers, against the powers, against the world forces of this darkness, against the spiritual forces of wickedness in the heavenly places.
>
> Ephesians 6:12

Satan employs two particularly effective means of deceiving us: First, he gets us to sin; then, once we have sinned, he keeps us mired in guilt.

To get us to sin, the master of deception
—convinces us that "it isn't so bad. It won't hurt,"
—convinces us that no one will find out, and that God will forgive us anyway,
—convinces us that what he is tempting us to do will actually satisfy us,
—saps our spiritual convictions so that we don't care,
—gets us overtired and frazzled so that we just want immediate relief and are willing to do whatever will give us that relief,
—twists our thinking so that we don't know what is right anymore.

Spiritual conflicts take two forms: temptation and spiritual opposition. When we are tempted to sin, we are to flee (2 Tim. 2:22). When we are confronted with spiritual opposition, we are to fight (James 4:7).

Most of us, however, have a genius for reversing the two. When we sense spiritual opposition in our life and ministry, we want to flee. And when presented with temptation to sin, we want to stand and fight. That is backward, and we will have little success until we get it straight.

Do you want to run away from your financial obligations?

> Stand and fight.

Is it too hard to improve family relationships?

> Stand and fight.

Are you tired of trying to grow spiritually?

> Stand and fight.

Is it tough being moral, ethical, and honest in the workplace?

> Stand and fight.

Are you tempted to toy with a relationship that isn't Christ-centered?

> Flee.

Are you tempted to buy something you can't afford?

> Flee.

Are you tempted to watch that questionable television program?

> Flee.

Are you tempted to put together a deal that isn't totally honest?

> Flee.

One of the keys to winning spiritual warfare is "to know when to hold 'em and to know when to fold 'em." We need to fight when we should fight, and flee when we should flee, and not confuse the two.

Deceiving us is not enough for this demon of death and darkness, however; for once we have sinned, he grabs the back of our heads and shoves our faces in the mud of guilt until we suffocate. By miring Christians in guilt, Satan keeps them from the joy of Christ and eliminates them as an effective force in leading others to Christ. To do this, Satan constantly accuses Christians of their sin, attempting to convince them that they have no business continuing their charade of Christian living. Of course he does all this in the first person, so you think you are just talking to yourself out of your own guilty conscience.

What a failure I am, what a disgusting piece of humanity, he screams in the daytime. *What a phoney. What a pitiful excuse for a Christian. Who do I think I am, anyway? I should have known from the beginning that I couldn't make it as a moral success. I was a fool to even try. I am a failure,* he whispers at night. *The Christian life might work for others, but it won't work for me. I'm inherently flawed. Give it up. Stop trying to fake it. Go back to the old life where I belong!*

If we believe this father of lies, he has us right where he wants us . . . defeated . . . convinced that our name brings a noxious odor to the nostrils of God.

The Power to Overcome

When I was a kid, I remember watching a western on television in which a huckster went from town to town with a huge rattlesnake in a glass cage. The man would cover the glass with a blanket and take it into a saloon. There he would tell the people what was under the blanket in the cage and would bet that the toughest, bravest man in town would not be able to hold his hand against the glass without jerking it back when the rattlesnake struck.

Well, the townspeople went wild with excitement. After deciding who they thought was the bravest, toughest man in town, they went to tell him about the bet. Of course, having everyone choose him as the toughest, bravest man in town made it impossible for the guy to resist the challenge. So he went to the saloon, where all the folks bet that he could hold his hand against the glass without jerking it back when the rattlesnake struck.

After all bets were taken, the huckster tore the blanket off to reveal the biggest, most menacing, evil-eyed reptile ever seen by man. Annoyed by the light and noise, the snake coiled to strike, his rattles buzzing nervously.

The toughest, bravest man broke out in a cold sweat. But prodded by the collective expectation of the townspeople, he moved his hand toward the glass.

The snake coiled even tighter. The rattler buzzed its lethal warning.

Slowly the man inched his hand toward the glass and finally touched it. As he did, the snake struck with fury. And reflexively, the toughest, bravest man jerked his hand away.

A stunned silence fell over the saloon. No one could believe it.

The man looked around in anguish and humiliation, then stormed from the saloon. The huckster collected his money and left town before the defeated man had a chance to collect his courage and come after him. Then the huckster moved on to the next town to repeat the scene and, once again, win the bet. And he almost always won.

Why? Because no matter how big and brave and tough the frontiersmen were, the threat of that striking reptile through the invisible glass was a fearsome thing. The only thing between them and certain death was a thin pane of glass. The huckster knew it would hold; they did not trust it. The huckster knew there was nothing to fear except fear itself, and he played on that fear to make his living.

I have often thought what a great metaphor that scenario was for spiritual warfare. The snake is Satan and the forces of evil. The glass is Jesus. As long as we stay on the right side of the glass, we have nothing to fear. Of course if we go sticking our hand inside the box, there is plenty of danger. But for those on the safe side of the glass, for those who live a life of faith and obedience to Christ, there is nothing to fear. The only ones terrorized by the evil inside the cage are those who do not trust the glass to keep them safe, or those who stick their hands inside the glass.

There are two important things we must understand about spiritual warfare: first, there is real danger on the wrong side of the glass; and second, we are safe on the right side of the glass, no matter how fearful things appear.

But what does that mean? Well, generally speaking, it means we must submit to God in all things and resist the devil (James 4:7). And specifically it means we must gird ourselves in the spiritual armor He has provided for us. We need

—the belt of truth, so that we can know, understand, believe, and obey the truth of God as revealed in the Bible and in Jesus.

—the breastplate of righteousness, so that we are not satisfied with known sin in our lives. We must confess any sin and, to the degree our spiritual maturity allows, live a godly lifestyle.

—the shoes of the preparation of the gospel of peace, so that we can rest in the truth of the promises God has given us.

—the shield of faith to ward off attacks of doubt, unbelief, discouragement, and temptation.

—the helmet of salvation, on which rests our hope in the future, and which enables us to live in this world according to the value system of the next.

—the sword of the Spirit, the Word of God, so that we can use the Scriptures specifically in life's situations to fend off attacks of the enemy and put him to flight.

God doesn't want us to sin, and certainly He doesn't take our sin lightly when we do. But He is also patient and loving and gracious. And no matter what we have done, we must not be afraid to come into His presence. God's grace is sufficient for all our sins.

We are often afraid to teach this because we think people will abuse it and go out and sin like crazy. However, when people truly understand the love of God . . . when they understand that our relationship with Him depends not on our own ability to cleanse ourselves, but on His grace . . . the result is just the opposite.

We drop down to our knees and cry out to God in gratitude that, in spite of all our shortcomings, He does not desert us. And this profound thanksgiving and understanding of God's grace produces an increased desire to be holy.

The secret to withstanding Satan's accusations is not what we do; it is what Christ did on the cross. The secret to withstanding Satan's accusations is to consciously rest in what Jesus did on the cross. If we truly understand that, we can stand against Satan's accusations.

As John White wrote in his book, *The Fight:*

> God's answer to your guilty conscience is the death of His Son. Your answer to a guilty conscience is usually something you do, like confessing harder, praying more, reading your Bible, paying more than your tithe in the offering and so on. Do you not understand? The Father does not welcome you because you have been trying hard, because you have made a thoroughgoing confession, or because you have been making spiritual strides recently. He does not welcome you because you have something you can be proud about. He welcomes you because His Son died for you. Are you blasphemous enough to suppose that your dead works, your feeble efforts can add to the finished work of a dying Savior? "It is finished!" he cried. Completed. Done. Forever ended. He crashed through the gates of hell, set prisoners free, abolished death and burst in new life from the tomb. All to set you free from sin and open the way for you to run into the loving arms of God.
>
> Now do you understand how "the brethren" overcame the Accuser by the blood of the Lamb? They refused to let his accusations impede their access to God. A simple confession was enough. They face the Accuser boldly saying, "We already know the worst you could ever tell us, and so does God. What is more the blood of Jesus is enough." Therefore, when you find the grey cloud descending, whether it be as you pray, as you work, as you testify or whatever, when you find the ring of assurance going from your words because of a vague sense of guilt, look up to God and say, "Thank you, my Father, for the blood of your Son. Thank you, even now, that you accept me gladly, lovingly in spite of all I am and have done—because of His death. Father and God, I come."[1]

Resist the efforts of Satan to accuse you, to bury you with guilt, to make you feel worthless and unqualified to come to Christ again. It is part of his warfare strategy to make you ineffective as a witness and unhappy as a disciple. Be on guard against his wiles. Recognize them. And stand firm against him in the strength God provides.

Focus Questions

1. Reflect on situations in your experience when you should have fought or fled, but you did the opposite. What can you learn from this?

2. In what area of your life are you most susceptible to Satan's deception? What can you do to avoid being deceived?

3. In what area of life are you most tempted to try to do the work of God while ignoring the work of man?

25

Truth Is the Basis of All Spiritual Victory

(Ephesians 6:14a)

Most Russian writers have been tremendously interested in Truth's exact whereabouts and essential properties. . . . Tolstoy marched straight at it, head bent and fists clenched, and found the place where the cross [of Christ] had once stood.

Vladimir Nabokov

*N*obody can tell bigger "lies" than fishermen. Exaggerating the size of the fish they "almost caught," the one that "got away," has given us the term "fish story." In fact, there is even a fishing contest which holds a lying contest afterward. The person who catches the biggest fish gets an award, but so does the person who tells the biggest lie, and often the size of the fish pales in comparison with the size of the lies. One contestant said that he had found a place where the fishing was so good that he had to stand behind a tree to bait his hook. Once when he wasn't paying close attention and forgot to stand behind the tree, a seven-pound largemouth bass jumped out of the lake, cleared thirty feet of shore, and bit the hook while the fisherman was still baiting it.

When it comes to promoting tall tales, Burlington, Wisconsin, boasts a Liar's Club, which anyone can join for one dollar and a good enough lie, and many whoppers have been submitted over the years. One aspiring member told how the fog was so thick that when they cut down a tree, it didn't fall over until the fog lifted. Another said his wife was so lazy that she fed the chickens popcorn so the eggs would turn themselves over when she fried them. Last year it was so dry, another claimed, that the bullfrogs born in the spring never learned how to swim. And one man said his wife's feet were so cold that every time she took off her shoes, the furnace kicked on.

Everyone knows and understands, of course, that this isn't really lying. It is "tall-tale telling" and is really just a form of entertainment. So we all laugh or smile, but never take it seriously.

However, there is a much more serious side to the issue of lying. In a magazine article entitled "A Nation of Liars?" Merrill McLoughlin writes:

> "I cannot tell a lie." It is a children's story, of course—and almost certainly apocryphal. Even so, for millions of Americans, the tale of how little George Washington confessed that he cut down the cherry tree is the prototypal lesson in truth, honor and the American way. The father of his country would not lie, even to avoid punishment, and his progeny should follow his example. The unmistakable moral: Good Americans tell the truth.
>
> Nevertheless, scandal is rocking the government, and voters have come off elections in which they were deluged with negative advertisement, much of it ridden with misleading innuendo. Wall Street is still reeling from revelations of unscrupulous business practices. There has been a rash of revelations about hyped and falsified scientific research: A study published last month accused 47 scientists at the Harvard and Emory University medical schools of producing misleading papers. A House subcommittee estimated last year that 1 out of every 3 working Americans is hired with educational or career credentials that have been altered in some way.
>
> What is going on here? Is America growing dishonest? Has something in the basic social fabric changed? There are many who fear that it has. "Duplicity and deception, in public and private life, are very substantially greater than they have been in the past," declares John Gardner, founder of the citizen's lobby Common Cause.[1]

A Grand Canyon of consequences lies between harmless tall tales and the plague of lies that is infecting our society. Nothing points up more clearly the need for the truth. And no one needs to be more aware of the truth than Christians, who must be committed to learning the truth and living it. We must be committed to truth and we must tell the truth with our actions as well as our words. About truth, the Bible is unambiguous. Truth is the first weapon in the believer's arsenal—the first piece in the full armor of God.

The Belt of Truth

Stand firm then, with the belt of truth buckled around your waist.

Ephesians 6:14a NIV

In preparing to do battle with the evil mastermind and his unholy hosts who are out to deceive and destroy us, Paul tells us, there are certain spiritual truths we must acknowledge and follow if we are to be victors. To vividly communicate these spiritual truths, the apostle uses the imagery of the armor of a Roman soldier. There are six pieces of armor, Paul says, and if we wear them we can be successful in the spiritual battle. Or, stated without the imagery, if we adhere to these six fundamental truths, we can be successful in the spiritual battle.

The first piece of spiritual armor is the belt of truth, which refers to the thick leather belt the Roman soldier wore to hold his tunic in place and to which was attached the sheath for his sword. When the Roman soldier "girded his loins," he tucked his long outer robe under his belt so that it would not hinder him in running or fighting.

In similar fashion, the Christian must prepare himself for spiritual battle by fixing in place his commitment to the truth of Scripture, and setting his mind to follow that truth. This keeps folds of falsehood from entangling his legs and tripping him, making him vulnerable in battle.

Peter used the same imagery in 1 Peter 1:13 when he wrote: "Therefore, gird your minds for action, keep sober in spirit, fix your hope completely on the grace to be brought to you at the revelation of Jesus Christ." This means, "Prepare your minds for action. Get ready for combat. Be self-controlled. Get focused."

The Christian must prepare himself for battle by making a total commitment to the truth of Scripture and by setting his mind to follow that truth.

Commitment to Truth

Semper Fidelis ("Always Faithful") is the official, etched-in-stone motto of the U.S. Marine Corps. Since 1775, Marines have been the first to fight in almost every major war of the United States. For over two hundred years, "from the halls of Montezuma to the shores of Tripoli," the Marines have stood for loyalty, discipline, and faithfulness.

Imagine the damage done to that image, then, when in a 1987 "spy-secrets for sex" scandal two Marine guards at the U.S. embassy in Moscow escorted Soviet agents into the most sensitive chambers of the consulate, including the "secure" communications center. The damage? Incalculable. Entire lists of secret agents were threatened, transmission codes were compromised, and plans were immobilized.

"When we can no longer depend on one another to do what we said we would do, the future becomes an undefined nightmare," says Ted Engstrom in his book *Integrity*. "What about our lawmakers? Do they obey their own laws? Have our preachers heard their own sermons on repentance? Is the business world sold on ethics? Are 'lovers' truly loving one another? Are parents producing character in their children or just raising characters?"[2]

Truth has great significance in our lives. Individual truth or falsehood affects everyone around us. Without a basic level of morality, without a basic level of trust and dependability, society breaks down. Business cannot be conducted without spending billions of dollars on legal fees to protect us from those who would take advantage of us. Billions of dollars of tax money must go to build prisons and house and feed prisoners. School systems break down, families break down, welfare and social aid breaks down . . . society breaks down.

Unless people are fundamentally true to their word, democracy does not work. The more people depart from truth, the more problems face us as a nation and the more society disintegrates.

"Do not be deceived," Paul wrote to the Galatians, "God is not mocked; for whatever a man sows, this he will also reap" (Gal. 6:7). If we sow lies and dishonesty, we will reap corruption and disintegration. It is a philosophical necessity to be true to our word.

But the believer's commitment to truth goes far beyond a philosophical understanding of the importance of truth in society. We must be committed to truth ourselves—committed to believing the truth and to telling the truth with our lives.

There is the truth (as in, telling the truth) and there is Truth. God is Truth. He is always true to His word. He always and only speaks and acts that which is true. And since we are created to be like God, we must speak and act according to what is true.

Can you imagine God's not being true to His word? . . .

Oh, yes, I know I said I would break into history and put an end to sin and pain and unrighteousness and set up a new heaven and a new earth where My children would live forever in love and joy and peace, but I lied. Or I got busy, and it doesn't look as if I'm going to get around to it. You'll have to make it on your own for a while. Good luck.

It is incomprehensible, isn't it? And a truly fearsome thought. We count on God to be utterly true to His word.

But, you may say, God is omniscient and omnipotent and can control everything, so He can be utterly true to His word. We are not omniscient and omnipotent. We cannot control everything; we can't even control our own lives. So how can we be utterly true to our word? We can't, of course—not as finite beings in a fallen world.

We may say, "I'll be there by 7:00," and then we get caught in traffic and we can't even keep our word on a simple thing like being on time for an appointment. That may be so. But did we mean it when we said we would be there by 7:00? If we did, our motives were true; we meant what we said—we told the truth—and we did our best to keep our word.

We must be true to our word because God is true to His word, and we are to be like Him. This means that
—we must embrace the total truth of Scripture;
—we must speak the truth and be true to our word;
—we must back up what we say with what we live.

When we are committed to believing the truth, we believe the promises of God and rest in them; we believe the commands of God and obey them; and we trust the truth of Scripture and order our lives according to it.

This is what it means to buckle on the belt of truth.

Telling the Truth in Word and in Deed

The results of a recent Gallup poll revealed that the ethical standards of Christians in the workplace were no higher than non-Christians. This included being honest about business facts and being true to one's word. This is alarming news. For if anyone should be standing apart from the crowd in the matter of truthfulness, it should be the Christian.

Now, I know that this issue is not an easy or a simple one. For centuries theologians and philosophers have debated whether or not it is ever proper to tell a lie. For example, is it all right to tell a lie to save a life—as Rahab did, in the time of Joshua, to save the lives of the Israelite spies? Or, as Winston Churchill once said, "In wartime, truth is so precious that she should be attended by a bodyguard of lies."

My goal is not to get into theoretical extremes, which would probably require a whole other book on the subject of truth and falsehood. My purpose in this study of Ephesians is to call the church to higher ground. We must step up to higher morals and ethics . . . in the way we do our work, the way we treat others, and the way we act . . . founded on our commitment to Christ. We must not be carriers of the disease that is infecting our society, for God hates lying.

"You shall not bear false witness against your neighbor," says the ninth commandment (Exod. 20:16). "There are six things which the Lord hates," says Proverbs, and one of them is "a lying tongue" (Prov. 6:16–17). "Therefore," says Paul, "laying aside falsehood, speak truth" (Eph. 4:25).

While the moral disintegration in society is a terrible thing, it does present an opportunity to face people with the truth of Christ and the Bible. And since they have no answers themselves for the dilemmas we face on every front, more and more people are willing to listen.

We must, therefore, be committed to the truth in what we say with our words as well as what we say with our lives. We must be people of the truth, not people of the lie. We must be people of integrity.

The word "integrity" comes from the root word *integer,* which means "whole." It is often used in mathematics, where an integer is a whole number. To be a person of integrity has come to mean an honest and ethical person, but this evolved from the idea of being a whole person.

To be a whole person, there must be unity between what we say and what we do. We cannot be duplicitous, two-sided, hypocritical; we cannot say one thing and do another. If we are people of integrity, then, our lives back up what we say. This means that if we say that evangelism is important but we are not engaged in evangelism, we are not yet whole. We are not yet integrated. It means that if we say that supporting Christian ministries is important but we don't give generously, we are not yet integrated. If we say that our families are important but do nothing to build them, we are not yet integrated. A person of integrity puts his life where his mouth is.

We are not teaching perfectionism, of course. We will all stumble and fall at times in our pursuit of truth, and God knows that. That's why He sent Jesus to die for our sin.

"If we say that we have no sin, we are deceiving ourselves, and the truth is not in us." But, "if we confess our sins, He is faithful and righteous to forgive us our sins and to cleanse us from all unrighteousness (1 John 1:8–9).

At times the belt of truth may get a little loose and slide around a bit. But we can always straighten it out and cinch it up tighter when that happens.

Whenever we function on anything that is not true, we place ourselves in jeopardy. Things are not true because the Bible says they are; the Bible says they are true because they are.

Remember: We cannot win the spiritual battle without the belt of truth.

Focus Questions

1. What are some of the greatest problems that have been created because people have failed to be true to their word (these may be in the personal, political, social, or other arenas of life)?

2. What problems might arise for a person who decided to always tell the truth?

3. What evidence do you see in your own life that you have put on the belt of truth? Is there any evidence that you may have let it slip a little? Explain.

26

Why the Straight and Narrow?

(Ephesians 6:14b)

*Holiness is not a series of do's and don'ts, but a conformity to
God's character in the very depths of our being. This conformity is possible only as we are united with Christ.*

Jerry Bridges

*W*hen Gary Richmond, a zookeeper at the Los Angeles Zoo, was given
master keys to every cage in the zoo, he was cautioned sternly to guard them
with his life and to pay exacting attention to which doors he opened and
which doors he closed.

"Richmond," the supervisor said, "these keys will let you in to care for
millions of dollars worth of animals. Some of them could never be re-
placed, but you could be, if you catch my drift. Some of the animals
would hurt themselves if they got out, and more significantly, they
might hurt and even kill somebody. You wouldn't want that on your
conscience."

I took him seriously, and performed flawlessly for four months.
Then, something happened with the most dangerous animal at the zoo.
Ivan was a polar bear who weighed well over nine hundred pounds and
had killed two prospective mates. He hated people and never missed an
opportunity to attempt to grab anyone passing by his cage.

I let him out of his night quarters into the sparkling morning
sunshine by pulling a lever to his guillotine door. No sooner had he
passed under it than I realized that, at the other end of the hall, I had
left another door opened. It was the door I would use to go outside if
Ivan was locked up inside. Now Ivan could walk to the other end of

the outdoor exhibit and come in that door I had left open, and, if he so chose, eat me.

In terror, I looked out the guillotine door. Ivan was still in sight. He was a creature of routine, and he always spent the first hour of his morning pacing. His pattern was L-shaped. He would walk from the door five steps straight out, and then turn right for three steps. He would then rock back and forth and come back to the guillotine door again, which he would bump with his head. He would repeat that cycle for one hour and then rest.

I timed his cycle and determined that I had seventeen seconds to run down the hallway and shut the open door. I staked my life on the fact that he would not vary his routine. He didn't seem to notice the wide open door, which is unusual. Animals tend to notice the slightest changes in their environment.

I decided that when he made his next turn, I would run down the hallway, hoping upon hope that I would not meet Ivan at the other end.

He turned and I ran. With every step my knees weakened. My heart pounded so hard I felt sure it would burst from fear. I made the corner and faced the critical moment. Ivan was still out of sight; I lunged for the door handle. As I reached out for the handle, I looked to the right. There was the bear . . . eight feet away. Our eyes met. His were cold and unfeeling . . . and I'm sure mine expressed all the terror that filled the moment. I pulled the huge steel door with all my strength. It clanged shut and the clasp was secured. My knees buckled and I fell to the floor racked with the effects of too much adrenaline. I looked up and Ivan was staring at me through the window in the door.[1]

Take care of these keys, Gary Richmond's supervisor had instructed him. Guard these keys. Pay strict attention to which doors you open and which doors you close. He held up a standard and exhorted Richmond, in gravest terms, not to fall short of that standard.

Why was that? Because he was a fussbudget? A worrywart? Because he wanted to limit his employee's freedom or stifle his enjoyment of life?

No, he held up a standard for Richmond to adhere to because, in doing so, he was protecting Richmond and the animals and all the visitors in the zoo. It was love and care and concern that set the standard, not a narrow, restrictive outlook.

So it is with God. He sets standards for us and exhorts us to adhere to them. Not because He is a cosmic kill-joy, a celestial fussbudget, or a heavenly worrywart. He sets standards and demands that we adhere to them because He sees reality clearly. He knows about consequences and cause-and-effect relationships. And He has built into His created order the necessary restrictions to keep us from harming ourselves and others.

Part of the reality He sees is the reality of spiritual warfare. He knows that our foes are not flesh and blood, but the powers of darkness, the "spiritual forces of wickedness" (Eph. 6:12).

We don't see or hear them. We can't touch, taste, or smell them. But they are here. This evil empire does the bidding of Satan, and its goal is to deceive and destroy those who follow God. And if it cannot destroy us, it at least wants to neutralize us so that we will not be of any consequence in leading others to follow Christ.

If we want to be effective in this spiritual battle, Paul tells us, we must put on certain pieces of spiritual armor. One piece of that armor is the breastplate of righteousness.

The Picture of Righteousness

Stand firm therefore, having girded your loins with truth, and having put on the breastplate of righteousness.

Ephesians 6:14

The breastplate was an important part of the Roman soldier's battle gear. It was a metal cast of a human torso which protected the upper part of his body, including his heart and lungs, from the arrows and spears of the enemy.

Using the analogy between literal armor and spiritual armor, we would say that the spiritual breastplate—the breastplate of righteousness—is for our protection. It is defensive armor that protects us in three ways . . . on three levels.

—Righteousness protects us from the consequences of sin, from the harm and damage and violent ravages of sin.

—Righteousness protects us from the hardening and choking of the spiritual arteries which kills the spiritual life more slowly and less violently than some of the more overt sins, but which renders us lifeless, nevertheless. It keeps us from drifting away from God and dying a slow, cold death.

—Righteousness protects us from Satan's deceptive methods by giving us discernment.

Righteousness protects us from sexual promiscuity and as a result protects us from venereal disease, AIDS, and other deadly consequences.

Righteousness protects us from drugs and other addictions that can destroy our minds and our bodies. Righteousness protects us from the dishonesty that can result in economic, social, and personal catastrophe and even prison. Righteousness protects us from the consequences of sin.

There is a tax on sin, and we must always pay it; there is no tax evasion in the spiritual realm. Sometimes sooner, sometimes later, but we always pay. The breastplate of righteousness is God's divine protection against the violent ravages of sin.

God demands that we live righteous lives because He loves us and wants the best for us.

Righteousness: Imputed and Imparted

Actually, righteousness has two layers to it. The first layer is the righteousness that is given to us, imputed to us, which means that Christ's righteousness has been applied to our heavenly account, when we become Christians. Imputed righteousness was affixed to us as a breastplate at the moment of salvation. It is a gift from God. On the basis of Christ's work in our behalf we have been made righteous . . . fit for heaven . . . acceptable to God. We are covered, protected, with the breastplate of righteousness.

As Christians, God has given us power over Satan and his hosts. We have Jesus living in us. We have the Holy Spirit living in us. The Bible says, "Greater is He who is in you than he who is in the world" (1 John 4:4).

So part of the daily spiritual warfare is realizing that we are God's children. Christ's righteousness has been imputed to our account. When Satan accuses us and condemns us, telling us we have no business trying to be a Christian . . . when he hisses at us that we are no good and that we are kidding ourselves by trying to live a good life, trying to bury us with guilt because we are not perfect . . . remember, it is all a lie—from the father of lies. We don't get to heaven by being good. We don't get to be a child of God by being good. We get to be a child of God by being born again into His spiritual family, and that happens by believing in Jesus and committing our lives to Him.

We are on one side of the glass. Satan is on the other side, preparing to strike. Christ is the glass in the middle, protecting us. We must trust the glass . . . we must trust the breastplate of righteousness. Satan has nothing that can hurt us except lies. Count on your imputed righteousness. It is important in the daily spiritual battle.

But the Bible also says, "Put on the full armor of God and then stand firm." It says, "Resist the devil and he will flee from you." In other words, we don't passively rest in God's protection; we must also actively engage the enemy in both offensive and defensive warfare, which means we need a second layer of protective righteousness, and that is imparted righteousness: the active living out of a righteous lifestyle as a result of the working of God in our lives.

We are on dangerous ground here, however, because the one thing we do not want to say is that we can earn favor with God by being good. We can't. We don't want to say that we increase our chances of going to heaven by being good. We don't. We don't want to say that God likes some of us better than others because we are better people. He doesn't. But we must say that when we become a child of God, He wants us to live like He does.

"Like the Holy One who called you, be holy yourselves also in all your behavior; because it is written, 'You shall be holy, for I am holy'" (1 Pet. 1:15–16). Or, as Paul wrote in Ephesians 4:1, "I . . . entreat you to walk in a manner worthy of the calling with which you have been called." Loosely paraphrased, that means, "Start living like committed Christians."

How do we do that? How do we don the breastplate of daily righteous living?

When we become Christians, we begin to desire to do good things and avoid bad things—that's the Holy Spirit working within us. This is often embryonic at first and will grow as we study the Bible and are challenged by the lives of others around us. The seeds of spiritual maturity must be watered and tended so that they take root and bear fruit, sometimes slowly, sometimes quickly.

We keep short accounts with God. Everyone sins, and when we do we confess it and He is faithful and just, through our advocate Jesus Christ the righteous, to forgive our sin and cleanse us from all unrighteousness.

As the grace of God allows us, we live as righteous a life as we can. And that imparted righteousness protects us from the wiles of Satan.

We must count on our imputed righteousness and live out on a daily basis the righteousness that Christ imparts to us. To fool around with sin, to knowingly and willingly tolerate known sin in our lives, is to open us up to spiritual dangers—a breach in our defenses—and make us vulnerable in the spiritual battle.

Twenty years ago, the Christian mandate consisted of a list of don'ts. Don't go to movies, don't dance, don't drink, don't play cards, don't wear long hair, don't listen to rock 'n' roll music. A lot of these prohibitions were rooted in thin air, not the Scriptures.

In the Christian circles in which I moved when I became a Christian, nothing was ever said about short tempers, but a lot was said about long hair. You couldn't see *The Sound of Music* in a movie theater, but you could watch anything you wanted on television. The Christian life was measured by the activities you didn't do, rather than by the Christlikeness of what you did do. If the sins were easily defined and visible, you couldn't do them. If they were not so easily defined or discernable, little was said.

In the last twenty years, that kind of legalism has been pretty much thrown off, except in some isolated circles. But in throwing out the bath water, we may have pitched the baby too. Now we want no one looking over our shoulders. We want no one telling us what to do. But have we, in the name of Christian freedom, gone too far? Are we, in the name of Christian freedom, embracing many of the values of the world we are trying to re-deem?

The Bible says it is a shame even to speak of the sins of immorality committed by the world. So is it legalism to exhort people not to watch those sins on television or in the movies?

The Bible says we are to think only about things that are true, honorable, right, pure, lovely, and of good repute. So is it legalism to encourage people to guard themselves against the unpure and the unlovely and the dishonorable?

The Bible says we are to speak only that which is edifying to those who hear. So is it legalism to encourage people to guard their tongues?

The Bible says the Lord hates dishonest business practices and a lying tongue. So is it legalism to exhort people to be honest and ethical in the workplace?

It is not legalism to exhort ourselves and others to righteous behavior based on biblical principles. God has given us standards of righteous behavior to protect us, to glorify Him, and to be a witness to the world around us.

We are in a spiritual war, and the battlefield around us is strewn with bleeding bodies. Couples are divorcing, children are rebelling, students are cheating, business people are stealing, politicians are peddling influence, and ministers are manipulating.

First, Satan pins us down on the battle front of doctrinal purity and wages war on that front. Then, when he sees that we are going to be able to hold our own there, he leaves half his troops to keep us pinned down. Then he outflanks us with the rest and attacks from the rear. We now find ourselves losing the battle, not on the front of doctrinal purity but on the front of personal piety.

Today, we are in a unique position in church history: We have a generation of Christians who believe the historically accepted orthodoxy while adopting lifestyles which deny the very truth they embrace. They sincerely believe one thing, but live another. The divorce rate among Christians is the same as among non-Christians. Alcoholism and sexual abuse are as prevalent within the church as without. Materialism is at an all-time high, and the "wealth and health" gospel commands a strong following. Meanwhile, personal discipline is at an all-time low. All of this and more has caused the church to lose its credibility as a significant force in American life. Many regard Christians as people locked in a commitment to an irrelevant way of life—a way of life they don't even exhibit themselves.

If we don't want to be a casualty, we must put on the breastplate of righteousness. Which means we had better quit playing fast and loose with the Christian disciplines and the commands of Christ. We had better stop saying, "What can I get away with?" and start saying, "What would Jesus do?" We had better stop crying "legalism" and start crying "righteousness."

Remember, in spiritual warfare we need the protection of the breastplate of righteousness.

Focus Questions

1. How have you seen God's commands protect your life? Have you experienced harm when you disobeyed His commands? Explain.

2. Do you see any areas in which, in the name of Christian freedom, you may have gone too far? Explain.

3. If Jesus were to visit you personally today, what do you think He would say about righteousness in your life?

27

The Path to Peace

(Ephesians 6:15)

This is a sane, wholesome, practical, working faith: That it is a man's business to do the will of God; second, that God himself takes on the care of that man; and third, that therefore that man ought never to be afraid of anything.

George MacDonald

*J*umping backward off a cliff can teach you a lot about yourself. At least I've certainly found it so. To be honest, the first time I didn't jump—it was more like a crawl. I was teaching at a college in Phoenix, Arizona, and one day several of my students approached me. "Mr. Anders," they said, "we are going up on Squaw Peak Mountain to do a little rappeling off some of the cliffs on Saturday. Would you like to go?"

It was hard for me to say no. For one thing, I didn't want to appear chicken. Besides, never having been rappeling before, I didn't understand how truly terrifying it would be. So I said, "Yes."

When we got to the mountain the next Saturday, my companions chose "a small cliff." I'll never forget walking over to the edge and looking down for the first time—that small cliff was only about the height of a ten-story building! They tied a hundred-foot rope around a rock at the top, hooked themselves into harnesses, and started rappeling down the cliff.

There were about a half a dozen of us, and because I wanted to be helpful, I let the others go first. Finally, I was the only one left. I muttered something about it taking longer than I expected and being a little short on time, but it didn't work. Before I knew what was happening, I was in a harness, and a rope the size of my first finger was threaded through and hanging off the cliff behind me.

By the time I got hooked up, most of the guys who had rappeled down had climbed back up to the top again, so there was a full house to witness my inauspicious descent.

"Just lean back against the rope, and walk backward off the cliff" they advised. Right . . .

I didn't trust the rope. Back in Indiana we used to swing on barn ropes that were as big around as my wrist. Those would hold a guy. This little thing might hold; it might not. And the aluminum safety pins (carabiners) that held me in my seat-belt diaper and attached me to the rope—well, they didn't look strong enough to hold a Thanksgiving turkey. I didn't have faith in my equipment, and I was terrified.

But there I was. Halfway over the edge. Too proud to climb back up; too scared to lean back and walk off. So I began to sort of shinny down, holding the ropes so tightly that I didn't even need any equipment. With my legs wrapped around the rope, hunched over in a strange, modified fetal position, down over the edge I squirmed. It was not a pretty sight, but it was the best I could do.

Before I had gotten a third of the way down, my arms were trembling uncontrollably and almost useless. My kneecaps were scraped raw from rubbing against the face of the cliff, my hands and elbows were bruised and aching. I hung there like a ham in a smokehouse, lips and cheek pressed against the face of the cliff, wondering if I would live to see another sunrise.

With infinite patience, the leader of the group said, "Mr. Anders, let the rope hold you. Lean back into the rope until your feet are flat against the cliff like you are walking. Then just feed the rope through your hand and you will walk down the face of the cliff."

Finally, when I concluded that I would never get out of that alive anyway, I did what he said. I leaned back against the rope until my feet were flat against the face of the cliff. Then I let the rope out . . . and I walked effortlessly down the face of the cliff!

What an exhilarating experience. I couldn't wait to get back up to the top and try it again. This time I leaned back into the rope and walked over the edge of the cliff backward. I pushed myself away from the face of the cliff and free-fell for fifteen to twenty feet; then I bounced back to the cliff, pushed away again, and fell another fifteen to twenty feet. In probably no more than thirty seconds I was at the bottom, unhooking, and racing to the top to go down again.

What I learned that day was that you have to trust your rope. You have to believe that it will hold you. If you trust in your own strength to get you down, it will sap every molecule of power before you even get close to the ground. But if you let the rope do the work, you can make it.

When it comes to the spiritual life, we are like rappelers. The cliff is life. The rope is God. If we try to make it in our own strength, it will sap the life out of us. But if we lean back on the rope, believing that He will hold us, we let God do the work of God and we make it down the cliff of life.

The apostle Paul tells us that there is an invisible army of evil beings which does the bidding of Satan and which tries to thwart the will of God in the lives of Christians. Paul describes this as a spiritual battle, and he says there are six pieces of armor we need if we are to be victors. Thus far we have discussed the belt of truth and the breastplate of righteousness. Now we are going to look at the shoes of the gospel.

The Footwear of God

Stand firm . . . having shod your feet with the preparation of the gospel of peace.

Ephesians 6:14–15

The Roman soldier needed good footwear. A soldier who couldn't keep his footing was a vulnerable soldier. Josephus, in the sixth volume of his major work on the Jewish Wars, described the soldiers' footwear as "shoes thickly studded with sharp nails." Thus, they could keep their footing in the worst conditions. The military successes of Alexander the Great and Julius Caesar were due in large measure to their armies' ability to undertake long marches at incredible speed over rough terrain. They could not have done this unless their feet were well shod.

The same holds true in the spiritual battle. We must keep our footing, no matter how treacherous the ground.

But what does that mean?

In the NIV, Ephesians 6:15 is translated, "and with your feet fitted with the readiness that comes from the gospel of peace." And the New Century Version reads, "On your feet wear the Good News of peace to help you stand strong."

So the next question is, what is the gospel of peace?

First, let's look at what it is not. It is not the gospel message of salvation by grace through faith in Christ. The context here refers to things we do on a daily basis in spiritual battle. We do not become Christians anew every day; that happens once.

What it does refer to, I believe, is the peace of God: the peace that is ours when we believe the promises of God and act accordingly. This is the peace suggested by Ephesians 2:14, which describes Jesus Himself as being "our peace." This is reinforced in John 14:27, where we read Jesus' own words: "Peace I leave with you; My peace I give to you; not as the world gives, do I give to you. Let not your heart be troubled, nor let it be fearful."

This peace is central to doing battle effectively in the spiritual war. So the truth here would be paraphrased: the peace of God in your heart helps you stand firm in spiritual battle.

When we believe God . . . when we believe what He says and trust Him . . . when we lean back against the rope, believing it will hold us . . . then we have the personal, inner peace that enables us to keep our footing in the daily spiritual battle. If we do not believe the promises of God, we will become agitated, weakened, and confused; when that happens, we are likely to lose our footing and be defeated in the daily spiritual battle.

So let's look at three of God's most important promises and see how they give us the inner peace we need to stand firm.

Promise #1: I will give you eternal life.

"For God so loved the world, that He gave His only begotten Son, that whoever believes in Him should not perish, but have eternal life" (John 3:16).

Everyone, at one time or another, thinks about death, and everyone, at one time or another, is afraid to die.

Pogo, the philosophizing possum who lives in the Okefenokee Swamp, says: "I hate death. In fact, I could live forever without it." Film director Woody Allen says: "It's not that I'm afraid to die. I just don't want to be there when it happens." And the little child says: "Dear God, what is it like when you die? Nobody will tell me. I just want to know. I don't want to do it."

Actually, most of the time it's the very young and the very old who tend to think about dying. Everyone in between thinks about it only when someone else dies or when he or she is very sick or when someone is in a bad accident. For most people, death is a big, swirling, yawing black hole at the end of the conveyer belt of life. People ride along on the conveyer belt, and when they get to the end, the belt drops them off into this black hole. It is the great unknown.

What happens then? This is, of course, the greatest question everyone asks. It is the question around which much of our literature and art are created and framed.

Is there life after death? Is there a God? Is there a heaven? Is there a hell? If there might be, where am I going to go? Is it safe to die? Is there the possibility of eternal torment? How can I escape it? How can I know for sure?

Someone has described death this way:

> Like a hen before a cobra, we find ourselves incapable of doing anything at all in the presence of the very thing that seems to call for the most drastic and decisive action. The disquieting thought, that stares at us like a face with a freezing grin, is that there is, in fact, nothing we can do. Say what we will, dance how we will, we will soon enough be a heap of ruined feathers and bones.[1]

Undertaker or comedian, lawyer or pipe fitter, admiral or homemaker, mechanic or movie star, cowboy or congressman . . . get them in a quiet moment when they will talk honestly and openly with you, and the one thing everyone fears most is death. The great enemy. The great unknown.

In the face of this reality, the great promise from Jesus is life. "I am the resurrection and the life," He says. "He who believes in Me shall live even if he dies, and everyone who lives and believes in Me shall never die" (John 11:25–26). That's a promise.

If we believe in Jesus, it is safe to die. We don't have to fear the great unknown any longer. We can have peace in the face of life's greatest enemy, death.

Promise #2: I will guide you in your daily life.

> Trust in the Lord with all your heart,
> And do not lean on your own understanding.
> In all your ways acknowledge Him,
> And He will make your paths straight.
>
> Proverbs 3:5–6

We don't have to know which way we must go through life. All we have to do is keep our hand in the hand of the One who does.

There is an old saying: "In order to be free to sail the seven seas, we must make ourselves a slave to the compass." When we make ourselves a slave to Christ, we are free to sail the seven seas of life. We don't have to be in bondage to ignorance or desires or lies. We can be free. There is no bondage in commitment to Christ, there is only freedom.

We don't have to stumble around in life. We don't have to stub our toe in the darkness, or walk off a cliff in blindness. The truth of the Scripture will give us light and sight and keep us from walking off the safe path.

When we commit ourselves to following all that we understand of God in the Scripture, we have peace . . . peace in knowing that we are doing the right thing with our life . . . peace in knowing that God is pleased with us . . . peace in knowing that we are being freed from slavery to things which hurt us. God's will is good.

Promise #3: I will give you peace in the midst of pain.

> And we know that God causes all things to work together for good to those who love God, to those who are called according to His purpose.
>
> Romans 8:28

All things aren't good in a direct sense, but indirectly God can use anything for our good.

Sooner or later, life will haul off and sock every one of us right in the stomach. And when we are standing there with searing pain stabbing through our whole body, knees buckling, mouth agape, struggling for air, we all ask ourselves, "Why? . . . Why did THIS happen to me? . . . Why did this happen to ME? What sense does it make? What good can ever come out of this? What purpose is there in it?"

It is at these moments that God seems both the closest and the farthest away.

Many different things cause pain, but much of it we bring on ourselves. Why? Because we do things the Bible warns us against. And so we reap what we have sown. But God is able to bring good even out of that kind of pain.

Maybe you have been foolish in the past. As a result, you have experienced more pain than you ever thought possible by suffering the consequences of your sin. Yet God can turn that into good by making you a strong, insightful, sensitive, wise person. He can turn that to good by using you in the lives of other people as you share the wisdom you have learned and help them not to make the same mistake. God can turn your life into a glorious tribute to His grace, no matter what you have done. He can bring good out of any pain.

Sometimes pain is the result of God's spanking us. This kind of pain hurts just as much as other pain, but God is able to bring good out of it too. Hebrews 12:7, 11 says: "God deals with you as with sons; for what son is there whom his father does not discipline? . . . All discipline for the moment seems not to be joyful, but sorrowful; yet to those who have been trained by it, afterwards it yields the peaceful fruit of righteousness."

Perhaps you started drinking, and before you knew it you were addicted. You were a Christian. You knew it was wrong. You knew you were in trouble. But you were too proud to ask for help . . . too proud to repent. So you tried to fight it yourself, but you lost. Pretty soon, you stopped trying to walk with God because you were convinced He was sick of you. You lost your friends, your job, even your family. You hit bottom.

Then, there on the bottom, you "found" God again. (Actually, He was there all the time.) You repented. You followed His lead and got the help you needed.

Now, years have gone by and you are still sober. God disciplined you. It hurt. But through it, God brought righteousness, strength, stability, and peace back into your life. And it was good.

Then, of course, there is the pain which no one can explain. The pain of a wayward child . . . the pain of disease . . . the pain of a physical disability. Yet those who have passed through this can testify that often when the pain is greatest, Jesus is the closest. They will tell you that when they reflect on the work God did in their lives as a result, it was worth it.

Sometimes this perspective and gratitude is not gained until afterward. At other times, fellowship with God is closest and sweetest in the very midst of it. But always, God can give peace for pain.

Standing Firm

God has given us many promises in His word—ropes for us to cling to and trust to hold us—but these are three of the most important ones.

Often when life gets heavy for us, when life feels as though it is going to crush us, it is because we are trying to carry a burden Jesus never intended us to carry. It is too heavy for us. Only He can carry it. We are trying to descend the cliff with our own strength, hanging on for dear life.

The burden of trying to take care of ourselves after we die is too heavy for us. If we believe His promise, we can have peace in the face of death.

The burden of trying to control all the people and possessions and circumstances to make life go the way we want it is too heavy for us. We cannot gain that much control. If we trust Him to guide us, to take us over the cliff in the darkness, we can have peace in the midst of life's uncertainties.

The burden of trying to cope with pain is often greater than we can handle by ourselves. It is too heavy for us. If we trust Jesus to carry that burden and give us the grace to face what comes, moment by moment, we can have peace in the midst of pain and beauty for ashes later.

When I began rappeling off that mountain, I didn't learn to trust the rope until I was so exhausted I couldn't do anything else. My guides told me to trust the rope. They told me to lean back against it and let it do the work. But I didn't believe them. I trusted my own strength—that was less threatening than trusting the rope. But I didn't have enough strength to get to safety. I wasn't sufficient for the circumstances. And when I finally got to the end of my own strength, I found that the rope would hold.

Many of us must be brought to the end of our own spiritual and emotional resources and strength before we will lean back into Jesus, believe His promises, and rest in them. When we do, He gives us the peace that puts our feet on solid ground and enables us to stand firm in the spiritual battle.

When we put on the shoes of the gospel of peace, we are saying: I believe the promises of God and count on them to be true for me. And when I do, I can have His peace in my life.

Focus Questions

1. What one thing do you fear most about totally trusting Christ? What would you need to do to reflect total trust in Him in that area?

2. Do you think it is "safer" to trust Christ and obey Him or to distrust Him and disobey Him?

3. Which one of the three promises in this chapter is hardest for you to trust? Which is easiest? Explain why.

28

Resisting Spiritual Brainwashing

(Ephesians 6:16)

He that will not command his thoughts will soon lose commmand of his actions.

Woodrow Wilson

*I*n his book *Beyond Survival,* Gerald Coffee tells of his experiences as a prisoner of war in Vietnam.

February 3, 1966, was a sparkler of a day. Bombardier-navigator Bob Hanson and I made our way across the flight deck of the USS *Kitty Hawk* and manned our vigilante aircraft for launch. I thrilled as the instantaneous surge took our 30 ton reconnaissance jet to 170 miles per hour in less than three seconds. "We're on our way," I said to Bob in the back seat while easing the nose up into a climbing turn over the deep shining blue of the Gulf of Tonkin. With the exception of the low cumulus clouds far to the north near China, the sky was absolutely clear. This was my second flight over North Vietnam and my adrenalin was pumping. I had joined the squadron over a month before in December of 1965, but all my other missions had been over South Vietnam or Laos. The mission went like clock work. I bracketed the husky steel and concrete bridge with my camera the way I had taught others as a reconnaissance instructor in Florida. I saw no flack but frequently changed directions to keep any ground gunners from tracking me. Then heading back toward the coast I felt a hit. It happened so fast, no tracers—no warning, first a vibration, then the illumination of my master warning light. The vibration became heavier and the control stick sluggish. Suddenly we rolled left. I tried to muscle the control stick into effectiveness. Nothing. The nose dropped and we picked up more speed. *May Day . . . May Day!* Rolling rapidly, warning lights flashing, no more sky ahead. Only the shimmering blue gulf shining in front like a propeller. "Eject Bob! Eject! Eject!"

As I came awake, I sensed my surroundings more than I saw them. I was in a stable. A water buffalo stood nearby with the chickens scratching at its feet. I was struck with the dreamlike scene—the serenity of the animals, the low bubbling of an opium pipe, the mixture of smells, and finally the incongruity of my own presence. Here I was, 31 years old, a prisoner of war among people we had been bombing and strafing. *God, I am going to need you a lot. Please stay with me.*[1]

Similar stories were repeated many times during the Southeast Asian conflict, and observers over the years have noted an interesting pattern. Of the many men who survived the horrors of captivity in Vietnam, those who survived well had at least two things in common: they had the ability to develop an inner world in which they lived, and throughout their ordeal they held on to the truth with bulldog tenacity.

One POW was a piano player. He played concert after concert in his own mind to help pass the time. Another was an architect. He designed houses, buildings, and entire cities in his mind during his long incarceration. Another man was an avid golfer. He played golf day in and day out on the golf courses in his memory. Curiously enough, after he got back to the United States and had recovered his health, he discovered that he was a better golfer than he was before he went to Vietnam.

These POWs constructed mental games and inner worlds to help them cope with both the horrors and the boredom of incarceration.

Standard operating procedure for the Vietnamese was to try to break their prisoners mentally. To do this, hour after hour they would pump propaganda into their cells via radio, loud speakers, and interrogators. Telling them that the United States government was a government of monsters . . . that the U.S. military had already forgotten them . . . that they were listed as killed in action and that no attempt whatsoever was being made to free them . . . that their families were no longer concerned about them . . . that their families didn't want to wait for them to get out of prison . . . that their wives had already divorced them and remarried.

The POWs who were able to resist this type of brainwashing were those who caught these lies in midair, slammed them to the ground, and kicked them out of their cell. Each time a lie would come into the POW's mind, he would kick it out again, forcing himself to cling to the truth, reminding himself of the truth and answering every lie with a corresponding truth.

No, they haven't forgotten me! . . . *No, they haven't given me up as dead.* . . . *They will come back and get me.* . . . *No, that isn't true. It's a propaganda ploy.* . . . *My wife hasn't remarried anyone else. She still loves me. She's going to wait for me till I get out.*

By focusing on their inner world and clinging tenaciously to truth, these men were not only able to survive a brutal captivity but were able, after their release, to put the war behind them, pick up their lives, and again become productive and happy members of society. Their battle was not just a physical battle; it was a battle of the mind and spirit—which is exactly what each believer faces in spiritual warfare.

We do not live solely in the physical realm. We are surrounded by the forces of darkness, poised to do whatever they can to thwart the will of God in our lives.

The Shield of Faith

. . . taking up the shield of faith with which you will be able to extinguish all the flaming missiles of the evil one.

Ephesians 6:16

Roman soldiers sometimes used a small, round shield, but the Greek word translated here describes a shield large enough for the soldiers to crouch behind to protect themselves from volleys of arrows coming from enemy archery divisions. The surface of these large shields was either metal or leather over wood, which could also repel or withstand flaming missiles. These were arrows that had been soaked in or wrapped with flammable material and were then set on fire and launched by the enemy—they were doubly lethal.

In spiritual warfare the enemy of our soul launches his deadly arrows at us, and it is faith that protects us. Faith is our shield.

So the next question we have to address is: What is faith?

Faith is believing what God has said and committing ourselves to what we believe.

The world's definition of faith is: believing in spite of the fact that there is nothing to believe. But that is not faith.

Faith is believing what God has said. For example, God has said He will never leave us or forsake us. He has said that He will take care of all our needs. So anytime we are believing something God has said, we are exercising faith.

But faith goes beyond belief. In fact, faith is not faith until it exercises commitment.

Do you believe in Jesus? That is intellectual belief, and it is not enough. That is believing ABOUT Jesus. You must believe IN Jesus. Only when you have committed your life to Him and to the truth He taught do you believe IN Him. That is faith.

The shield of faith means that we are protected by the truth of Scripture and the power of God when we have believed what God says and committed ourselves to it.

The Flaming Missiles

The Bible does not tell us what the flaming missiles are. Most commentators say they are discouragement, doubt, fear, hate, desire, lust, and possibly procrastination and carelessness. With the shield of faith we can extinguish these flaming missiles of the evil one. So if we find ourselves in the middle of something that we cannot extinguish, it is probably not a flaming missile.

For example, I read in one commentary that many Christians died during the persecution of the Jews in Nazi Germany. That persecution was described as a flaming missile. However, great faith was exercised in the midst of that persecution, yet the persecution was not extinguished. It went on for years. Therefore, I would suggest that this persecution was not in itself a flaming missile.

The flaming missiles could have been doubts and discouragement and bitter thoughts against God in the midst of that persecution. Those are the kinds of fiery darts that Satan would delight in hurling at believers in the midst of such extreme suffering. And those are the kinds of satanically flaming missiles which can be extinguished/vanquished by faith: doubt, discouragement, bitterness, and hate.

Using the Shield

Faith is believing what God has said and committing ourselves to it. Flaming arrows are thoughts and feelings which Satan projects into our minds to get us to doubt what God has said. Usually Satan hurls his flaming darts in the first person so that when they enter your mind, you end up saying, "I think this . . ." or "I feel that . . ."

Use faith as a shield, then, *calling the lie a lie, and telling yourself the truth!* Let's look at several examples.

Discouragement

You have been married for five years and things are not going just the way you would like. Satan comes along and says, "I'm discouraged. My marriage is not as rewarding as I thought it was going to be. Maybe I married the wrong person. Maybe God really wanted me to marry someone else. I would be better off if I were married to someone else."

The shield of faith says, "No. That is a lie. I prayed for God's guidance before we got married. Our parents and pastor gave us their blessing. I was not living in any known sin. So I must accept that it was God's will for me to marry my spouse. I vowed to remain faithful, and God expects me to keep that vow. And since He will strengthen me to do His will, I can trust Him to do that. If I am honest, I will have to say that many of the problems in our marriage are my own fault, and I must uphold my end of the relationship better. If I trust and obey God, He will use this time of testing to build my spiritual maturity."

That's the shield of faith. It catches Satan's lies in midair, kicks them out, and tells the truth.

Temptation

You are traveling on business for your company, and you have an expense account of $150 a day for food and lodging. You got a good deal on a hotel room, you ate one meal on the plane, so for today you have only spent $100. When you asked for a receipt from the taxi driver, he tore off a blank receipt form and told you to fill in the amount yourself. You ate at the hotel restaurant, and when you asked for a receipt, the waitress simply tore off the bottom of the check and gave it to you blank. Now you are sitting in your room at the end of the day, tallying up your records and considering the $50 you could put in your pocket by padding your expense account.

Satan says, "Go ahead, for heaven's sake. It's only $50. It's not like I'm going to break the company. Besides, everyone does it. The president of the company does it. So why in the world wouldn't it be okay for me to do it? Nobody is going to know, and $50 isn't going to hurt anything in a $100 million operation."

The shield of faith says: "No! The Bible says I should not steal. God hates dishonesty and falsehood. The Bible says the person who conceals his or her sin will not prosper. The Bible says God will supply all my needs in Christ Jesus. I will not steal this money."

That's the shield of faith in operation. It catches Satan's lies in midair, kicks them out, and tells the truth.

Immorality

You have been traveling all day. You've checked into your hotel, had a bite to eat in the coffee shop, and now you're relaxing in your room for a couple of hours before hitting the sack. You turn on the TV and start flipping through the channels. NBC, CBS, ABC, Playboy. What's this? The Playboy channel. There's no box on top of the TV, which means you don't have to pay for it. It's just on there, like ABC and all the rest.

Satan says, "There it is—two hours of free lust. Go ahead. The door is locked. The curtains are pulled. No one will ever know. After all, I'm just a healthy, red-blooded American boy. Everybody from congressmen to businessmen to some preachers watch this kind of stuff. I've always been curious . . . I'll just check this stuff out and see what it's like. Besides, no one will ever know. And a couple hours can't hurt. It's just like watching a movie."

The shield of faith says, "It's a sin against my wife. It's a sin against God. It will make me more susceptible next time, and it can become an addiction. It will inhibit my relationship with my wife. The Bible says, 'Be holy for I am holy.' The Bible says I must love my wife as Christ loved the church. The Bible says, 'Whatever a man sows, that shall he also reap.' I would be sowing infidelity, dishonesty, and lust. What possible good can come from that? Besides, it will not satisfy. It will only create a desire for more, and I cannot satisfy that desire without getting in deeper and deeper and deeper, and in the end I will be addicted and destroyed."

That's the shield of faith. It catches Satan's lies in midair, kicks them out, and tells the truth.

Doubt

Life is a mess. It's so unfair. After you had two children, your husband divorced you. Now he is out running around after as many women as he can. He doesn't even pay his child support regularly. You are working two low-paying jobs just to make ends meet. During the day you have to leave your children with strangers in a day-care center, and when you do have time with them, you are so tired there is no chance of meaningful interaction. You are getting old before your time. You'd like to remarry, but none of the men you are interested in are interested in you.

Satan comes along and says, "God doesn't love me. There's something wrong with me. If God really loved me, He wouldn't treat me this way. What have I done to deserve this? Life just isn't fair. Christianity doesn't work. It's a religion for suckers, and I've been suckered long enough. My ex is out there, carefree, living the good life. Why shouldn't I go out and get myself a piece of the action for a change? If I don't look out for myself, no one else will."

The shield of faith says, "No! That's a lie. It is true that my life hasn't been a bed of roses, but much of my trouble I have caused myself. I knew I shouldn't have married Jim; I knew he wasn't a committed Christian. Besides, I wasn't the perfect wife. And since the divorce I haven't really gotten involved in a church where I could have some spiritual accountability and relationships with godly people. I have not worked at trying to find out what the Bible says, and I have not been as careful as I should have been in doing what the Bible says. God does not hate me. He loves me, and He has sent people to help me—like my parents—but I didn't listen to them. I have made bad choices, and I am paying the consequences for those choices. But I can begin to walk a different path. I can begin by committing my life totally to Christ. When I do, God will bring His truth and His people and His blessing into my life and help me get it turned around."

That's the shield of faith. It catches Satan's lies in midair, kicks them out, and tells the truth. Anything that we are tempted to do that is short of total commitment to Christ is a lie. It is Satan's spiritual brainwashing. He wants to deceive us in order to destroy us. When he offers us something, it never satisfies—it never gives us the peace we long for. It only makes us want the next level he has to offer. Then, when that doesn't satisfy—which it never does—it leads us to the next level. And so it goes, on and on, until he has us addicted and destroys us.

When faced with his lies, we must say, "NO. That is a lie. I am not going to believe it. I am tired of getting yanked around by your lies and promises of better things if I take shortcuts. It's not true, and I am going to do what I know is right. I'm going to tell myself the truth, and for once and for all in my life, I am going to do what is right."

When you do that, you come under the umbrella of God's protection and guidance. And though it may take some time to clear up all the messes, God will straighten out your life and make something beautiful out of it.

Don't settle for anything less than believing God and doing what He says. You're worth far too much to waste yourself on anything other than Him.

When we take up the shield of faith, we are saying: Whenever I feel like doubting or sinning or quitting, I will reject those thoughts and feelings because I deeply believe in God's truth.

Focus Questions

1. Can you think of any areas in your life where you have been believing Satan's lies?

2. What is the truth that contradicts those lies?

3. Do you think you know the Bible well enough to use Scripture to counter Satan's lies? What is the most important thing you could do to improve your command of Scripture?

29

Live for the Next World and Get This One Thrown In

(Ephesians 6:17a)

Aim at heaven, and you will get earth thrown in. Aim at earth, and you get neither.

C. S. Lewis

*C*harles Dickens's *A Christmas Carol* is, aside from the Advent narrative in the Gospels, probably the most beloved of all Christmas stories. Whether being read aloud by the glow of Christmas lights or enjoyed in one of its many film versions, the story of old Scrooge, frail Tiny Tim, sturdy Bob Cratchit, and the three Christmas ghosts warms our hearts and renews our spirits.

Scrooge, led by the Ghosts of Christmas Past, Present, and Future, was able to see where he had been, what he had become, and what the future held for him unless he changed his ways. In a sense, it makes a nice metaphor for the Holy Spirit, who has been sent to guide us into all truth—and the source of that truth, the Word of God.

The Bible makes clear that who we are now and what we do now has eternal consequences. We must project ourselves into the future. We must fix that picture in our minds and live today in light of who we have become and who we will be when we get to heaven. We must live in this world according to the value system of the next.

Alexander Solzhenitsyn said, "The only way to survive in prison is to abandon all expectations for this world and live for the next." The only way to have consistent joy in this life is to place our values, our hopes, our expectations, and our affections in the next world, not this one.

The Helmet of Salvation

And take the helmet of salvation.

Ephesians 6:17a

The head is a particularly vulnerable spot on the human body. A blow to the arm or leg may be painful; but take a blow to the head and suddenly the stars are out and the birds are singing. A sharp blow to the arm or leg might break a bone; a sharp blow to the head can kill. That is why football players and bicycle riders wear helmets. That is why construction workers wear hard hats.

Roman soldiers wore helmets for obvious reasons. A blow from a sword or spear or club could cause injury or death, so the soldier preparing for battle had to have his head protected with a helmet.

In developing his metaphor of spiritual armor, Paul indicates that the helmet is one of the most important pieces, for it is the helmet of salvation.

Salvation has three different dimensions: past, present, and future.

—Past: "For by grace you *have been saved* through faith; and that not of yourselves, it is the gift of God; not as a result of works, that no one should boast" (Eph. 2:8–9, italics added).

This carries with it the idea that at some point in the past we were forgiven and cleansed of our sins, spiritually reborn, and made eligible for heaven. We were justified—declared righteous—by God.

Past salvation delivered us from the penalty of sin.

—Present: "For the word of the cross is to those who are perishing foolishness, but to us who *are being saved,* it is the power of God" (1 Cor. 1:18, italics added).

This carries with it the idea that we are being freed more and more from the power of sin in our everyday lives. Jesus said, "You will know the truth, and the truth will set you free" (John 8:32 NIV). As we come to know more and more truth, we are more and more set free from the negative effects of sin. As we live in faithful obedience to God, He frees us from the power and bondage of sin.

When God asks us to be faithful in marriage to only one person and not to be sexually promiscuous, He is freeing us from deadly diseases. When He asks us not to get drunk, He is freeing us from the devastation of alcohol abuse. When He asks us to control our anger, He is freeing us from the effects of physical abuse.

While many think only of the high cost of being a disciple, they forget about the high cost of NOT being a disciple.

Present salvation delivers us from the power of sin.

—Future: "Christ also, having been offered once to bear the sins of many, *shall appear* a second time, not to bear sin, to those who eagerly await Him, *for salvation*" (Heb. 9:28).

When Christ comes again, He will deliver us to our final salvation, and we will go to heaven. The present heaven and earth will be destroyed in a cosmic flash, and a new heaven and earth will be created. All sin will be destroyed, and we will live forever in the presence of God, unaffected and untouched by sin, never again knowing anything of sin.

Future salvation will deliver us from the presence of sin.

If you would stand firm in the spiritual battle with the powers of darkness, the apostle Paul says, keep your mind fixed on your final and ultimate salvation. Put your heart in the next world while keeping your hands in this one.

Living Today in Light of Tomorrow

Creation is groaning under the weight of sin (Rom. 8:22–23), and we as human beings groan under the weight of sin.

On a global scale, we wish we could have peace. We wish that armies would not march against armies. We wish terrorists would not plant bombs and take hostages. We wish totalitarian governments would not oppress their own people.

But Scripture warns us to expect wars and rumors of wars in this world . . . it warns of man's inhumanity to man. There will never be peace on earth. If we hope only in this world, we will be bitterly disappointed.

On a social scale, we wish we could have harmony. We wish we could end prejudice and bigotry. We wish we could end corruption in government and business. We wish we could end crime and abuse. We wish people would not destroy the environment and pollute the water and poison the air. We wish we could have a greater sense of community and be more willing to look out for each other.

But Scripture tells us to expect persecution and bigotry . . . it tells us to expect selfishness and crime and vice. Corrupt actions come from corrupt hearts.

On a personal level, we wish we could get people and possessions and circumstances to go the way we want them to. We wish we could get our job to be as satisfying and pay us as much as we would like. We wish we could get our kids to be mature and resist the pull of their peers to sin. We wish we could lose weight on ice cream and conquer illnesses with chocolate fudge.

But Scripture teaches us that circumstances will fly up in our faces . . . it teaches us that possessions will rust before our eyes and that money will take wings and fly away. Solomon said that he had tried everything that this world had to offer . . . fame, money, pleasure, achievement, alcohol . . . and none of it satisfied. It was like trying to bottle wind or eat sand. If we look to this world for satisfaction or fairness or healing, we will be continually disappointed.

Yet God does give us hope. For He says that this world is not all there is. This world is not our home; we are just passing through. We don't belong here, any more than a fish belongs in the desert or a camel belongs in the sea. We belong to God. We belong in heaven. That is where our hope and our home is.

Certainly, we can experience joy and satisfaction and peace in this world, but it is a gift of God and a mere foretaste of heaven. Certainly, we can have a sense of purpose in this world, but it is a gift of God and a mere foretaste of heaven. Certainly, we can have satisfying relationships in this world, but they are a gift of God and a mere foretaste of heaven. Anything that is pleasant and right and just and good is a mere foretaste of heaven. Anything that is harmful and bad and unjust and evil is a mere foretaste of hell—of eternity without God.

Live, then, for the things of the next world. Put your hope in the things of the next world. Change your values to the things of the next world. Develop your taste for the things of the next world. Not because everything is bad in this world. It isn't. But because nothing in this world satisfies in the end, and nothing in this world offers any permanent solutions to anything.

What are you trusting in this life to give you meaning and joy and satisfaction and peace?

If you are single, do you think a spouse will give your life meaning? Not without Christ it won't.

If you are struggling financially, do you think more money will give you satisfaction? Not without Christ it won't.

If you are stuck in a deadend job, do you think a career change will give you joy? Not without Christ it won't.

That doesn't mean you can't pursue these things if God gives you the freedom. Just don't expect them to give you the final meaning and joy and satisfaction and peace in life.

If you try to find your basic, foundational meaning in life from the people, possessions, and circumstances of this world, you will be kicked, scratched, punched, and tripped. You will be hurt, disappointed, exhausted, and confused. Oh, things may go well for a while, but eventually you lose control.

But, if you get your basic, foundational meaning in life from God—

if you get your longing for love met in the awareness that He, and He alone, can love you perfectly and unendingly;

if you get your sense of significance from the fact that He has called you to the greatest cause of the ages—to know Him and make Him known;

if you get your sense of purpose from the fact that He has gifted you to do certain things that only you can do, and that He wants to use you as a major player in His plan for the ages, both now and forever—

THEN, the heartache and disappointment of life do not destroy you. They may hurt, but they do not destroy. And the good things of life can be truly enjoyed. Only the Christian who is walking closely with God has the capacity to truly enjoy the good things in life.

If you are looking to people, possessions, and circumstances to give your life meaning and satisfaction, then you will become confused and hurt and angry with God because He refuses to give you the things you feel you need in life. But if you find your meaning and satisfaction in Him, then in good times AND bad, life has meaning and purpose.

So, put on the helmet of the hope of salvation. Fix your mind, your hopes, your values on the world to come. It will protect you from the deadly blows of the enemy in this world.

Focus Questions

1. Imagine that you have been visited by your own ghosts of Christmas past, present, and future. What might you learn from such a visit?

2. What are you aiming for in life that you believe will give you happiness? What if you don't get it? Will Jesus and what He chooses to give you be enough? Ask Him for grace that it will be.

3. What is the most appealing thing about heaven that helps you put your hope in the next world?

30

The Sword in Spiritual Combat

(Ephesians 6:17b)

Defend the Bible? I would just as soon defend a lion. Just turn the Bible loose. It will defend itself.

Charles H. Spurgeon

*A*t 7:00 P.M. on Monday night, April 14, 1986, thirteen fighter jets came screaming in off the Mediterranean Ocean toward the Libyan city of Tripoli. Hurtling along near the speed of sound, no more than five hundred feet above the ground, these metal lightning bolts delivered their deadly cargo, then pulled up in a breakneck angle and turned back toward the Mediterranean and the safety of home base.

Later evaluation would show that every major target they had gone in for was hit. Barracks, communication centers, a naval site, a terrorist headquarters, and on-ground planes and helicopters. President Reagan's retaliatory strike against Muammar al-Qadhafi's global terrorism was complete. Mission accomplished.

Hitting such small targets while traveling six hundred miles an hour only five hundred feet above the ground is like running down a steep hill as fast as you can and spitting on an anthill.

How did they do it? What made it possible?

Laser beams! Pencil-thin laser beams spotted the target electronically and then locked on to it with computer-controlled mechanisms. The bombs themselves also had a laser-sensing device which guided them to the target.

Laser-beam technology is revolutionizing warfare. Reagan's "Star Wars Initiative" called for putting satellites into orbit over the earth which would be able to direct laser beams on incoming missiles and knock them out of the

279

sky. Tanks, anti-aircraft guns, and even personal infantry weapons are being fitted with lasers to increase efficiency and minimize human error. Laser beams have a formidable future in modern warfare.

But laser beams are also a potent force for healing. At the fertility center at Northside Hospital in Atlanta, Dr. Cameron Nezhat uses a laser beam to remove endometriosis and increase a woman's chances for conception. In Colorado Springs, an ophthalmologist uses the tiny beam to tack a detached retina back in place for an Olympic athlete. At Roswell Park Memorial Institute in Buffalo, New York, Frank Rauscher reports that lasers are being used to destroy cancerous tumors.

Lasers (Light Amplification by Stimulated Emission of Radiation) produce an intense, penetrating beam of light which has awesome power both to destroy and to heal, to protect and to attack, for defense as well as offense.

In the apostle Paul's day the laser of offense and defense, the weapon of both attack and protection, was the soldier's sword.

The Sword of the Spirit

And take . . . the sword of the Spirit, which is the word of God.

Ephesians 6:17b

The final piece of armor in the believer's arsenal is the sword of the Spirit, and it is different from the previous five. Like the laser, it is extremely powerful, and has both an offensive and defensive capacity.

The Roman soldier's sword (*machaira*) was short and double-bladed. This cut-and-thrust weapon, wielded by the heavily armed legionary, was distinct from the large Thracian broadsword (*rhomphaia*). The smaller weapon was used in hand-to-hand combat. It was a weapon of last resort, used in intense warfare.

The believer's sword is the Word of God

There are two different words for the "word" of God in the Bible. One is *logos*, which refers to the collection of words embodying the whole body of God's revealed truth. For us this is synonymous with the Bible.

The second word, *rhema*, which is the one used in this verse, refers to specific, individual words. When we get involved in spiritual combat, we do not appeal to the entire Bible; we use specific, relevant passages.

For example, when you are tempted to get angry and really blow your top, it is not effective to say, "I believe the whole Bible." Instead, you counter temptation with: "The anger of man does not achieve the righteousness of

God"; "A fool always loses his temper, / But a wise man holds it back"; "An angry man stirs up strife, / And a hot-tempered man abounds in transgression" (James 1:20; Prov. 29:11, 22). The specific words of God are those which will help you do the right thing and, thus, be successful in the spiritual battle.

Commitment to the whole Bible is important in the spiritual warfare, but this occurs when we don the first piece of armor, the belt of truth. When we do that, we accept the truth of the Bible and choose to follow it with integrity. Then, when we take up the sword of the spirit, we use those Scriptures specifically in life's situations to fend off attacks of the enemy and put him to flight.

But why, you may ask, does Paul also call it "the sword of the Spirit"? Why doesn't he simply call it the sword of the Word?

Well, he calls it the sword of the Spirit for two reasons: first, because the Holy Spirit gave us the Word; and second, because the Holy Spirit helps us to understand it.

Second Timothy 3:16 says, "All Scripture is inspired by God." The word *inspired* means, literally, "God-breathed." And in 2 Peter 1:20–21 we are told that "no prophecy of Scripture is a matter of one's own interpretation, for no prophecy was ever made by an act of human will, but men moved by the Holy Spirit spoke from God."

Now, theologians admit that we don't know exactly what this means, but somehow the Holy Spirit influenced the prophets and writers of Scripture to write and speak only what God wanted. Therefore, these are God's words, not theirs.

So, the Word of God is called the sword of the Spirit because the Spirit of God is the One who gave it to us. Not surprisingly then, we need the Holy Spirit to help us to understand it.

In the frustrating days just before I became a Christian, I tried reading the Bible, but I got nothing out of it. So I put it away in defeat. Then, months later, I became a Christian, and suddenly I could not get enough of it. I not only wanted to read it, but I could understand it. I read and read and read and gradually understood more and more.

Mark Twain once said, "Many people are troubled by the things in the Scripture that they don't understand. Frankly, the ones that bother me are the ones that I do understand."

I can identify with that. I don't understand everything and never will. But what I do understand teaches me what I need to know about the Christian life and provides protection against the wiles of Satan.

The Sword for Defense

Each piece of the armor of God is closely linked to the next. For example, the defensive use of the sword of the Spirit is closely linked with the shield of faith. Every time we feel like doubting or sinning or quitting, we take up the shield to reject those thoughts and tell ourselves the truth by brandishing the sword of the Spirit.

When Satan tempted Jesus with physical comfort, Jesus blocked that temptation with the shield of faith, calling it a lie. Then He countered with the sword of the Spirit, telling the truth: "It is written, 'Man shall not live on bread alone, but on every word that proceeds out of the mouth of God'" (Matt. 4:4). Jesus knew the specific portion of Scripture that addressed the temptation He was facing, and this defense gave Him the strength to overcome the enemy.

When Satan tempted Jesus with power, Jesus blocked that temptation with the shield of faith and countered it with the sword of the Spirit: "Begone, Satan! For it is written, 'You shall worship the Lord your God, and serve Him only'" (Matt. 4:10).

Satan was vanquished in the battle because Jesus wielded the sword of the Spirit.

The same protective armor is ours. Satan tempts. And because we know the Bible specifically, we can spot the error in what he is promising us and act accordingly.

The Sword for Offense

A teacher at Newton Massachusetts High School, one of the better high schools in the nation, quizzed a group of college-bound seniors before a "Bible as Literature" course he was planning to teach. In that quiz, according to the students' answers, he learned some astounding things about the Bible: Sodom and Gomorrah were lovers, Jezebel was Ahab's donkey, the New Testament gospels were written by Matthew, Mark, Luther, and John, Eve was created from an apple, Jesus was baptized by Moses, and Golgotha was the name of the giant who slew the apostle David.

It's funny. But it's also sad. In the past, biblical knowledge was foundational to American education. Even the great Ivy League schools of Harvard, Princeton, and Yale were founded primarily for the training of ministers of the gospel. Today, however, our nation is almost totally ignorant of the Bible.

At the same time, our nation is being ravaged by broken homes, drug and alcohol abuse, physical and sexual abuse, runaway children and teenage pregnancies, venereal disease and AIDS in epidemic proportions, crime and graft in business and government, and illiteracy in a nation where education is compulsory. We are a nation in crisis.

Why? Because we do not know the Bible. Because we do not care to know the Bible. And sadly, even many Christians are almost totally ignorant of the Bible.

We simply must learn the Bible. No matter how well we know it, we must get to know it better. And there are a multitude of ways to do this: Christian books and study guides, commentaries and other aids, Sunday school classes, home Bible studies, growth groups, community Bible studies, seminars, discipleship ministries. There are countless ways to study the Bible, and you must find the ways that work for you.

But remember . . . the Bible is not to be studied as an end in itself. It is to be studied as a revelation of God and His truth to us so that our thinking is changed, our values are changed, our habits are changed, our actions are changed, our words are changed . . . so that our lives are changed.

Change! That is the grand purpose of the Bible. Changing us so that we become more than the person we were yesterday—less like a fallen person and more like God. The Bible speaks to every facet of our lives, either directly or indirectly.

God isn't merely a safety net or a lifeboat. He isn't just walking behind us to rescue us from problems so that our lives will go smoother. He requires active participation from us. He demands our commitment, our allegiance, our worship, and our obedience. To do that, we need the power of the Word. "For the word of God is living and active and sharper than any two-edged sword, and piercing as far as the division of soul and spirit, of both joints and marrow, and able to judge the thoughts and intentions of the heart" (Heb. 4:12).

When we learn the true Word and follow it:
—hurting people are helped;
—abused people are healed;
—angry people are soothed;
—depressed people are encouraged;
—fearful people are given courage;
—weak people are given strength;
—confused people are given insight;
—foolish people are given wisdom;

—ignorant people are given knowledge;

—selfish people are given generosity;

—hateful people are given love;

—doubting people are given faith;

—aggressive people are given gentleness;

—proud people are given humility.

It isn't quick and it isn't easy, but it is sure.

So take up the sword of the Spirit, which is the word of God, and gain victory in the spiritual battles you face.

Taking up the sword of the Spirit means: I will use the Scriptures specifically in life's situations to fend off attacks of the enemy and put him to flight.

Focus Questions

1. The Bible, like a laser beam, can be used for defensive or offensive purposes. Jesus quoted Scripture to Satan in answer to his temptations. What subject would you like to know more about to be able to use that truth to defend yourself against temptation? How will you pursue that information?

2. What pain in the world do you wish you could help alleviate? How could you learn more about the Bible in that area?

3. In what area of your life would you like to experience the most change? What first step could you take toward that end—after praying about it?

31

Contact with the Spiritual Commander

(Ephesians 6:18–24)

We cannot all argue, but we can all pray; we cannot all be leaders, but we can all be pleaders; we cannot all be mighty in rhetoric, but we can all be prevalent in prayer. I would sooner see you eloquent with God than with men.

Charles H. Spurgeon

*T*wo Quaker ladies were discussing the relative merits and prospects of Abraham Lincoln and Jefferson Davis during the Civil War.

"I think Jefferson will succeed because he is a praying man," said one.

"But so is Abraham a praying man," said the other.

"Yes," rejoined the first lady, "but the Lord will think that Abraham is joking."

While Abraham Lincoln told this humorous story on himself many times, it may strike a responsive chord in many of us; for many have the nagging suspicion that when they pray, the Lord thinks they are joking. The reality is, many of us are uneasy about prayer. To one degree or another we feel unworthy and inadequate. We're not sure if we are qualified to pray. We're not even sure we know how to pray.

On the other hand, we all feel pulled to pray. Even those who say they are "not very religious" or those who have never made a commitment to Christ instinctively find themselves thanking the Lord for good things and— especially—calling on Him in times of trouble.

As believers, we see the inherent virtue in prayer, and we wish that we were better at it. We were created by God for fellowship with Him, and without it we feel a sense of void. God is calling us. Nothing else will satisfy. We want to draw near to God and have Him draw near to us (James 4:8).

Paul has just told us that if we want to be victorious in spiritual warfare, we must obey six biblical principles—pictured as six pieces of armor. Then he follows these principles with a summary principle: pray.

Making Contact with the Commander

> With all prayer and petition pray at all times in the Spirit, and with this in view, be on the alert with all perseverance and petition for all the saints.
>
>   Ephesians 6:18

Paul gives us four "alls" to guide us in understanding his instructions on prayer:

1. With all prayer and petition = the scope of prayer

2. At all times in the Spirit = the attitude of prayer

3. With all perseverance and petition = the fervency of prayer

4. For all the saints = the target of prayer

Prayer comes from the word *proseuche,* which refers to general requests, while petition comes from *deesis,* referring to specific requests. This includes thanks and praise to God, confession of sin, pouring out to God the thoughts and feelings of our mind and heart, general prayer for things that are on our minds, and requests for specific things that are of concern to us.

Praying at all times does not mean that we walk around with our hands folded or that we spend all our time on our knees. Rather, prayer is to be our attitude as we go through the events of everyday life. And praying in the Spirit means that we do not recite meaningless prayers. It means that we depend on God's guidance in what we pray for. It means a recognition and dependence upon the fact that, as stated in Romans 8:26–27, "we do not know how to pray as we should, but the Spirit Himself intercedes for us with groanings too deep for words; and He who searches the hearts knows what the mind of the Spirit is, because He intercedes for the saints according to the will of God."

Praying at all times in the Spirit means we have an attitude of submission to, dependence on, and guidance from the Holy Spirit in our praying.

We are members of the body of Christ; therefore, what other Christians are doing is of interest to us. When Billy Graham preaches to thousands in

Moscow, it is important to us. When Christian leaders gather in the Philippines for a conference on world evangelization, it is important to us. When friends, missionaries, and ministry leaders are involved in ministry and outreach, it is important to us. And we should pray for them.

Based on this teaching, Paul appeals for the Ephesian church to pray for him. But when he does, notice his request. He doesn't ask for material things. He asks that he may be given boldness in witnessing.

Left to themselves, the Ephesians might have prayed—as would we—that he be released from prison. They might have prayed that God would give him health. They might have prayed that God would comfort him and allow him to be freed to go back to Jerusalem to live a normal life.

But that is not what Paul wanted. He had accepted his circumstances as being from God, and said, "Pray that I might be an effective witness for the cause of Christ. That is why I am here."

Getting a Response from the Commander

In an old "Peanuts" cartoon I saw many years ago, Linus is looking quizzically at his folded hands. Lucy comes up, and Linus says, "I have just made an important theological discovery. I have discovered that while you are praying, if you hold your hands upside down, you get the opposite of what you pray for."

Many of us have suspected that all along. We have been holding our hands upside down and are getting just the opposite of what we are asking for!

There are a lot of things we don't know and understand about prayer, but we must not let that keep us from praying. We must not let the things we don't understand destroy the things we do.

First of all, we must understand that God wants us to pray. He is waiting for us to pray. Not in the same way that the IRS wants and waits for us to file our income tax—with hands on hips and ready to box our ears if we don't—but like a loving parent wanting and waiting to hear His child's requests, with an earnest desire to answer.

Which brings us to the next point: God does answer our prayers. Not all prayers, but He will answer those that are answerable.

Now, I can hear you shouting at me, "But how do I know which ones are answerable?"

Well, we can't get too detailed in answering this, but we can say that there seem to be several levels of restriction on receiving answers to prayer.

One verse says, simply, that we should ask and we will receive (Matt. 7:8). Period. No qualifications. Taken in isolation, this verse seems to indicate that no request will be denied us.

However, there are other verses that add qualifications to our asking. For example, in James 1:6, we see that we must "ask in faith, without any doubting." In John 14:13 it says we must ask in Jesus' name. And in John 15:7 we learn that we must abide in Him, and His word must abide in us, and THEN we can ask what we will, and it will be given to us. So, it seems that there are levels of restrictions on prayer that we can observe when we put all the verses on prayer together:

Level 1: Ask and you shall receive—no qualifications

Level 2: Ask in faith, without doubting; ask without unconfessed sin—specific qualification

Level 3: Abide in Me and My Word in you—general qualification

Level 4: Thy will be done—final qualification

This chart is not exhaustive, but it is representative of the levels at which we might analyze our prayers.

First, we are given the open invitation to simply ask.

If we do not receive an answer, we may check ourselves on level 2. Are we asking in faith? Do we have any unconfessed sin that could be hindering the answer? Does the request conflict with anything in the Bible (which would assure that it is not in God's will)? Are we asking with proper motives?

If that level seems to check out, then we may need to move on to level 3, where we check on our overall spiritual maturity. Are we abiding in Christ, and is His Word abiding in us? Perhaps God is delaying the answer to prayer because He wants to drive us to a deeper walk with Him.

If we gain no insight or receive no answer on this level, we move to level 4, where we simply pray, "Thy will be done." This is, of course, the prayer Jesus prayed in the Garden of Gethsemane when He asked that the Father would take this cup (being crucified) from Him . . . but then said, "Nevertheless, not My will but Thine be done."

In reality, of course, we cannot compartmentalize our prayers to this degree. We ought to make a simultaneous check of all these things as we are praying. However, spelling them out this way helps us see if we have overlooked something. And by going back through each of these qualifications, the Holy Spirit may help us see something we didn't see before.

Sometimes, God is simply delaying the answers to our prayers. Why? Well, there may be several reasons:

1. The timing is not right. He may answer it, but later.
2. The request may need to be clarified. When the answer comes, God wants us to be able to recognize it. Often we don't even recognize an answer because we did not crystallize the request in our own minds.
3. God might delay to create a sense of expectation and to call attention to the fact that it was He who answered and not just good luck or natural consequences.
4. He might delay an answer to prayer to deepen our understanding of Him and His Word.
5. He might delay to draw us into a deeper relationship with Him. Things that come easily are often taken lightly. God does not want prayer to be taken lightly. Therefore, answers to prayer do not come easily.

Our Relationship with the Commander

The relationship between parent and child gives us great insight into the relationship between the children of God and our heavenly Father. When a child is young, uneducated, and immature, he asks for things that are preposterous and even dangerous. He wants to have only candy for lunch. He wants to drive the car and run the vacuum—things he clearly cannot or should not do. The loving and perceptive parent would surely not grant all the requests of a two-year-old.

As the child grows older, the requests he makes become less ridiculous and impossible. His whole life becomes more in line with the parent's will. Yet even in the teenage years, parents cannot grant all their child's requests. Some are still foolish; others are selfish and manipulative.

As the child grows into enlightened adulthood, there are few requests that a parent cannot grant, because they are asked with a knowledge and understanding that is consistent with the parent's will. And the adult child understands—especially if he has children of his own—that his parents did not refuse childhood requests because they didn't love him . . . but because they did. Their denial of the request was rooted in greater knowledge and wisdom.

God is not a Cosmic Customer Service, where every order will be filled according to your request if you just learn how to fill out the form properly.

If we envision Him as He really is—our heavenly Father who loves us and wants the best for us in all His sovereign wisdom, and who answers or doesn't answer based on His superior, all-knowing will—then we can avoid a sense of failure or doubt or disappointment when our prayers aren't answered in just the way and at the time we prescribe.

If we understand that God is good, that He loves us, that He wants the best for us, and that He is, in fact, our heavenly Father, then rather than eyeing Him like some Heavenly Vending Machine, "What in the world is wrong with this thing?" and being tempted to give it a good swift kick, we can say, as we would of a loving parent, "Well, I guess that request is not what is best for me at this time. And since I want what is best for me, I will accept the denial."

The bottom line in prayer is that God wants a relationship with us. That is His ultimate desire. So He refuses any approach that will allow us to simply go through an equation to get what we want. Equations won't work. The only thing that will work is personally drawing closer to Him.

That is why no one fully understands prayer in a way that can be communicated to others as a "system." There is a very personal and intimate dimension to prayer. There is no "system." It is you and God alone in a room, looking for what is best for you, and learning to trust and follow Him. Only by getting to know Him better will prayer begin to make sense.

So pray! Risk praying poorly. Pray the best way you know how. Don't allow that which you don't understand about praying to keep you from praying. And do not let that which you don't understand about prayer to destroy that which you do understand. PRAY! God will lead you into fuller understanding over time.

Remember:

1. We can pray to God because Christ has made us acceptable to Him. We are completely free to enter the Most Holy Place (a metaphor for worshiping and praying directly to God) without fear because of the blood of Jesus' death (Heb. 10:19–22 NIV). So we can come to God with a sincere heart and a sure faith, for we have been cleansed and made free from guilt.

2. Because God knows everything, we can be completely and utterly honest, totally transparent, before Him and know that we will be accepted, understood, and helped.

3. When we hurt, God hurts. Therefore, we cannot accuse Him of not caring or of being distant when our prayers for relief are not answered.

4. To pray effectively, we must know the Scriptures well, because to know God's will, we must know His Word and be obedient to it.

5. Gratitude should be our attitude in prayer for all that God does for us.

6. Learning to pray well takes time.

I've often been amazed by dogs and how they absolutely love to do that for which they were bred. Bird dogs love to hunt birds. Put them in the truck and start driving toward the fields, and they quiver with excitement. Sled dogs live to pull sleds. They bark and howl in anticipation as they are hitched to the traces. And when the whip cracks and they hear their master shout "Mush!" their ecstasy is undisguised. When these dogs do what they are created to do, they are filled with joy.

And so it is with us. God created us for fellowship with Him. And when that communication takes place, there is a deep joy and satisfaction that nothing else can duplicate . . . it is our direct source and hookup to His power . . . it is our access to His guidance and peace . . . and created within us is a longing for it that nothing else will satisfy.

As we have discussed throughout this book, God created us for eternity with Him, which is where our inheritance and our riches lie. Thus, in this never-enough world we must always remember who we really are and where our true wealth, purpose, love, and power really lie.

Ray Stedman, well-known and beloved pastor, knew this well. A year before his death in 1992, he preached these words:

The world tells us, if you don't take it now, you're never going to get another chance. I have seen that misunderstanding drive people into forsaking their marriages after 30 or 40 years and running off with another, usually younger, person, hoping they can still fulfill their dreams because they feel life is slipping away from them. Christians are not to think that way. This life is a school, a training period where we are being prepared for something that is incredibly great but is yet to come. I don't understand all that is involved in that, but I believe it, and sometimes I can hardly wait until it happens. . . . Don't succumb to the philosophy that you have to have it all now or you will never have another chance. You can pass by a lot of things now and be content because you know that what God is sending you now is just what you need to get you ready for what he has waiting for you when this life is over.[1]

Focus Questions

1. Are there any prayers you have prayed that God did not answer? If so, are you now glad that He didn't? What does that tell you about future prayers?

2. What would life be like if God always answered everyone's prayers?

3. How important is prayer in your life? When, why, and how do you pray? What does this tell you?

Notes

Chapter 1—The Vault Is Open

1. John Piper, *Desiring God* (Portland, Oreg.: Multnomah Press, 1986), 19.

Chapter 2—Treasures from God the Father

1. Taken from Charles Colson, *Against the Night* (Ann Arbor: Servant, 1989), 144–46.

Chapter 5—The Giver Behind the Gift

1. Chuck Swindoll, *Growing Deep in the Christian Life* (Portland, Oreg.: Multnomah Press, 1990), 99.
2. James Packer, *Knowing God* (Downers Grove, Ill.: InterVarsity, 1973), 32.
3. Albert Wells, *Inspiring Quotations* (Nashville: Thomas Nelson, 1988), 143.

Chapter 8—The Riches of Our Spiritual Resources

1. Dr. Paul Brand and Philip Yancey, *Fearfully and Wonderfully Made* (Grand Rapids, Mich.: Zondervan Publishing House, 1980), 17–18.

Chapter 10—Enjoying People and Using Things

1. Alan McGinnis, *The Friendship Factor* (Minneapolis: Augsburg Publishing House, 1979), 20–21.
2. Martin Lloyd-Jones, *Christian Unity: An Exposition of Ephesians 4:1–16* (Grand Rapids, Mich.: Baker Book House, 1980), 52.
3. Dr. Paul Brand and Philip Yancey, *Fearfully and Wonderfully Made* (Grand Rapids, Mich.: Zondervan Publishing House, 1980), 26.

Chapter 11—Building a House of Bricks, Not Sticks

1. "Points to Ponder," *Reader's Digest,* May 1989, excerpted from *Timberlake Monthly.*

Chapter 12—Walk Which Way?

2. John F. MacArthur, Jr., *Ephesians,* The MacArthur New Testament Commentary (Chicago: Moody Press, 1986), 164.
2. William Golding, *The Lord of the Flies* (New York: Capricorn Books, 1955), 187.
3. Corrie ten Boom, *Tramp for the Lord* (New York: Jove Books, 1978), 45–46.

Chapter 13—What We Look Like When We Look Like Christ

1. Erwin Lutzer, *Managing Your Emotions* (Wheaton, Ill.: Victor Books, 1983), 92.
2. Chuck Swindoll, *Three Steps Forward, Two Steps Back* (Nashville: Thomas Nelson, 1980), 149.

Chapter 14—The Imitation of God

1. Harvey Mackay, *Swim with the Sharks Without Being Eaten Alive* (New York: William Morrow & Co., 1988), 141–42.

Chapter 15—People with Purpose

1. Chuck Yeager and Leo Janos, *Yeager* (New York: Bantam Books, 1986), back cover.
2. Charles Swindoll, *Growing Strong in the Seasons of Life* (Portland, Oreg.: Multnomah Press, 1983), 182.

Chapter 16—The Fountain of Love

1. Corrie ten Boom, *Tramp for the Lord* (New York: Jove Books, 1978), 29.

Chapter 17—Singing in the Rain

1. Dr. Paul Brand and Philip Yancey, *Fearfully and Wonderfully Made* (Grand Rapids, Mich.: Zondervan Publishing House, 1980), 167–68.
2. John Haggai, *Winning Over Pain, Fear, and Worry* (New York: Inspirational Press, 1991), 414–15.
3. Ibid.

Chapter 19—The Character of a Godly Wife

1. James Hurley, *Man and Woman in Biblical Perspective* (Grand Rapids, Mich.: Zondervan, 1981), 151.
2. Ibid., 154.
3. James Dobson, *What Wives Wish Their Husbands Knew About Women* (Carol Stream, Ill.: Tyndale House, 1975), 183.

Chapter 20—The Character of a Godly Husband

1. James Dobson, *What Wives Wish Their Husbands Knew About Women* (Carol Stream, Ill.: Tyndale House, 1975), 35.
2. Charlie Shedd, *Letters to Philip* (Old Tappan, N.J.: Fleming H. Revell, 1968), 32.
3. Jack Mayhall, *Marriage Takes More Than Love* (Colorado Springs: Navpress, 1978), 130.

Chapter 21—The Character of a Godly Family

1. Jay Kessler, *Ten Mistakes Parents Make with Teenagers* (Nashville: Wolgemuth and Hyatt, 1988), vii–viii.
2. Charles Kuralt, *On the Road with Charles Kuralt* (New York: Ballantine Books, 1985), 350–53.

Chapter 22—How Would You Work If Jesus Were Your Boss?

1. Peter Kreeft, *Making Sense Out of Suffering* (Ann Arbor, Mich.: Servant Books, 1986), 142–43.
2. Bruce Olson and Susan DeVore Williams, *Charisma and Christian Life,* November/December, 1989.

Chapter 23—How Would You "Boss" If Jesus Were Your Employee?

1. Tom Peters, *A Passion for Excellence* (New York: Warner Books, 1985), xvi–xvii.
2. Joe Aldrich, *Life-style Evangelism* (Portland, Oreg.: Multnomah Press, 1981), 15–16.
3. Peters, *Excellence,* 341–43.

Chapter 24—Spiritual Power

1. John White, *The Fight* (Downers Grove, Ill.: InterVarsity Press, 1976), 87–89.

Chapter 25—Truth Is the Basis of All Spiritual Victory

1. Merrill McLoughlin, "A Nation of Liars?" *U.S. News & World Report,* 23 February 1987, 54–61.
2. Ted Engstrom, *Integrity* (Waco, Tex.: Word Books, 1987), 3–4.

Chapter 26—Why the Straight and Narrow?

1. Gary Richmond, *A View from the Zoo* (Waco, Tex.: Word Books, 1987), 25–27.

Chapter 27—The Path to Peace

1. Tom Howard, quoted in *Illustrations for Biblical Preaching* (Grand Rapids, Mich.: Baker Book House, 1982), 90.

Chapter 28—Resisting Spiritual Brainwashing

1. Gerald Coffee, "Beyond Survival," *Reader's Digest.*

Chapter 31—Contact with the Spiritual Commander

1. *Christianity Today,* 14 December 1992, 11.